The Honest Politician's Guide to Crime Control

The University of Chicago Press · Chicago and London

Norval Morris and Gordon Hawkins

the honest politician's guide to crime control

Chapter 1 appeared in condensed form in *Midway,*
Winter 1969, © 1969 by The University of Chicago.
Chapter 3, in slightly adapted form, appeared in *Midway,*
Summer 1969, © 1969 by The University of Chicago.

Standard Book Number: 226-53901-6
Library of Congress Catalog Card Number: 76-101467

The University of Chicago Press, Chicago 60637
The University of Chicago Press, Ltd., London

To Elaine, the Tuesday cook

Contents

We offer a cure for crime — not a sudden potion nor a lightning panacea but rather a legislative and administrative regimen which would substantially reduce the impact of crime.

Crime is man's second fear. The cataclysm of war is the first. Crime, not disease, is the second; it has a quality of aggression, generative of fear, which disease lacks.

Crime is our major domestic problem and much of the world shares in it. A third of the people of America are afraid to walk alone at night in their communities. In cities of more than half a million some 40 percent of the inhabitants confess to this fear. One in every six of our male children will be referred to juvenile courts for an act of delinquency, other than traffic, before his eighteenth birthday.

Our problem is to reduce both crime and the fear of crime. Our cure does both. And in a situation where conventional wisdom offers little in the way of a solution. One of our respected political scientists, Daniel P. Moynihan, said recently: "Nobody knows a damned thing about crime." There are others who suggest that only a multibillion-dollar program designed to eradicate all social inequity and achieve a near millennium can be effective in dealing with it. But for the most part a malaise compounded of fear, apathy, and inertia prevails.

If ingenuous utopianism would be unhelpful, so also is that posture — cynical dystopianism — which knows that nothing can change. Crime is not a natural phenomenon nor does it consist of inevitable episodes which can in no way be foreseen and guarded against. The history of the Volstead Act demonstrates that the development of crime on an unprecedented scale, and in an enormous variety of forms, can be stimulated by legislative action. We shall demonstrate that this is a process which can most effectively and beneficially be reversed.

We shall argue further that, far from its being true that we know nothing about crime, there is available now a fund of information on the subject which were it acted upon responsibly and steadily would substantially reduce crime and curtail the fear, suffering, and unhappiness it entails. Much of that information can be found in the report of the President's Commission on Law Enforcement and Administration of Justice (*The Challenge of Crime in a Free Society*) together with the task force reports, research studies, and consultants' papers which cover the detailed research and analysis underlying the general report.

We have addressed ourselves to the general reader without any specialized knowledge of the criminal justice system. But we do not, as some writers do, assume that the general reader is a naïve simpleton capable only of absorbing predigested material served with a dressing of rhetoric. We assume, what will in many cases undoubtedly be true, that he is better read and intellectually more sophisticated than we are.

How to present our cure? Let us not hedge; let us assume dictatorial powers limited only by the realities of the budget which press alike on all. It is not uncommon for would-be reformers to put forward an extensive "laundry list" of proposals based on the assumption that unlimited men, money, and materials will be made available. This is too facile. In the real world a case has to be made for even a modest increase in resources particularly in the field of social welfare. In that respect we have tried to be realistic. Nevertheless, if we are heeded, crime and the fear of crime will be reduced impressively without treasury flutters, though, of course, the refashioning of such a complex system as the criminal justice system cannot be achieved without transitional costs.

Our proposals are put in the form of dictatorial

ukases for purposes of exposition. No doubt we thus gain vicarious satisfaction for latent political ambitions; but such despotism is no threat to social order. No massive resistance is required to halt our hegemony. The reader has merely to close the book and we are instantly deposed. But if you are interested, here is our cure for crime.

We acknowledge our grateful indebtedness to such snippets of man's accumulated wisdom as we have been able to ingest and to plagiarize and to the purveyors of such insights, living and dead, whom we have encountered. Many have led us astray and, doubtless, are responsible for any infelicities or weaknesses in our work. If such blame is to be made specific, however, Hans W. Mattick, Karl Menninger, Anthony M. Platt, Hans Zeisel, and Frank Zimring bear a peculiar burden. Contrary to long-standing tradition we accept responsibility for any virtues in this book.

1

The Overreach of the Criminal Law

The first principle of our cure for crime is this: we must strip off the moralistic excrescences on our criminal justice system so that it may concentrate on the essential. The prime function of the criminal law is to protect our persons and our property; these purposes are now engulfed in a mass of other distracting, inefficiently performed, legislative duties. When the criminal law invades the spheres of private morality and social welfare, it exceeds its proper limits at the cost of neglecting its primary tasks. This unwarranted extension is expensive, ineffective, and criminogenic.

For the criminal law at least, man has an inalienable right to go to hell in his own fashion, provided he does not directly injure the person or property of another on the way. The criminal law is an inefficient instrument for imposing the good life on others. These principles we take as self-evident, though we shall soon consider some of the consequences of their neglect. They must receive priority of attention in our cure for crime since only when they are applied will we have both the resources and the clarity of purpose to deal with the serious problems of crime — injury to the person, fear in the streets, burglaries, muggings, and the larger incursions on our property rights.

Hence, our first series of dictatorial ukases deals with law reform. They are not an academic refashioning of minutiae of the law; they are rather a determined return to the proper, more modest and realistic role of the criminal law. It is fortunate that we have dictatorial powers, since this type of law reform is distasteful to politicians and probably commands less than majority popular support. Politicians rely heavily on the criminal law and like to invoke criminal sanctions in connection with most social problems, if only to indicate their moral fervor and political virtue. They take little interest in the consequences of the invocation. Moreover, support for the removal of a sanction is often interpreted as support for the behavior previously punished; if you vote for the legalization of consensual adult homosexual conduct you must be either a faggot or a homosexual fellow traveler. Few votes are so gained. Likewise, the public often cherishes criminal sanctions as an expression of their virtuous inclinations as distinct from the squalid realities of their lives.

It is necessary, however, if we are to be serious about the crime problem, to clear the ground of action of the criminal law. This is essential to the police, to the courts, and to the correctional agencies. They must deal only with those problems and those people for whom their services and their capacities are appropriate; not those who are merely being sacrificed to prejudice and taboos. Public sacrifice, throwing virgins off the rocks, to reinforce the group superego, to placate the ancient gods, is not the job of the criminal justice system.

We provide, initially, a bare statement of our program; the rationale follows.

1. **Drunkenness.** Public drunkenness shall cease to be a criminal offense.

2. **Narcotics and drug abuse.** Neither the acquisition, purchase, possession, nor the use of any drug will be a criminal offense. The sale of some drugs other than by a licensed chemist (druggist) and on prescription will be criminally proscribed; proof of possession of excessive quantities may be evidence of a sale or of intent to sell.

3. **Gambling.** No form of gambling will be prohibited by the criminal law; certain fraudulent and cheating gambling practices will remain criminal.

4. **Disorderly conduct and vagrancy.** Disorderly conduct and vagrancy laws will be replaced by laws precisely stipulating the conduct proscribed and defining the circumstances in which the police should intervene.

5. **Abortion.** Abortion performed by a qualified medical practitioner in a registered hospital shall cease to be a criminal offense.

6. **Sexual behavior.** Sexual activities between consenting adults in private will not be subject to the criminal law.
   Adultery, fornication, illicit cohabitation, statutory rape and carnal knowledge, bigamy, incest, sodomy, bestiality, homosexuality, prostitution, pornography, and obscenity; in all of these the role of the criminal law is excessive.

7. **Juvenile delinquency.** The juvenile court should retain jurisdiction only over conduct by children which would be criminal were they adult.

The last ukase — the removal of, in effect, half the jurisdiction of the juvenile courts — will be discussed in a later chapter. It is mentioned here as an important part of the law-reform component of our cure for crime, encompassing one-sixth of all "criminal" cases. Our rationale of the other planks in our legislative program follows and culminates in an eighth ukase.

The consequences of our program for adults emerge from the statistics. There are six million nontraffic arrests of adults per year in the

United States. Counting most conservatively, the reforms listed above account for three million of those arrests. Indeed, the report of the President's Commission on Law Enforcement and the Administration of Justice (hereafter referred to as the President's Crime Commission) states, "Almost half of all arrests are on charges of drunkenness, disorderly conduct, vagrancy, gambling, and minor sexual deviations." The consequent reduction of pressure on police, courts, and correctional services would have a massive impact on the criminal justice system.

"We may start with the obvious observation that not every standard of conduct that is fit to be observed is also fit to be enforced." Ernst Freund's words define the theme of this chapter. There are two senses in which the criminal law causes crime. It is the formal cause of crime. If we had no criminal law we would have no crime. It is also an efficient cause of crime in that some of our criminal laws foster, encourage, sustain, and protect crime – in particular, organized crime. It is therefore necessary to begin with the question of what constitutes and what ought to constitute a crime? Or to put it another way: when should we use the criminal law in an effort to regulate human conduct?

This is not the place to make a contribution to a classic debate between John Stuart Mill and Sir James Fitzjames Stephen in the nineteenth century and between Professor H. L. A. Hart and Lord Devlin in recent years. We are broadly in agreement with the definition of the proper sphere of the criminal law given by Mill in his essay *On Liberty*:

> The principle is, that the sole end for which mankind are warranted, individually or collectively, in interfering with the liberty of action of any of their members is self-protection. That the only purpose for which power can be rightfully exercised over any member of a civilized community against his will, is to prevent harm to others. His own good, either physical or moral, is not a sufficient warrant, he cannot rightfully be compelled to do or forbear because it would be better for him to do so, because it will make him happier, because, in the opinion of others, to do so would be wise or even right.

The function, as we see it, of the criminal law is to protect the citizen's person and property, and to prevent the exploitation or corruption of the young and others in need of special care or protection.

We think it improper, impolitic, and usually socially harmful for the law to intervene or attempt to regulate the private moral conduct of the citizen. In this country we have a highly moralistic criminal law and a long tradition of using it as an instrument for coercing men toward virtue. It is a singularly inept instrument for that purpose. It is also an unduly costly one, both in terms of harm done and in terms of the neglect of the proper tasks of law enforcement.

Most of our legislation concerning drunkenness, narcotics, gambling, and sexual behavior and a good deal of it concerning juvenile delinquency is wholly misguided. It is based on an exaggerated conception of the capacity of the criminal law to influence men. We incur enormous collateral disadvantage costs for that exaggeration and we overload our criminal justice system to a degree which renders it grossly defective as a means of protection in the areas where we really need protection — from violence, incursions into our homes, and depredations of our property.

The present "overreach" of the criminal law contributes to the crime problem in the following ways, which will be more fully documented as we deal with particular areas of that overreach:

1. Where the supply of goods or services is concerned, such as narcotics, gambling, and prostitution, the criminal law operates as a "crime tariff" which makes the supply of such goods and services profitable for the criminal by driving up prices and at the same time discourages competition by those who might enter the market were it legal.

2. This leads to the development of large-scale organized criminal groups which, as in the field of legitimate business, tend to extend and diversify their operations, thus financing and promoting other criminal activity.

3. The high prices which criminal prohibition and law enforcement help to maintain have a secondary criminogenic effect in cases where demand is inelastic, as for narcotics, by causing persons to resort to crime in order to obtain the money to pay those prices.

4. The proscription of a particular form of behavior (e.g., homosexuality, prostitution, drug addiction) by the criminal law drives those who engage or participate in it into association with those engaged in other criminal activities and leads to the growth of an extensive criminal subculture which is subversive of social order generally. It also leads, in the case of drug addiction, to endowing that pathological

condition with the romantic glamour of a rebellion against authority or of some sort of élitist enterprise.

5. The expenditure of police and criminal justice resources involved in attempting to enforce statutes in relation to sexual behavior, drug taking, gambling, and other matters of private morality seriously depletes the time, energy, and manpower available for dealing with the types of crime involving violence and stealing which are the primary concern of the criminal justice system. This diversion and overextension of resources results both in failure to deal adequately with current serious crime and, because of the increased chances of impunity, in encouraging further crime.

6. These crimes lack victims, in the sense of complainants asking for the protection of the criminal law. Where such complainants are absent it is particularly difficult for the police to enforce the law. Bribery tends to flourish; political corruption of the police is invited. It is peculiarly with reference to these victimless crimes that the police are led to employ illegal means of law enforcement.

It follows therefore that any plan to deal with crime in America must first of all face this problem of the overreach of the criminal law, state clearly the nature of its priorities in regard to the use of the criminal sanction, and indicate what kinds of immoral or antisocial conduct should be removed from the current calendar of crime.

Drunkenness

One of every three arrests in America — over two million each year — is for the offense of public drunkenness; more than twice the number of arrests in the combined total for all of the seven serious crimes which the FBI takes as its index crimes (willful homicide, forcible rape, aggravated assault, robbery, burglary, theft of $50 or over, and motor vehicle theft). The cost of handling each drunkenness case involving police, court, and correctional time has been estimated at $50 per arrest. We thus reach a conservative national estimate of annual expenditure for the handling of drunkenness offenders (excluding expenditure for treatment or prevention) of $100 million. In addition, the great volume of these arrests places an enormous burden on the criminal justice system; it overloads the police, clogs the courts, and crowds the jails.

The extent to which drunkenness offenses interfere with other police activities varies from city to city, but in the majority of cities it involves a substantial diversion of resources from serious crime. Thus, in

Washington, D.C., during a nine-month period, it was found that 44 percent of the arrests made by the special tactical police force unit used "to combat serious crime" was for drunkenness. A similar situation exists in relation to correctional systems. In one city it was reported that 95 percent of short-term prisoners were drunkenness offenders. One-half of the entire misdemeanant population consists of drunkenness offenders. Yet the criminal justice system is effective neither in deterring drunkenness nor in meeting the problems of the chronic offenders who form a large proportion of those arrested for drunkenness. All that the system appears to accomplish is the temporary removal from view of an unseemly public spectacle.

We think that the use of the police, the courts, and the prisons on this scale to handle unseemliness at a time when one-third of Americans are afraid to walk alone at night in their own neighborhoods is so ludicrously inept and disproportionate that we need no more than point it out to justify the removal of drunkenness from the criminal justice system. This is not to say that if a person while drunk causes damage to property, steals, or assaults another person he should not be arrested under the appropriate statutes dealing with malicious damage, theft, or assault. But there should always be some specific kind of offensive conduct in addition to drunkenness before the criminal law is invoked.

It is sometimes argued that we have a choice between the criminal law model and the medical model in the treatment of drunkenness. And there is a considerable literature which deals with the dangers of medical authoritarianism. To us this is a false dichotomy; our choice need not be so narrowly restricted. A social welfare model may, in the present state of medical knowledge, be preferable to either the criminal law or the medical model.

For the police lockups, courts, and jails we would substitute community-owned overnight houses capable of bedding down insensible or exhausted drunks. For the police and the paddy wagons we would substitute minibuses, each with a woman driver and two men knowledgeable of the local community in which the minibus will move. A woman is preferred to a man as the driver–radio-operator because it is our experience that the presence of a woman has an ameliorative effect on the behavior of males, even drunken males.

The minibus would tour the skid row area, picking up the fallen drunks and offering to help the weaving, near-to-falling drunks. If there be a protest or resistance by a drunk, cowardice and withdrawal must control our team's actions; if there be assaults or other crimes, a police transceiver will call those who will attend to it; if there be unconsciousness or drunken consent, the minibus will deliver the body to the overnight house.

If there be talk by the drunk the next day of treatment for his social or alcoholic problem, let him be referred, or preferably taken, to whatever social assistance and alcoholic treatment facilities are available. Indeed, let such assistance be offered if he fails to mention them; but let them never be coercively pressed.

The saving effected by abolishing the costly and pointless business of processing drunkenness cases through the criminal justice system would vastly exceed the cost of providing such facilities and treatment programs for those willing to accept them.

Such a system may be less effective than a medical detoxification model of the type now operating in New York and Saint Louis, but it is clearly cheaper and more humane than our present processes and does not distract the criminal justice system from its proper and important social functions.

Narcotics and Drug Abuse

As in the case of drunkenness, so in regard to the use of other drugs, the invocation of the criminal process is wholly inappropriate. Yet at present, although drug addiction itself is not a crime in America, the practical effect of federal and state laws is to define the addict as a criminal. According to FBI arrest data, 162,177 arrests for violations of the narcotic drug laws were made in 1968. As the President's Crime Commission report puts it, ". . . the addict lives in almost perpetual violation of one or several criminal laws." Neither the acquisition nor the purchase nor the possession nor the use of drugs should be a criminal offense. This elimination of criminal prosecution provisions should apply to the narcotics (opiates, synthetic opiates, and cocaine), marihuana, hallucinogens, amphetamines, tranquilizers, barbiturates, and the volatile intoxicants.

Those who support the present laws and the traditional methods of enforcement commonly claim a causal connection between drug use and crime. Yet leaving aside crime to raise funds to support the inflated costs of purchasing legally proscribed drugs, the evidence of a causal connection between drug use and crime is slight and suspect.

As with alcohol, the fact that drugs not only release inhibition but also suppress function is commonly ignored. They may well inhibit more crime than they facilitate; heroin for example has a calming depressant effect, and the "drug crazed sex fiend" of popular journalism has no counterpart in reality although the myth dies hard. The proto-typal headline, "Addict Rapes Widow" is misleading — the truth would be "Addict Nods While Widow Burns."

There seems to be no doubt, however, that the policy of criminaliza-tion and the operations of criminal justice agencies in this field have in themselves been criminogenic without measurably diminishing the extent of the drug problem or reducing the supply of narcotics entering the country. There is substantial evidence that organized criminals en-gaged in drug traffic have made and continue to make high profits. There is evidence, too, that criminalization of the distribution of drugs has caused much collateral crime with drug addicts, "to support their habits," as the President's Crime Commission puts it, "stealing millions of dollars worth of property every year and contributing to the public's fear of robbery and burglary."

The one certain way totally to destroy the criminal organizations engaged in the narcotics trade and to abolish addict crime would be to remove the controls and make narcotics freely available to addicts. As Harvard economist Thomas C. Schelling puts it, "If narcotics were not illegal, there could be no black market and no monopoly profits, and the interest in 'pushing' it would probably be not much greater than the pharmaceutical interest in pills to reduce the symptoms of common colds."

We do not propose the abolition of all controls over the importation, manufacture, and distribution of drugs, nor the abolition of penalties against those unauthorized persons who trade in drugs for profit; but we are convinced that if addiction were treated as a medical matter this would undercut the illicit traffic and largely eliminate the profit incentive supporting that traffic. The British approach to this problem, which involves the maintenance of strict control over the supply of drugs but leaves the treatment of addicts (including maintenance doses to addicts) in the hands of the medical profession, has resulted in a situation where no serious drug problem exists.

Certain difficulties in the British approach have recently emerged. Heroin addiction has increased with immigration of groups having larger addict subcultures within them and for other reasons. But though the increase, stated as a percentage, seems great, it starts from a base so very much smaller than that in the United States that the figures showing increase misstate the problem. It remains a problem of little social significance. Further, the outlets for medical prescription and administration of drugs need to be better controlled to avoid the development of a black market. But these are details in a scheme of incomparably sounder structure than we have evolved in this country.

With regard to marihuana, it is necessary to say something further. At present marihuana is equated, in law, with the opiates although its use does not lead to physical dependence nor does tolerance and the desired dose increase over time. Further, the risks of crime, accident, suicide, and physical or psychological illness are less than those associated with alcohol.

At the moment the law, by treating marihuana as equivalent to opiates, may well foster the belief that there is no difference between them. Yet as marihuana can be relatively easily obtained in most states and found not to have the dramatically deleterious effects advertised, graduation to the use of heroin, which *is* addictive and harmful, could be stimulated by this policy. Worse still, because marihuana is bulky and detection is thereby facilitated, youthful experimenters are encouraged to move to dangerous and addictive drugs which are more easily concealed. As with alcohol, controls relating to the sale or other disposition of the drug to minors are necessary, but that is all.

One of the principal advantages of the decriminalization and the pathologization of addiction is that the "image" of drug taking as an act of adventurous daring conferring status on the taker as a bold challenger of authority, convention, and the Establishment will be destroyed. With punitive laws and the brunt of law enforcement falling heavily on the user and the addict rather than on traffickers, we have created a persecuted minority with its own self-sustaining myths and ideology. The alcoholic, on the other hand, is nowhere seen as a heroic figure in our culture but quite commonly as a person to be pitied and treated as sick. Consequently, no addict subculture with a morale-enhancing, self-justifying ideology and recruitment process has developed in this area.

Gambling

Gambling is the greatest source of revenue for organized crime. Estimates of the size of the criminal revenue from gambling in the United States vary from $7 to $50 billion, which means that it is huge but nobody knows how huge. Because statutes in every state, except Nevada, prohibit various forms of gambling, criminals operate behind the protection of a crime tariff which guarantees the absence of legitimate competition. This has led to the development of a powerful and influential vested interest opposed to the legalization of gambling.

Despite sporadic prosecution, the laws prohibiting gambling are poorly enforced and there is widespread disregard for the law. We do not face a choice between abolishing or legalizing gambling; the choice is between leaving gambling and the vast profits which accrue from it in the hands of criminals or citizens taking it over and running it for the benefit of society or, by licensing and taxation measures, controlling it.

The position regarding betting on horse races is highly irrational. In many states those who attend races are allowed to bet on horses and a portion of the money wagered is paid as a tax to the state treasury. Yet it is illegal to accept off-track wagers. But as most people cannot find time to go to the track, such wagers are placed on a scale far exceeding the legitimate ones. The President's Crime Commission cites "estimates by experts" which state that the total involved in off-track betting "is at least two or three times as great" as the total of $5 billion involved in legal betting at race tracks. Yet of the sum of from $10 to $15 billion wagered off-track, nothing at all is forfeit to the state treasury.

It has proved impossible to enforce the laws against betting, and all attempts to make the laws effective have failed. In this situation a major step toward insuring rational and socially beneficial control of gambling would be the institution of state lotteries, such as operate in New Hampshire and New York. More than twenty-five governments, from the Kenyan, which makes $42,000 a year, to the Spanish, which makes $70 million, run national lotteries. Norway, Sweden, France, and Australia all have such lotteries with a substantial levy on gross revenue going to state treasuries.

In addition to the provision of state lotteries, off-track betting can be controlled by the establishment of state-run betting shops as in Australia. Insofar as gambling is harmful, the harm can at least be reduced by fixing limits to wagers and other measures of control. As for other forms of gambling, the Nevada solution whereby the state tax commission administers gambling by supervising a license system under which all applicants have to be cleared by the commission — and state, county, and city taxes and license fees represent a substantial revenue — has operated with success for many years. The infiltration of organized criminals has been blocked by screening all applicants for criminal records. The tax commission employs inspectors and has held hearings and revoked several licenses. The principal lesson to be learned from Nevada is that gambling can be kept clean and does not have to be run by criminals.

Disorderly Conduct and Vagrancy

According to the Uniform Crime Reports, there were nearly six hundred thousand arrests for disorderly conduct in 1968. This represents more arrests than for any other crime except drunkenness. Disorderly conduct statutes vary in their formulation, and the conduct dealt with as disorderly includes a wide variety of petty misbehavior including much that is harmless, although annoying, and not properly subject to criminal control.

Criminal codes and statutes should prohibit specific, carefully defined, serious misconduct so that the police can concentrate on enforcing the law in that context. Disorderly conduct statutes allow the police very wide discretion in deciding what conduct to treat as criminal and are conducive to inefficiency, open to abuse, and bad for police-public relations.

Similar considerations apply to vagrancy. It is a criminal offense in all states, with over ninety-nine thousand arrests in 1968. Here, however, it is not a question of more rigorously defining the type of behavior to be prohibited but rather of entirely abandoning the vagrancy concept. The commentary to the American Law Institute's Model Penal Code states: "If disorderly conduct statutes are troublesome because they require so little in the way of misbehavior, the vagrancy statutes offer the astounding spectacle of criminality with no misbehavior at all." And the fact is that those statutes, which frequently make it an offense for any person to wander about without being able to give a "good account of himself," burden defendants with a presumption of criminality and constitute a license for arbitrary arrest without a warrant.

Vagrancy laws are widely used to provide the police with justification for arresting, searching, questioning, and detaining persons whom they suspect may have committed or may commit a crime. They are also used, according to the President's Crime Commission task force report on the courts, "by the police to clean the streets of undesirables, to harass persons believed to be engaged in crime and to investigate uncleared offenses." These laws often make possible the conviction of persons without proof of antisocial behavior or intention and in general confer unbounded discretion on the police.

In our view the police need authority to stop any person whom they reasonably suspect is committing, has committed, or is about to commit a crime and to demand his name, address, and an explanation of his behavior — to stop and frisk, now clearly constitutionally permissible. The police need such powers of inquiry to control crime and to protect themselves in dealing with persons encountered in suspicious circumstances, and they should have these powers without having to resort to the subterfuge of vagrancy arrest.

As for such behavior as begging, which is included in many vagrancy statutes, we agree with the American Law Institute's Model Penal Code commentary that "municipalities may properly regulate the use of sidewalks to safeguard against annoying and importunate mendicants and merchants; but such legislation does not belong in the penal code."

Abortion

It is estimated that a million abortions are performed every year in America and that criminal abortion is the third most remunerative criminal enterprise in the United States — following gambling and narcotics. The arrest rate is certainly less than one per thousand abortions performed. No other felony is as free from punishment as illegal abortion, particularly when it is performed by a medical practitioner.

Nevertheless it would be incorrect to say that the laws relating to abortion have no effect on behavior. The commentary to the American Law Institute's Model Penal Code states that "experience has shown that hundreds of thousands of women, married as well as unmarried, will continue to procure abortions . . . in ways that endanger their lives and subject them to exploitation and degradation. We cannot regard with equanimity a legal pattern which condemns thousands of women to needless death at the hands of criminal abortionists. This is a stiff price to pay for the effort to repress abortion."

The principal effect of the abortion laws appears to be that whereas women of higher socioeconomic status can usually receive competent and even legal termination of pregnancy — "therapeutic abortion on psychiatric grounds" — those less fortunately placed are forced to resort to the backstreet abortion with its grim train of consequential shame, misery, morbidity, and death. It is a law for the poor.

Abortion may be sinful or immoral, but it is not the function of the law to enforce the whole of morality. It is difficult to understand what religious or moral principle, what divine or human purpose, is served by compelling underprivileged women to undergo pregnancy for the full term and to bear unsought and frequently unwanted children or to risk sickness or death at the hands of incompetent and frequently lecherous and importunate abortionists. No doubt the fact that the price of maintaining this principle is paid almost exclusively by the poor has delayed its critical examination.

We, as criminologists, have a professional reason for advocating a rational approach to abortion legislation. We have been impressed by observation in many countries of the disproportionate number of unwanted children we find in orphanages, reformatories, correctional institutions for youth, and on through the correctional treadmill to institutions for habitual criminals. We believe that the single factor most highly correlated with persistent delinquency and crime would be, if properly tested, being unwanted.

The principle which is most often invoked in this connection is that designated by the phrase "the sanctity of life." It is ironical that in defense of the sanctity of life we pursue a policy which tends toward the maximization of maternal mortality. The highest mortality rates occur in cases of illegal abortion, followed next by cases of confinement (i.e., parturition after at least twenty-eight weeks of pregnancy) and finally by cases of legal abortion where the rate in some countries is as low as 0.01 percent. Thus by confining legal abortion to a minimum, so that for the vast majority the alternatives are either confinement or illegal abortion, we ensure that the incidence of maternal mortality is maximized.

The sanctity of life is often also taken to refer to the life of "the unborn child." Yet the use of this expression is as if we referred to the reader as "an adult fetus." To say that a fertilized ovum or an embryo is a human being and therefore entitled to the full protection of the law is a prejudicial abuse of language. Nor do those who take this position ever maintain it consistently, for they never embrace the logical corollary which is that all abortive operations are murders and should be so treated in law.

For our part, in view of the fact that human reproduction is a continuum, such questions as "When does life begin?" are unanswerable, except perhaps in metaphysical or theological terms. Nevertheless it is quite practicable to draw objective distinctions between abortion, infanticide, and homicide; and in terms of these well-recognized distinctions we say that abortion should not be regarded as criminal as long as the woman desires its performance. We see no reason to regard some other arbitrarily selected point prior to parturition, in what is a continuous process, as having any particular significance.

In regard to this problem we adopt what Professor Glanville Williams calls "the short and simple solution" of permitting abortions to be conducted by qualified legal practitioners in certified hospitals when requested by the pregnant woman. We believe that the woman herself should have the full right to decide whether she will go through with the pregnancy or not, although there should be formal provisions to ensure that she is protected from undue pressure from other persons and that her request represents what she on some advised reflection really wants. In short, we regard the total legalization of abortion performed by a licensed physician as the answer. We see no advantage to be gained by a protracted piecemeal approach in this area.

Sexual Behavior

With the possible exception of sixteenth-century Geneva under John Calvin, America has the most moralistic criminal law that the world has yet witnessed. One area in which this moralism is most extensively reflected is that of sexual behavior. In all states the criminal law is used in an egregiously wide-ranging and largely ineffectual attempt to regulate the sexual relationships and activities of citizens. Indeed, it is as if the sex offense laws were designed to provide an enormous legislative chastity belt encompassing the whole population and proscribing everything but solitary and joyless masturbation and "normal coitus" inside wedlock.

It is proper for the criminal law to seek to protect children from the sexual depradations of adults, and adults and children from the use of force, the threat of force, and certain types of fraud in sexual relationships. Further, there is some justification for the use of the criminal law to suppress such kinds of public sexual activity or open sexual solicitation as are widely felt to constitute a nuisance or an affront to decency. But beyond this, in a post-Kinsey and post-Johnson and Masters age, we recognize that the criminal law is largely both unenforceable and ineffective, and we think that in some areas the law itself constitutes a public nuisance. We shall deal with some of the principal areas of conduct from which the criminal law should be withdrawn in whole or in part; types of behavior which although at present adjudged criminal are more properly regarded as matters of private morals.

Adultery, Fornication, and Illicit Cohabitation

Extramarital intercourse is punishable in the majority of states with penalties ranging from a $10 fine for fornication to five years' imprisonment and a $1,000 fine for adultery. Mercifully, prosecutions are rare. The vast disparity between the number of divorces on the ground of adultery and the minute number of prosecutions for that offense reveals that enforcement is deliberately kept at a microscopic level.

A situation of this kind constitutes a double threat to society. In the first place it provides opportunities for victimization and discriminatory enforcement often provoked by jealousies. In the second place the promulgation of a code of sexual behavior unrelated to actuality (according to Kinsey, 95 percent of the male population is criminal by statutory standards), and its enforcement on a derisory scale, and in arbitrary fashion, cannot but provoke contempt and resentment.

It is one thing to retain laws which, because of difficulty of detection, cannot be rigorously enforced, quite another to preserve those which are not seriously intended to be applied. At a time when it is of considerable importance that the law should mean what it says, anything likely to make citizens take it less than seriously can only be harmful. It is at least a reasonable assumption that anything which provokes cynicism, contempt, derision, indifference, resentment, and hostility toward the law and law enforcement agencies is likely to have undesirable repercussions on behavior. At this time it seems unwise to incur the risk of such costs and for no discernible gain.

Statutory Rape or Carnal Knowledge

Sexual intercourse with a willing female under the statutory age of consent is sometimes referred to as "carnal knowledge," sometimes as "statutory rape." It is usually a felony. The statutory age of consent varies from ten years of age (in Florida, South Dakota, and New Mexico) to eighteen years of age (in New York and thirteen other states) and, in Tennessee, twenty-one years of age. Such variations must confuse the divining rod of the natural lawyer! The maximum penalties range from death (in fifteen states) to ten years' imprisonment (in New York). In general these penalties are exceeded only by those for murder and equaled only by those for forcible rape and kidnapping. In North Carolina and Washington sexual intercourse between an adult female and a male under the age of consent is also statutory rape on the part of the female, but in general, as one textbook puts it, "the criminality of statutory rape seeks to protect the purity of young girls."

A great deal of statutory rape legislation is totally unrealistic in a number of respects. Most age limits were fixed at a time when physical maturity was attained later than it is now. Furthermore, nowadays teen-age girls are far more knowledgeable and sophisticated than the law appears to recognize, and the assumption that in cases of consensual intercourse the male is necessarily the initiator and the female always plays a passive, bewildered role is unlikely to correspond closely to reality. Moreover, even if the male genuinely believes, on reasonable grounds, that the girl is over the age of consent, he has, except in California, no defense to a charge of statutory rape; it is thus clear that not only rationality but also justice is sacrificed in the pursuit of purity.

The offense of statutory rape should clearly be abolished and since in all such cases the girl has given her consent — otherwise it would be rape, viking rape not statutory rape — the man's offense should be that of intercourse with a minor. In our view, the function of the law in relation to sexual behavior of this nature should be restricted to providing protection for the immature in cases where there is significant disparity of age between the male and the female.

An abuse of a relation of trust or dependency should be regarded as an aggravating circumstance. This need would be adequately met if the age of consent were fixed at sixteen. The accused should be acquitted if he can establish that he reasonably believed the girl to be past her sixteenth birthday. It should be added that we are speaking of adult criminal liability here; that is, we are not talking about problems of sexual experimentation by youths and criminal liability within whatever is the juvenile court age in any jurisdiction.

Bigamy

Bigamy, the triumph of hope over experience, is contracting a second marriage during the existence of a prior marriage and is a statutory crime. It does not constitute a serious part of the crime problem. We mention it only as an interesting example of the legal stigmatization and punishment of conduct which may (as when both parties are aware of the previous marriage, which is the general situation) harm no one although it offends some religious and moral codes. It may be that a certain amount of wrath on the part of the Deity is engendered but his appeasement is no longer regarded as a function of the criminal law. The bigamous marriage itself is legally a nullity.

In many cases the only antisocial consequences of bigamy are the falsification of state records and the waste of time of the celebrating officer. This problem would be better handled by penalties for false declarations in relation to ceremonies of marriage. Sanctions are to be found in all criminal codes for giving false information in relation to official processes, and deceiving the woman would be an aggravating circumstance relevant to sentencing. If necessary, the maximum punishment for such false declarations could be statutorily increased.

The great value of such a low-key approach to a practical problem is that it avoids the trails of ecclesiastical glory that accompany the crime of bigamy at present. Commonly all that is involved in bigamy is, as Glanville Williams puts it, "a pathetic attempt to give a veneer of respectability to what is in law an adulterous association," and prosecution serves no purpose and achieves no object other than increasing the sum of human misery.

One Australian judge, impressed with this analysis, in sentencing a convicted bigamist upbraided him thus: "Wretched man! Not only have you and this young lady deceived your friends. Worse, you have thrown Her Majesty's records into confusion."

Incest

Incest is sexual intercourse between persons related within prohibited degrees which vary widely. In some societies the interpretation of incest is so broad as to exclude half the available population. In America, a number of states prohibit the marriage of first cousins and few if any permit the marriage of those more closely related than that.

Incest is an ecclesiastical offense. In England it did not become a criminal offense until 1908. In America it has also generally been made a crime by statute and usually includes affinity (i.e., relationship by marriage) as well as consanguinity.

The statutory prohibition of marrying one's deceased brother's wife was designed to reduce fratricide, suggesting a somewhat cynical estimate of the nature of brotherly love. By contrast, marrying one's deceased sister's husband is generally not proscribed, revealing the law's gallant misjudgment of female determination. In some gentler societies it is thought admirable and is sometimes obligatory to assume matrimonial responsibilities for one's brother's widow and children.

Although incest figures prominently in the literature of psychoanalysis, all available evidence indicates that it is rare, and certainly prosecutions for it are exceptional. We mention it here merely as an example of the law trying to enforce morality, for where both parties are adult and commit incest with full consent, no other purpose is served. Insofar as children need protection from adults, or force or the threat of force is involved, protection is already provided by other statutes. Incest between consenting adults in private is not a proper subject for the criminal law.

Sodomy and Crimes against Nature

Statutes concerning sodomy and crimes against nature include within their scope such sexual behavior as bestiality, both homosexual and heterosexual, anal and oral copulation, and mutual masturbation. These laws receive only capricious and sporadic enforcement, usually, although not exclusively, in regard to such relations outside marriage. Obviously laws of this kind are peculiarly liable to abuse because of the wide discretion involved.

No social interests whatsoever are protected by desultory attempts to impose upon persons adherence to patterns of sexual behavior arbitrarily selected from the great variety which forms our mammalian heritage. Bestiality would be more properly dealt with under statutes relating to cruelty to animals where any cruelty is involved; otherwise, there is no reason to include it within the criminal law.

Homosexual Acts

Homosexual offenses are treated under such titles as sodomy, buggery, perverse or unnatural acts, and crimes against nature; homosexual practices are condemned as criminal in all states but Illinois, usually as a felony. Penalties vary enormously. A consensual homosexual act which is legal in Illinois is a misdemeanor in New York and can be punished as a felony by life imprisonment in some states. The Kinsey report states: "There appears to be no other major culture in the world in which public opinion and the statute law so severely penalize homosexual relationships as they do in the United States today."

Our primacy in this field is purchased at a considerable price. Although the Kinsey report maintains that "perhaps the major portion of the male population, has at least some homosexual experience between adolescence and old age," only a small minority are ever prosecuted and convicted. Yet the law in this area, while not significantly controlling the incidence of the proscribed behavior, not only increases unhappiness by humiliating and demoralizing an arbitrarily selected sample of persons every year and threatening numberless others, but at the same time encourages corruption of both the police and others who discover such relationships by providing opportunities for blackmail and extortion.

As far as the police are concerned, a great deal has been written both about corruption in this area and the degrading use of entrapment and decoy methods employed in order to enforce the law. It seems to us that the employment of tight-panted police officers to invite homosexual advances or to spy upon public toilets in the hope of detecting deviant behavior, at a time when police solutions of serious crimes are steadily declining and, to cite one example, less than one-third of robbery crimes are cleared by arrest, is a perversion of public policy both maleficent in itself and calculated to inspire contempt and ridicule.

In brief, our attitude to the function of the law in regard to homosexual behavior is the same as in regard to heterosexual behavior. Apart from providing protection for the young and immature; protection against violence, the threat of violence, and fraud; and protection against affronts to public order and decency, the criminal law should not trespass in this area. If all the law enforcement agents involved in ineffectual efforts to control buggery were to be diverted to an attempt to improve the current 20 percent clearance rate for burglary it is unlikely that there would be an immediate fall in the burglary rate. But it is utterly unlikely that there would be an increase in buggery; for people's sexual proclivities and patterns are among the least labile of their responses, as the almost total failure of "cures" and treatment programs for homosexuals should have taught us. And in the long run such a strategic redeployment of resources could not but be beneficial to society.

Prostitution

According to Kinsey almost 70 percent of the total white male population of the United States has some experience with prostitutes. But many of them have never had more than a single experience, and relations with female prostitutes represent a very small part of the total sexual outlet of the male population. It would appear that the incidence and importance of prostitution in this country have been greatly exaggerated in the literature, much of which seems to be the product of a prurient interest in the subject. In fact, professional prostitution is said by some authorities to be declining as a result of increasing sexual permissiveness which eliminates some of the need for such outlets. The Uniform Crime Report shows 42,338 arrests for "prostitution and commercialized vice" in 1968 but many arrests of prostitutes are included in the four hundred thousand yearly arrests for "disorderly conduct," so that the figures cannot be regarded as a meaningful index.

Prostitution is commonly statutorily defined as the indiscriminate offer by a female of her body for sexual intercourse or other lewdness for the purpose of gain and is a criminal offense in all states. The penalties most commonly imposed are fines or short prison sentences.

At one time it was widely believed that most prostitutes were unfortunate women who had been "driven" to a life of prostitution by poverty, bad upbringing, seduction at an early age, or broken marriages, but some research sponsored by the British Social Biology Council suggests that in the majority of cases this way of life is chosen because it offers greater ease, freedom, and profit than available alternatives. There is no evidence that the incidence of neurosis or psychological abnormality is greater among prostitutes than among housewives.

Prostitution is an ancient and enduring institution which has survived centuries of attack and condemnation, and there is no doubt that it fulfills a social function. It is often asserted that prostitution provides an outlet for sexual impulses which might otherwise be expressed in rape or other kinds of sexual crime. No research has been done in this area but the notion has a certain plausibility. It is undeniable, however, that prostitutes are sought out by some men who, because of a physical deformity, psychological inadequacy, or (in the case of foreigners and immigrants) unfamiliarity with the language and customs, find great difficulty in obtaining sexual partners. The Kinsey report states that prostitutes provide a sexual outlet for many persons who without this "would become even more serious social problems than they already are."

The costs of attempting to enforce our prostitution laws have been admirably summarized by Professor Sanford Kadish:

. . . diversion of police resources; encouragement of use of illegal means of police control (which, in the case of prostitution, take the form of knowingly unlawful harassment arrests to remove suspected prostitutes from the streets; and various entrapment devices, usually the only means of obtaining convictions); degradation of the image of law enforcement; discriminatory enforcement against the poor; and official corruption.

Once again it is our view that the use of law enforcement resources in this way, in a fruitless effort to promote moral virtue, is wasteful and socially injurious. Insofar as prostitution itself is responsible for social harms like the spread of venereal disease, regular compulsory medical inspection would provide better protection than our present haphazard enforcement policies. Moreover, all the evidence indicates that it is ordinary free promiscuity which is more largely responsible for the spread of venereal disease. Insofar as public solicitation constitutes an affront to some persons' susceptibilities, it would be perfectly possible (as has been done in some German cities) for municipal regulation to confine the activities of prostitutes to certain prescribed areas. As in many cases they are already largely confined in this way for purely commercial reasons, this would create few enforcement problems.

With regard to the pimp, procurer, and brothel keeper or operator we face a problem about which John Stuart Mill was for once somewhat equivocal. Thus he says, "Fornication, for example, must be tolerated, and so must gambling; but should a person be free to be a pimp or to keep a gambling house?" In his view "there are arguments on both sides." But he concludes by saying that he "will not venture to decide" whether there is sufficient justification for "the moral anomaly of punishing the accessory, when the principal is (and must be) allowed to go free; of fining or imprisoning the procurer, but not the fornicator."

Currently the punishment of those who live on immoral earnings is often justified on the ground that the pimp may exploit the prostitute. On balance we incline to the view that the criminal law is improperly used in this area. There is no evidence that exploitation is in fact a serious problem.

In this connection the Wolfenden committee states: "Such evidence as we have been able to obtain on this matter suggests that the arrangement between the prostitute and the man she lives with is usually brought about at the instance of the woman and it seems to stem from a need on the part of the prostitute for some element of stability in the background of her life. . . . We have no doubt that behind the trade of prostitution there lies a variety of commercial interests. . . . The evidence submitted to us, however, has disclosed nothing in the nature of 'organized vice' in which the prostitute is an unwilling victim coerced by a vile exploiter." The President's Crime Commission task force report on organized crime states that in America prostitution plays "a small and declining role in organized crime's operations." Apparently it "is difficult to organize and discipline is hard to maintain."

It is relevant here to mention also the call girl who caters to a more exclusive clientele than the ordinary prostitute. These girls are largely immune to the law. Possibly this is because, as Harold Greenwald says in his social and psychoanalytic study *The Call Girl*, "to arrest one call girl generally requires the services of a number of highly trained men for many days and involves expensive wire-tapping equipment." It may also be that there is a certain reluctance on the part of law enforcement agencies to invade privacy on the social levels where these girls operate. However that may be, it can only be to the benefit of society if the highly trained men and expensive equipment employed in this field are diverted to dealing with crime which really injures and frightens the public.

Pornography and Obscenity

The law relating to obscenity has remained virtually the same since 1873, although it has lately been interpreted more liberally. On the whole, sparing and only occasional use has been made of the legal sanctions in recent years although their minatory force cannot be and is not disregarded. The only consequence of censorship for which there is any solid evidence is that a number of works of literature and art have had their circulation severely restricted.

It is still confidently asserted in many quarters that exposure to erotica and pornography leads to moral degeneration and sex crime. But the exhaustive Kinsey Institute study of 15,000 sex offenders found no evidence that pornography was a causal factor in the offenses. Indeed, their findings suggest that it may rather be inability to secure fantasy release of impulse by means of pornography which distinguishes sex offenders from other people. If prurience can find satisfaction by reading books or looking at pictures, it is difficult to conceive anything less harmful to society. It is those who cannot achieve satisfaction in this way who may constitute a danger.

If controls are felt to be necessary in this area, we think that they should be limited to providing "protection" for the "immature" and preventing affronts to public decency. The former might be partially met — no more can be expected — by prohibiting the sale of pornography to minors; the latter, by the prohibition of the public display of pornographic material in the streets.

Other Areas: Moral and Social Welfare

There are a number of other areas in which we feel that the criminal law's interference in matters of morals is unwarranted. Fond as we are of Blackstone's justification for the rule treating suicide as a felony — "the suicide is guilty of . . . evading the prerogative of the Almighty, and rushing into his immediate presence uncalled for" — we do not think it the proper function of the law to enforce ancient eschatological doctrines. Therefore, in those few states which still treat attempted suicide as a crime and the larger number where the altruistic abetment of suicide is a crime and the survivor of a genuine suicide pact is guilty of murder, we submit that the law goes beyond its proper sphere. We are not impressed by the argument that the police must have power to prevent a suicide from killing himself and that only the criminal prohibition of attempted suicide can provide that power. As Glanville Williams says, "So far as is known, no inconvenience has been felt to arise from the absence of specific powers in those American jurisdictions that do not punish attempted suicide." But if it is felt to be necessary, it would be perfectly possible to enact legislation allowing any person some right of interposition to prevent a suicide without resorting to the criminal law.

Some years ago the American Bar Foundation conducted a pilot survey of the administration of criminal justice in the United States which was designed to identify some causes of "breakdown, delay and ineffectiveness" in the systems which administer criminal justice in the United States. The report of that study indicates two other areas in which it is evident that the resources of the criminal justice system are employed to perform tasks which have no relevance to the crime problem and should be handled by other agencies.

In the first place a large number of states have special statutes dealing with the issuance of worthless checks; that is, checks which have the genuine signature of the drawer but are drawn upon a bank in which he has neither sufficient funds nor any arrangement for payment. A considerable amount of police time is involved in investigating and processing these cases. In our view the conduct involved should be regarded as unethical rather than criminal (except where there is a genuine attempt to defraud) and should be handled by debt-collecting agencies and through the civil rather than the criminal process.

An analogous case is that of failure to support one's family. Nonsupport is commonly prosecuted under disorderly conduct statutes as a misdemeanor although the conviction and the imprisonment of the offender mean that he is thus legally prevented from fulfilling the obligation which he is being punished for neglecting. There is no doubt that the invoking of the criminal process may ultimately become necessary in some cases. But to employ the police and prosecutors to pursue husbands who are errant in this way is not only a wasteful use of their time but also exceedingly maladroit. For matters of this kind are clearly the province of welfare or social service agencies equipped to handle family problems. In this connection the President's Crime Commission task force report on the courts is clearly right when it says that insofar as using the criminal process serves to provide legal aid to indigent families, "the explicit provision of more legal aid services for civil proceedings is plainly preferable." Certainly the use of the police as agents of both social and moral welfare and crime control represents a confusion of purposes which inevitably results in neither being adequately fulfilled.

Conclusion: Some Objections and the Eighth Ukase

We are of the opinion that if the employment of the criminal justice system's resources were to be curtailed and restricted along the lines we have suggested in the seven major fields of action indicated, and the means thus made available were devoted to protecting the public from serious crime, such a redeployment would result in a substantial accession of strength to law enforcement which would help appreciably to reduce the crime problem to manageable proportions.

We recognize, however, that so radical a program as that proposed may be regarded by some as unacceptable and that it could justifiably be said that we have so far ignored a number of legitimate objections to the repeal of criminal laws. Thus Rupert Cross in his admirable paper "Unmaking Criminal Laws" says, "In general the criminal law has selected as proper subjects for its attention those parts of the moral law which are suitable for enforcement by the infliction of punishment following upon a judicial enquiry, and in general the criminal law disregards those parts of the moral law which are unsuitable for enforcement in this way."

He goes on to say that "whenever the repeal of a criminal law is mooted, it is proper to ask" a number of questions, which he lists as follows:

> Would the repeal of the relevant law lead to an increase in the prohibited practice? Would it weaken the moral condemnation of that practice? Is the prohibited practice harmful to other individuals? Is it actually or potentially harmful to society? Is the practice strenuously condemned by public opinion? And, is the criminal sanction effective?

We agree that these are all in some degree relevant questions. They are not, however, questions to which it is possible to give categorical answers in every case. And even if answers can be given it is by no means clear what the practical implications of any particular answer or combination of answers might be. Indeed, it is evident that if one accepts Mill's doctrine that "the only purpose for which power can rightfully be exercised over any member of a civilized community against his will is to prevent harm to others," then the crucial question in this context must be: Is the prohibited conduct harmful to other individuals or to society? If the answer to that question is negative, then questions about whether a repeal of the relevant law might lead to an increase in the prohibited conduct or weaken moral condemnation of it are otiose.

It should be clear, then, that in the light of our definition of the function of the criminal law, in terms of the protection of the lives and property of citizens and the preservation of public order and decency, the sort of restrictions on the use of the criminal sanction we have proposed are not only unobjectionable but desirable. Moreover, we have suggested that even those who do not accept our definition must face the question whether the collateral social costs of endeavoring to preserve the particular prohibitions we have discussed are not excessive.

We have argued that they are excessive, not only in terms of human suffering and the loss of freedom, but also in that in many cases the attempt to use the criminal law to prohibit the supply of goods and services which are constantly demanded by millions of Americans is one of the most powerful criminogenic forces in our society. By enabling criminals to make vast profits from such sources as gambling and narcotics; by maximizing opportunities for bribery and corruption; by attempting to enforce standards which do not command either the respect or compliance of citizens in general; by these and in a variety of other ways, we both encourage disrespect for the law and stimulate the expansion of both individual and organized crime to an extent unparalleled in any other country in the world.

We are not writing for the law technician; we therefore ask you to accept our eighth ukase largely on trust:

> **8. A Standing Law Revision Committee.** Every legislature must establish a Standing Criminal Law Revision Committee charged with the task of constant consideration of the fitness and adequacy of the criminal law sanctions to social needs.

Our present criminal law is a product of a series of historical accidents, emotional overreactions, and the comforting political habit of adding a punishment to every legislative proposition.

The American Law Institute in its Model Penal Code blazed a path of codification in this country which had earlier been traced by Sir James Fitzjames Stephen in England and Lord Macaulay in India. That Occam's razor should be brought to bear on the jungle of criminal sanctions none will doubt; that the steps toward consolidation, codification, and constant critical observation of the body of the criminal law are suitable steps in this direction few will controvert. All movements toward codification have rapidly revealed the facility with which the deadwood of the criminal law may be chopped away and sanctions designed comprehensible to the interested layman, clear even to the potential criminal, and more suited to our regulatory purposes than our present criminal law jungle. The American Law Institute's Model Penal Code, emulated in the Illinois Code of 1961 and being followed to a greater or lesser extent by the present codification efforts in several states of this country, provides an excellent model but this is not a task that can be done once and then left. It needs continuing attention.

The complete reform and rationalization of the criminal law is a long-term task. Our immediate concern in the present context is to increase its effectiveness by reducing its overreach. In the President's Crime Commission task force report on the courts it is said: "Only when the load of law enforcement has been lightened by stripping away those responsibilities for which it is not suited will we begin to make the criminal law a more effective instrument of social protection." This primary phase of our program is designed precisely to achieve that end, by that method.

Herbert Packer's *The Limits of the Criminal Sanction* (Stanford University Press, 1968), published after this chapter was written, is a comprehensive and, since we heartily agree with him, wise study of the issues discussed in this chapter.

2

Incidence, Costs, Victims, and Causes of Crime

O, horrible! To what a height of liberty in damnation hath the devil trained our age!

John Ford, 'Tis Pity She's a Whore (1633)

We begin, *tout court*, with our ukases:

1. In that we lack a reasonable estimate of the incidence of crime in this country, immediate steps must be taken to obtain realistic measures as a basis for planning and action.
2. No federal, state, or local criminal justice agency, nor anybody in receipt of public funds, shall devote any resources to investigating the "cost of crime" in America. By contrast, the application of systems analysis techniques to determining the costs of alternative strategies for repressing, controlling, and preventing crime shall be energetically pursued.
3. In that the victims of violent crime bear the costs of such crime to an inequitable degree, schemes for their compensation shall be established in all states.
4. Research into "the causes of crime" by those working in the criminal justice system shall be prohibited. By contrast, research studies evaluating the effects of crime prevention and control programs will be mandatory, it being required that a minimum of 5 percent of the budget of *all such programs* shall be devoted to this research.

The need and justification for these edicts derive in part from the fact that we are entering a province of knowledge and action only recently developed as a scientific discipline. Criminology has not yet shed all its prescientific swaddling bands. Alchemic myths, shibboleths, liturgies, and rituals out of the prenatal past still exercise an influence on theory and practice, on both the questions we ask and the programs we pursue. We must both exorcise demons and expound the rationale of our decrees.

Fifty years ago a British criminologist, Charles Mercier, wrote, "There is no subject on which so much nonsense has been written as this of crime and the criminal." This was an inaccurate statement because there are few disciplines which have not produced a substantial quantum of nonsense, in most cases vastly in excess of the criminological contribution, if only because they started earlier. But Mercier had a point. There has been a lot of nonsense written about crime and criminals. And it is significant that, as in other fields of study, a great deal of that nonsense has been produced in the attempt to answer large general questions like: What is the volume of crime? What is the cost of crime? What are the causes of crime? "The most natural and frequent question people ask about crime," says the President's Commission report, "is 'Why?'" The report goes on to say that "it is an almost impossible question to answer." So it is; but it is equally impossible flatly to ignore questions of this kind and we shall not attempt to do so. Let us face them now.

Incidence of Crime

There is too much crime, far too much avoidable human suffering from crime, and grossly too much fear of crime. This is true whether or not crime has been increasing of recent years. Loud and sometimes scholarly disagreement might suggest that the question is of central importance — which it is not. Increase or not, there has always been too much avoidable crime. We offer a program to reduce it but do not, as some do, seek to make the case for our program by a political use of unreliable statistics. The Uniform Crime Reports (UCRs), published annually by the Federal Bureau of Investigation, are the best tool so far developed in this country to assess the incidence of crime and delinquency, particularly of those more serious types of criminal behavior which are called the index crimes: willful homicide, forcible rape, aggravated assault, robbery, burglary, larceny of $50 and over, and motor vehicle theft. These reports are the product of a nationwide system under which some 8,000 local police agencies, covering 92 percent of the total population, report offenses they know of to the FBI. Each year the reports carry a summary "for the general reader interested in the general crime picture." The theme that emerges over the past two decades is one of increasing gloom deepening to catatonic depression. Is the UCR analysis of burgeoning criminality compelling?

The "general crime picture" presented to the "general reader" is far from general; it is highly selective and invariably emphasizes increases in serious crime. Thus: the "last year of the fifties registered a new all-time high"; the "first year of the sixties recorded a new all-time high"; "in 1961 a 3 percent increase over the previous all-time high." Thereafter the phrase "all-time high" was dropped, but from 1962 to 1968 increases of from 6 to 17 percent were monotonously reported. In 1968 it was pointed out that in 1967 there were nineteen victims of serious crime per one thousand inhabitants, an increase of 15 percent over 1966. It was further reported that the risk of being a victim of one of these crimes had risen 71 percent since 1960. From the figures for 1968 it appears we then suffered a further 17 percent increase over 1967.

The reports also contain random obiter dicta on a variety of contentious topics. For example:

The professional law enforcement officer is convinced from experience that the hardened criminal has been and is deterred from killing based on the prospect of the death penalty.

[L]aw enforcement machinery is impaired and policing is hampered as a result of the increasing restrictions being placed on enforcement operations.

[M]any impassioned and articulate pleas are being made today on behalf of the offender tending to ignore the victim and obscuring the right of a free society to equal protection under the law.

It would be convenient if one could distinguish between the statements of fact as providing hard objective data and the dicta as expressions of mere opinion. This is not always possible. What appear to be categorical factual statements are often extremely dubious inferences from unreliable data. Consider, for example, the statement in the Uniform Crime Reports, 1960, that the "first year of the sixties recorded a new all-time high, with 98 percent more crime than in 1950."

Such a statement is patently liable to mislead any "general reader" who fails to reflect that there was a substantial increase in the United States population between 1950 and 1960. When the crime rates, i.e., crimes per 100,000 inhabitants, are calculated and adjustments necessary for valid comparison are made, the actual increase was only 22 percent. And this increase was almost entirely confined to property offenses. In relation to population, murder remained unchanged, and in proportion, aggravated assault and robbery decreased.

It is even more important to note that the figures on which these statements are based are not figures for criminal acts that occurred but for "crimes which are counted by the police as they become known to them." Moreover surveys carried out for the President's Crime Commission confirmed what a variety of earlier studies had indicated, that the actual amount of crime is several times that reported and recorded in the UCRs. Thus, to infer from an increase in reported crime that there is "98 percent more crime" is to take a wild leap in the dark.

On the basis of the President's Commission figures it would be possible for the amount of forcible rape reported to increase by 250 percent, for reported burglaries to increase by 200 percent, for reported aggravated assaults and larcenies of $50 and over to increase by 100 percent — all without any increase in the amount of crime committed.

It is perfectly possible that the substantial changes and developments in reporting and estimating and recording procedures which occurred between 1950 and 1960 merely brought out into the light more of what is called the dark figure of crime and thus produced an increase purely statistical in character without any real increase in crime having taken place at all. Yet all the statements in the UCRs about increases in the volume of crime suggest that the FBI accepts the specious assumption, made by the nineteenth-century Belgian pioneer criminal statistician Adolphe Quetelet, that the amount of known crime bears a constant relation to the amount unknown.

A recent study of the apparent increase in crimes of violence in postwar England demonstrates that an increase in reported crime may also be due to a variety of other factors apart from greater uniformity and efficiency in recording. The development of better facilities for obtaining help from the police, such as emergency telephone systems and an increased number of radio-equipped police vehicles; greater readiness on the part of the police to record incidents as crimes which in the past might have been ignored; and a decrease in the public toleration of criminal behavior (particularly aggressive and violent behavior) may all lead to an artificial statistical increase in crime. In the English study it is estimated that a substantial part of the increase — "perhaps as much as half of the total" — is attributable to a greater readiness on the part of the public to report aggressive behavior. In such circumstances it is quite conceivable that in reality standards of behavior may have improved rather than declined.

Similar considerations apply to the statements in the UCRs about criminal victimization. Assertions such as that the "risk of becoming a victim of serious crime increased 16 percent in 1968" which are based on police statistics, can scarcely be regarded as possessing any significance at all in the light of the President's Commission surveys of crime victimization. These surveys revealed victimization in respect of serious crime on a scale ranging, depending on the offense, from two to ten times more than the number contained in the police statistics. In these circumstances it is impossible on the basis of the police figures to draw any valid inference at all as to variations in the risk of becoming a victim of serious crime.

We lack reliable methods for measuring the volume of crime. This applies to both the UCRs and to all presently available victim studies. Statements about the trend of crime may reflect no more than that each year we dip deeper into the well of criminal behavior to fill the tank of criminal statistics a little higher. Observers at the tank side (with their backs to the well) become increasingly alarmed as the level rises. Hearing their shrill cries relayed across the land, many citizens are convinced that America faces "a rising tide of crime and lawlessness." They fear that one day the well, fed by numberless springs, may overflow and we shall all be engulfed in a flood of criminal anarchy.

Should we then transfer our attention from the tank to the well? To ask how much water there is in the well poses a pointless question. Propositions regarding "the volume of crime" hardly belong to the realm of significant discourse, for crime is not a unitary phenomenon; it is a label applied to a thousand diversities of behavior. Their aggregation is a pointless exercise in mixing the immiscible, and quantification only lends a spurious air of precision and clarity to statements which are inherently confused.

Must we then conclude, since our present criminal statistics are an undefined sample of an artificial universe of heterogeneous elements, that we are dealing with a phenomenon beyond the reach of rational assessment by scientific methods? Clearly not. We do not abandon all attempts to measure temperature because of one deficient thermometer, nor would we if all existing thermometers proved inadequate. We would search for better thermal measuring methods. And in the case of crime the national census approach to assessment is not the only one possible; the use of a limited sample rather than census survey techniques holds great promise, as has been demonstrated to the commercial world in the sphere of market research. Sample surveys of victims of crimes similar to those initiated by the President's Commission should be instituted on a regular basis. Intensive studies in depth of defined crime problems in limited areas will, when combined with census data and victim studies, begin to provide reliable information on the dimensions of the problem we face.

The regularly published UCR percentage changes in the volume of crime from one year or decade to another can serve no purpose beyond alarming and frightening the public, and facilitating congressional acceptance of FBI budgetary requests. Even rates computed per 100,000 population are an extremely crude measure, for they are based on the tacit and erroneous assumption that all human beings are equally capable of committing crimes. As we shall show, there are demographic and ecological variables disproving that assumption.

Though it is impossible to rely on the presently available crime statistics to assess the incidence and trends of crime in America today, from other evidence it seems clear to us that both the volume and the rate of crime in America has indeed increased, is increasing, and, unless preventive measures like ours are followed, will continue to increase. Four important strands of evidence are the size of the population, the age structure of the population, urbanization, and increased affluence.

As to the first of these it is obvious that, assuming the proportion of crimes to the population remains stable, the total volume or absolute amount of crime will increase every year as the population increases. In other words the increase in the population of the United States from approximately 150 million in 1950 to approximately 200 million in 1968 might be expected, other things being equal, to produce a 25 percent increase in the total amount of crime. Moreover, if the official population projections of approximately 217 million in 1980 and 256 million in 1990 are realized, further absolute increases in crime may be anticipated. This in itself may be criminogenic in that it will result in greater concentrations of population; and increased density of population is commonly associated with higher crime rates.

But even more important to crime rates than the absolute increase in population is the changing age structure of the population. Three-quarters of the 1968 arrests for the index crimes plus petty larceny and negligent manslaughter were of people under 25. This is not a novel development. For as far back as criminal statistics are available the ages from 15 to 24 have been the high-risk group — the most crime prone group in the country. Because of the unusual birth rate in the postwar years the size of this group has been increasing much faster than other groups in the population and will continue to grow disproportionately for at least fifteen more years. Each year since 1961 nearly a million more youths have reached the ages of maximum risk than did so in the previous year. Between 1960 and 1970 the 15–19 age group has increased by 45 percent and the 20–24 age group by 56 percent. Thus the volume of crime and the overall rate can grow without any increase in the rate for any given age. Indeed, the President's Commission studies based on 1960 arrest rates indicate that between 40 and 50 percent of the total increase in arrests reported between 1960 and 1965 could have been expected as the result of increases in population and changes in the age composition of the population.

No less significant than the size and age composition of the population is its distribution between rural, suburban, urban, and inner-city areas. Rates for most crimes are highest in the big cities and with few exceptions average rates increase progressively as the size of the city becomes larger. Of the nearly 4.5 million index crimes known to the police in 1968, over 4 million occurred in cities. The average rates for those offenses are at least twice as great in cities of more than one million as in the suburbs or rural areas. By far the greatest proportion of the increase in those crimes recorded in America over the past thirty years has taken place in the cities of more than half a million which, though with less than 18 percent of the total population, account for over half the reported index crimes against the person and almost a third of all reported index property crimes. It may be that the explanation of this is not just that cities have large populations but that urban population is often concentrated in the poorer areas which have high delinquency and crime rates. But there are too many unexplained variations in crime rates between cities for this to be the whole explanation. Nevertheless, though the relationship between crime rates and the degree of urbanization is not a simple one, the increase in the urban population by more than 50 percent since 1930, while the rural population has increased by less than 2 percent, has clearly been a major factor in the rising national crime rates, and the figures may therefore reflect a real increase in crime.

We shall comment later in this chapter on the fact that as societies grow more affluent the amount of crime tends to increase. Here it is necessary only to observe that this has been an almost universal experience and that many criminologists maintain that affluence itself, and certainly unevenly distributed affluence, is a causal factor in increasing crime rates. Nor can there be any doubt that increasing criminal opportunities (more goods to be stolen) and increasing material aspirations (beyond the reach of legitimate access) have been reflected in increased offenses against property — which constitute over 90 percent of all index crimes in the United States. It is also possible that increased affluence has led to a breakdown in parental control both because of greater juvenile independence and because of an increase in divorce and separation in rich industrial societies, but this is somewhat speculative. Indeed, the whole area is speculative in that we do not know to what degree increased affluence leads to increased expectations of police protection and hence more reporting of crime. Nor do we know how far affluence may engender higher expectations regarding the behavior of others and lower toleration of antisocial activities.

The four developments we have enumerated — increasing size and changing composition of the population, urbanization and affluence — are such as to lend support to the view not only that there has been an increase in the volume and rate of crime in America but also that unless drastic and rigorous action is taken this trend will continue.

Even if our gloomy assessment of present crime rates and our predictions of further increase in crime and delinquency are erroneous, it is undeniably true that there is an increasing fear of crime. This fear not only diminishes the amenity of life, just as much as a real increase in crime, by reducing confidence and freedom in social interaction, but, by keeping people off the streets, facilitates the commission of such crimes as mugging. As the President's Commission report puts it: "As the level of sociability and mutual trust is reduced, streets and public places can indeed become more dangerous. Not only will there be less people abroad but those who are abroad will manifest a fear of and a lack of concern for each other." This increased fear of crime is in some areas turning the American dream into a nightmare.

But even increased fear may have some social value. It may generate and help to launch and support better methods of preventing and treating crime. It may provide a climate in which every change in social arrangements, every program that is introduced into the criminal justice system which purports to have an effect on reducing crime or delinquency or reducing the fear of crime or delinquency, is critically tested. This is one of the ways in which we shall exercise our dictatorial powers. Whereas we will not in any way seek to impede the further development of UCRs (other than rigidly to prohibit the budgetary self-serving commentary on them provided by the FBI), we will seek to put many more resources into victim studies, sample surveys, and other means of seeking to understand the incidence of crime in given defined communities and the attitude of people to it. But the compilation and publication of essentially meaningless total crime figures will be prohibited. The dissemination of misleading information in this way constitutes a serious disservice to the public. It is clear that if we are to control crime we require a reasonably reliable view of the incidence of crime and delinquency in our country. We must promptly take steps, quite other than our present reliance on UCRs, to gain such a view. We need a series of surveys, soundings in time and place, making use of sample as well as census techniques, if we are to begin to measure changes in the extent of crime and delinquency with precision sufficient for social planning.

The Cost of Crime

The position is much the same in regard to the question of "the cost of crime" in the United States. This has been variously estimated at from some hundred million dollars to twenty-two billion dollars (the latter figure being the FBI director's estimate). What do these estimates mean? They are reached by adding together all sorts of costs related to crime and presenting the total as the cost of crime to the community. Yet to aggregate such varied items as the fees paid for illegal abortions, the potential earnings of prisoners, the actual earnings of policemen, and money spent on burglar alarms is an economic absurdity. It makes no sense to add the estimated national bill from vandalism to the estimated total spent on prostitutes and commercial vice. Whereas the former does represent a loss to the economy, the latter is a matter of the supply of services on a commercial basis which may be morally deplorable but represents an *addition* to the national income in just the same way as does the production of legitimate goods and services. Nor can we assume that all victims' losses represent a loss to the community, for stolen money and goods do not usually cease to exist and may be even more productively employed after the transfer. Such transfer costs represent an individual but not necessarily a public cost and may stimulate production.

A concrete example will illustrate what may be involved in a simple property crime and the difficulty of its economic analysis. One of the authors visited New York for a lugubrious criminological conference, taking with him a portable IBM dictating machine. Having established himself in his hotel room, he left the room for some criminological research. On his return he found that some of his chattels had been tampered with and on a full search discovered that the IBM dictating machine and a small bottle of sleeping pills had been stolen. This selectivity indicated at least the likelihood that the crime had been perpetrated by an addict; but since, as with most other such crimes, the criminal was never discovered, one can never be sure of the matter. Appropriate protestations were made to the hotel and subsequently through the university (the true owner of the dictating machine) to the insurance company. Without too great a delay a substitute, equally effective IBM dictating machine was delivered. This chattel costs more than $425. The usual means of assessing the costs of crime would multiply this private loss by the number of such recorders stolen in the year — say, 1,000 — and conclude that such crimes had cost the community $425,000. This is, of course, nonsense. What is the reality? It is likely that the thief sold the recorder to a fence for approximately $30. It is likely that the fence subsequently sold the machine to someone who wanted to use it for, say, $100 to $150. That purchaser probably knew or suspected that the recorder had been stolen. It is highly likely, in economic terms, that the purchaser used this dictating machine at least as productively as its original owner. It may be true, however, that, generally speaking, stolen chattels are used less productively than those legitimately purchased; for the purchaser of the recorder may be hesitant to take it to the office and probably keeps it for his work at home, thus imposing on himself some restrictions on the full productivity of the chattel. Has IBM suffered? Certainly not; it is delighted. Has the insurance company suffered? We doubt that insurance rates are responsive to minor changes in the incidence of loss. In any event that is the business they are in; they seem to prosper and invest their money broadly in productive and useful enterprises so that there is no necessary economic loss to the community from a larcenous method of redistribution of property. It is a transfer cost. One can deplore the immorality of the seizure, but its economic consequences to the community are not necessarily harmful.

Some of the costs of this theft were generated by its being reported to the police and the consequent use of their time and manpower. The costs would be increased in the unlikely event of their catching the criminal and processing him through the criminal justice system to ultimate parole-discharge. This is not for a moment to suggest that the system should not be activated; it merely argues that the values leading us to use it are incapable of assessment solely in economic terms. What is sometimes called "the ultimate cost of crime" — a global total of national income as it would be if there were no crime — involves making so many cosmic assumptions that realistic economic analysis is impossible. To talk of the total cost of crime is even more absurd than to talk of the total volume of crime. But, as with the volume, so with the cost of crime: while the macrocosmic question is unanswerable, it is possible to ask and wise to seek answers to questions of more limited scope. We can ask and should seek answers to specific questions about public expenditures on law enforcement, the costs of the administration of justice and of the treatment of offenders. Such information is essential to national policy making. In regard to the assessment of victims' losses it would be pointless to calculate a total composed of such incommensurable items as death, insurance premiums, psychological injury, and the costs of medical care. But, here too, special research projects should be designed to obtain information about particular kinds of losses as a measure of the impact of crime on society; the sensible deployment of crime prevention and law enforcement resources depends upon the availability of such assessments.

The Victims of Crime

The brunt of crime in the United States, other than "white collar" or business crime, is borne by individual persons. Yet the victim of crime is largely ignored in most of the standard criminological texts. Police statistics relate principally to arrested offenders and include little about victims. Only in postprandial and political speeches is the plight of the victim mentioned; he has been grossly neglected both as a subject of study and as a class of person entitled to public aid.

Such research as has been done in this area indicates that the role of the victim is frequently crucial to the criminal act, not only in regard to the part he could have played in preventing it, but also because of the part he frequently plays in the act itself. Expressions like "victim proneness," "victim precipitation," and "victim instigation" have been used to refer to the fact that the victim is often a contributor to the act in varying degrees ranging from simple carelessness or negligence through to deliberate provocation.

Thus Marvin Wolfgang's *Patterns in Criminal Homicide*, based on the study of the records of the police homicide squad in Philadelphia over a five-year period, reveals that, of the 588 cases of criminal homicide which occurred during that period, 150 or 26 percent were victim precipitated in that the victim was a direct, positive precipitator of the crime by being the first to show and use a deadly weapon, to strike a blow in an altercation, or in other ways to make a physical assault. In such cases Wolfgang also found that the victim is more likely than the offender to have a previous record of assault. In short, in one out of every four criminal homicides the familiar stereotype of a weak passive victim facing a strong and brutal aggressor is wildly astray. Similarly, research on sex crimes and delinquencies carried out on behalf of the California legislature in the 1950s found that the child victims of adult sex offenders "are generally themselves willing or active participants" and not infrequently initiate the sexual relationship.

Another important finding of Wolfgang's study was that the greatest threat as a murderer is not the marauding stranger; only 12 percent of the murders were committed by strangers. In over two-thirds of the cases there was a preexisting close victim-offender relationship of a direct, personal, intimate character. His findings were subsequently supported by an English study made for the Home Office Research Unit by Evelyn Gibson and S. Klein. Their analytical survey of murders known to the police in England and Wales over a ten-year period revealed that for nearly 70 percent of women victims the murderer or suspect was either the husband, another relative, or a lover. Moreover, for about 75 percent of all child victims, the murderer or suspect was a parent or older relative. Wolfgang further found that 68 percent of females slain were killed in the home rather than outside. This suggests that both women and children have more to fear from whoever may be waiting for them at home than anyone they are likely to meet in the streets, however dark and ill-lit they may be.

Unfortunately relatively little is known about the relationships between victims and offenders in crimes other than homicide. Surveys made by the District of Columbia Crime Commission show that victim-offender relationships in rape and aggravated assault closely resemble those for homicide. Thus 81 percent of the aggravated assault victims were previously acquainted with their assailants, as were almost two-thirds of the rape victims.

Another source of public alarm about crime concerns the degree to which it involves interracial attacks. The President's Crime Commission found that assaultive crimes against the person other than homicide are overwhelmingly intraracial. The offender who attacks a white person is most likely to be white and Negroes are most likely to assault Negroes. In Chicago it was found that a Negro man runs the risk of being the victim of a crime against the person nearly six times as often as a white man; a Negro woman nearly eight times as often as a white woman. Thus, although Negro males account for two-thirds of all assaults, Negroes also constitute the vast majority of the victims of assault. We tested the prototypal interracial fear in the Chicago statistics for 1966: in that year two white women murdered Negro males, and no white woman was murdered by a Negro male!

Such information as is available about the relations between victims and offenders indicates that there are fewer alarming incursions by outsiders or strangers than is generally thought, and many more interactions between persons who are both racially homogeneous and related to or acquainted with one another. Yet exaggerated fear of victimization by strangers and decreased mutual trust lead to a widespread impoverishment of social life which represents a very real "cost of crime" to society. It is clearly necessary to collect more adequate data on victim-offender relationships, not only so that the public may be able to assess the nature of personal risks more accurately and realistically, but also so that appropriate measures of prevention and control may be initiated.

Compensation to Victims of Crime

If in some cases there may be some responsibility for the act on the part of the victim, in most the victim will have done nothing to precipitate the crime. And such innocent victims suffer losses which are rarely compensated in any way. The criminal law, except in rare instances, fails to ensure restitution to victims and often makes a civil remedy out of the question by incarcerating the offender. The idea of victim compensation is ancient, going back to the Law of Moses and the Code of Hammurabi; but in Western civilization, since the Middle Ages, the victim has had to rely on an illusory civil process which, because of the poor financial situation of the offender, usually proves inadequate. After trial and conviction the offender is rarely worth suing. His counsel may be, but not he. Recently, however, in New Zealand, Great Britain, California, Hawaii, Maryland, Massachusetts, New York, four (soon five) of the ten Provinces of Canada, and the State of New South Wales in Australia, victim compensation programs of various kinds have been established. All these programs have in common that they are confined to the compensation of victims of crimes of violence. The rationale of these programs takes the form either of an argument to the effect that the government, having failed to prevent crime and provide physical security for its citizens, should be responsible for compensating the victims of crimes it has failed to prevent; or alternatively of an appeal to the welfare principle that people incapacitated or in need through no fault of their own are entitled to public aid. Sometimes it is also argued that "growing interest in the reformation of the criminal is matched by decreasing care for the victim," and that the balance needs to be redressed by ensuring that equal or greater care be expended on the victims of criminals. It may be added here that the English penal reformer Margery Fry, to whose writings the present revival of interest in victim compensation is directly attributable, argued that the not unnatural desire of victims to have the offender "suffer by law" was a major obstacle to the rational treatment of offenders. And she maintained that the provision of restitution to victims would to some extent neutralize the demand for vengeance and thus diminish opposition to more positive and constructive penal methods.

None of these arguments is compelling. It is unreal to expect the government to prevent all crime, nor can it be regarded as having failed or being at fault for not doing so. Similarly, it cannot be assumed that the victims of crime are entitled to prior consideration among all those who suffer from inadvertent and fortuitous deprivations. Nor, despite its rhetorical appeal, should the argument that there is some injustice "in the expenditure of public funds for the benefit of 'bad' persons to the neglect of 'good' people" be allowed to pass. Governmental expenditures on the rehabilitation of criminals and on the compensation of their victims need independent justification as quite separate and different ways in which to use public funds. A sounder approach, it seems to us, is to recognize that crime is endemic in our society and that it is only proper for a society so organized that crime is endemic to share the burden which is by chance imposed on particular (unfortunate) individuals. The analogies with workmen's compensation and with compulsory third-party motor vehicle insurance are of some relevance; perhaps a closer analogue in this country is the extensive medical and social welfare provisions of the Veterans Administration legislation by which the community shares in the loss to the individual who has suffered for us from the external aggression of war. We should likewise share the loss to those who suffer for us from the internal aggression of crimes of personal violence.

It is also important that the compensation scheme should cover those injured in coming to the aid of a potential victim of a crime or assisting the police in the prevention of crime or making an arrest. Some have suggested that at least one factor in the reluctance of citizens to come to the aid of victims of crime or of the police is the realization that in the event of their being injured, disabled, or killed — however substantial a loss they may suffer — neither they nor their dependents will receive financial assistance or compensation for their loss. The case of

Kitty Genovese in New York in which thirty-eight people watched or listened for an extended period while a young woman was being repeatedly knifed immediately outside their apartment building was the occasion of a great deal of pious breast-beating, moralizing, and sermonizing about the callousness of contemporary society. There has never been a shortage either of such sermons or of callousness. What is required is that some practical steps be taken to ensure that those who do not hurry by on the other side of the road past the Kitty Genoveses and other victims of crimes, but render active assistance, are not alone made to bear a burden which is essentially a community responsibility.

In view of what we have said above about victim precipitation, it is clear that provisions for the reduction or elimination of compensation in the case of victims who have precipitated their own loss are necessary as are safeguards against fraudulent claims. All present compensation schemes incorporate such mechanisms. One difficult question which arises in this connection is whether compensation should be paid not only in respect of physical injury and its economic consequences but also for the "pain and suffering" attendant upon the injury. Our position is that we would not include such an element in our compensation scheme. We cannot bear the knife for the victim nor endure his pain; the limit of our collective responsibility seems to us to be the removal of the sharper pains of financial suffering from his physical suffering. And from his dependents. Let us take an example: Should there be compensation for "pain and suffering" in a rape case? Many of the present schemes include such compensation and some of the legislative debates make much of the woman's suffering and the appropriateness of financial recompense. One can agree with the suffering and yet properly raise the question whether compensation should be paid. If, of course, in the course of the rape she has suffered physical injury that requires hospitalization, obviously there should be compensation for these losses. It is also possible that she has physical or psychological trauma which will reduce her earning capacity in the future and these too would be compensable. Also, if she is married, there may be extra costs in the family for housekeeping and child care while she is receiving medical attention and these too should be reimbursed. But for the misery, pain, and degradation of the rape, we take the rather hard line that no compensation should be paid. Otherwise, we move into areas of assessment of suffering in which money is not a possible balance and in which any payment we make can only be of the heart balm or symbolic nature. When we move into that area we exaggerate the proper role of compensation schemes.

It is necessary to add a word about property crimes. Victims of crimes against property are commonly insured against such loss. Victims of crimes of violence, who are disproportionately poor, are but rarely insured. Nor are they in a position to enter into a privately financed insurance scheme. State compensation schemes are in effect state insurance schemes protecting victims of crimes of violence to the person.

In sum, from consolidated revenues we should ensure that those victims of crimes of violence who have not been the precipitants of their own suffering do not suffer *financially* as a result of the crime. If such schemes work without political criticism from either side and to the general satisfaction of the citizens of such relatively poor countries as New Zealand and the United Kingdom, arguments of impecuniosity should not preclude their adoption in this country.

The Causes of Crime

To speak of a cure for crime suggests an analogy with disease which like all analogies can be both illuminating and misleading. It is illuminating because it implies that crime, like disease, is not a unitary phenomenon, and thus no single explanatory theory applicable to all crimes is feasible any more than a single theory can be found to explain all diseases. One of the best definitions of crime is Lord Atkins's statement, "The domain of criminal jurisprudence can only be ascertained by examining what acts at any particular period are declared by the State to be crimes, and the only common nature they will be found to possess is that they are prohibited by the State and that those who commit them are punished."

Crime consists of a great variety of human acts which in many cases have little more in common than that they are violations of the criminal law. This has not always been clearly recognized and the search for *the* cause of criminality was still being assiduously pursued at the time Lord Atkins wrote, less than forty years ago. Today, however, it is generally thought to have been an illusory quest, not unlike the eighteenth-century chemists' search for the elusive hypothetical substance, phlogiston, believed to be the principle of fire and the cause of combustibility of all inflammable bodies. The essential point is that the concept of crime, like the concept of tort, is a legal concept. Indeed very frequently the same act is both a crime and a tort. Yet — and this is significant — there is scant literature on the causation of tort. No research projects have been conducted to search for the primary cause of tort. Apart from problems of traffic safety, no one inquires what social or psychological pathologies underlie the incidence of tort in our society. No one has suggested that those who commit torts are biologically inferior to their fellows. In the late 1930s, however, a great deal of money was spent on a research project at Harvard which reached the conclusion that "the primary cause of crime is biological inferiority." Although the procedures of that investigation have been criticized and its conclusions rejected, all the criticism has been directed at technical matters, such as the selection of control groups. It is like criticizing the alchemists who sought the "philosopher's stone" for having faulty research designs or defective laboratory equipment.

Equally, the search for *the causes* of crime is illusory, though recommended in some otherwise respectable criminological texts and pursued by many expensively outfitted criminological safaris. Shifts in the location of the causes of crime have varied with theoretical fashions in allied fields. Currently, psychiatric and sociological explanations have a wide following. Psychiatric theory tends to emphasize the emotional background and personality characteristics of the offender, while sociological theory stresses the role of group factors such as social norms, social roles, and urbanization. Psychiatric theories, based largely on individual case studies, have implications for the treatment of the individual offender, and they bulk large in presentencing reports. Sociological theories, being concerned with crime as a social phenomenon, have, on the other hand, more significance for social planning with regard to delinquency and crime control.

It is probably true that at this general level of abstraction there is a fair amount of information available about the factors associated with crime. These explanations, however, offer no guides concerning different responses to the same conditions. After all, by no means all children in "delinquency areas" do in fact become delinquents, officially labeled so at any rate, and few enter upon a life of crime. And although attempts have been made to relate general psychiatric and sociological explanations to the individual case and to explain how it comes about that certain children and adults in certain environments do in fact come to behave in an antisocial manner, none of them has been formulated in terms susceptible of empirical verification. An alternative and possibly more fruitful approach might be to ask how it is that certain individuals subject to those adverse sociological, psychological, or psychiatric pressures do not behave in an antisocial manner.

What many of these theories have in common is an acceptance of the view that most criminal behavior is learned in a particular social context and that it is not different in nature from other behavior; criminals and delinquents cannot be distinguished from noncriminals on the basis alone of their physical constitution, intelligence, or economic background. And although many different factors have been shown to be associated to a greater or lesser degree with crime, it has not proved possible to organize and integrate them in a causal theory of criminal behavior. This point is sometimes concealed by suggesting that the causes of crime are multifactorial or multifactorial-dynamic. But no matter what linguistic artifices are employed, the truth is there are no more causes of crime than there are causes of human behavior. Or, perhaps put more accurately, the causes of human behavior are the causes of crime.

It is sometimes suggested that on the basis of a sufficiently refined taxonomy we might hope to arrive at causal explanations of particular types of criminal behavior. An ingenious attempt to do something of this kind is Professor D. R. Cressey's study of embezzlement, *Other People's Money*, in which he takes a rigorously defined category of behavior and claims to provide an explanation of it. One critic has suggested that apparent universality is achieved "largely by formulating the explanation so that it can hardly fail to be true of all cases, rather like the fortune-teller's prediction that her client's life will be altered by a fair person of the opposite sex." In fact Cressey's "explanation" is a "definition" of a particular type of embezzlement, and although causal homogeneity is asserted the definition does not provide a basis for empirical prediction or provide any means of identifying embezzlers prior to embezzlement. Cressey's analysis instructs us about embezzlement but does not provide a causal explanation.

But to return to the analogy with disease: if the analogy is illuminating in some respects it can also be grossly misleading insofar as it suggests that crime in either its individual or epidemiological aspects is necessarily pathological or dysfunctional. Crime is human behavior which is in violation of the criminal law, but a large part of it is perfectly "normal" behavior both in the statistical sense and in the sense that it occurs naturally. This is not to say, as some sociologists seem to suggest, that all criminal behavior is a normal response to a bad environment, or that persistent serious criminality may not be related to psychopathy or neurosis. But the truth is that almost all adults have at some time in their lives committed criminal acts and it is those who have not who are abnormal. Almost all the acts which are defined as criminal in our society have at some time in some society been tolerated and even socially approved. The line between legitimate and illegitimate means of acquiring property is both arbitrary and difficult to define precisely. There are wide differences between states in regard to what sexual behavior is criminal, and considerable variation in the same state at different historical periods. There is no evidence that the bulk of criminal behavior is the result of some pathological mental or somatic condition which distinguishes criminals in general from noncriminals. It has, of course, been suggested that some loosely defined psychopathology can in every case be inferred from the criminal behavior for which it is then proffered as an explanation — an interesting example of vacuous circularity.

In much the same way it is often asserted that crime is a symptom of social disorganization or an indication of some kind of social pathology. From this perspective crime can be viewed as serving the social function of indicating the existence of social maladjustment. This is very similar to Emile Durkheim's theory of "anomie" (or normlessness). Durkheim argued that some forms of crime are the product of rapid social change and its attendant breakdown of traditional means of social regulation. But Durkheim was speaking here of periods when crime rates were exceptionally high and his name is also associated with the rather different and in a sense antithetical view that crime should be regarded as functional insofar as it is a dynamic factor which contributes to or is at least an essential feature of the development of society. In this view crime is not abnormal but a normal part of society "bound up," as Durkheim put it, "with the fundamental conditions of all social life and by that very fact it is *useful*." It might be possible to abolish crime, but the kind of stringent and ruthless control this would require would make society so rigidly inflexible that change and progress would be impossible. A contemporary of Durkheim, Gabriel Tarde, independently asserted that crime is the price we pay for "our enlightenment and our discoveries." This view is by no means as paradoxical as it might appear at first sight.

One of the authors of this book was at one time director of the United Nations Asia and Far East Institute for the Prevention of Crime and Treatment of Offenders in Tokyo. In that position he was occasionally questioned by trainees from rather backward Asian countries with low delinquency rates, who, seeing signs of increasing delinquency rates in their countries, wished his advice on how this trend might be inhibited. He found the answer not difficult. He urged them to ensure that their people remained ignorant, bigoted, and illeducated; that on no account should they develop substantial industries; that communications systems should be primitive; and that their transportation systems should be such as to ensure that most of the citizens lived within their own small, isolated villages for their entire lives. He stressed the importance of making sure their educational systems did not promise a potential level of achievement for a child beyond that which his father had already achieved. If it was once suggested that a child should be able to grow to the limit of his capacity rather than to the ceiling of his father's achievement, he pointed out, the seeds of the gravest disorder would be laid. He stressed the universal human experience that village societies are entirely capable of maintaining any discordance or human nonconformity within their own social frameworks and never need to call on centralized authority to solve their problems. He would take time to sketch, with a wealth of detail, the horrors of increased delinquency and crime that would flow from any serious attempt to industrialize, urbanize, or educate their communities. He would conclude with a peroration against the establishment of an international airline.

This advice was ironical, but only because it reflected the irony of history. The evidence is substantial that social, industrial, and commercial progress is accompanied by an increase in criminal activity. For as you expand the bounds of human freedom and economic and social potential, you equally expand the bounds of potentiality for nonconformity and delinquency and crime. As legitimate opportunities increase so also do illegitimate opportunities. As our economic insights now stand, industrialization seems to carry with it urbanization, which in turn carries with it the anonymity, isolation, frustration, discontent, and the enormous criminogenic potential of the city. Therefore, for the dictator of an Asian country or an African country south of the Sahara, it might well be a wise policy decision to set a course of action knowing that it would increase juvenile delinquency and crime. He would of course count the cost of applying resources toward the minimization of juvenile delinquency and crime and their more effective treatment. In this sense juvenile delinquency and crime are functional and not dysfunctional; they are, at the present level of our knowledge, costs that must be paid for other socially valuable development processes in the community.

This is not at all to say that we should not use our best endeavors to reduce crime and delinquency so far as we can. It is only to say that we should realize that they are, at least in part, inevitable concomitants of other desirable social developments. In short, the pain and distress associated with crime should be seen not so much as symptomatic of disease but rather as growing pains.

It might be suggested that even if this perspective is valid it is useless for the purpose of understanding and controlling criminal behavior, that what we need is more research into causation to determine the etiology of particular criminal behaviors and patterns of behavior, for ignorance about causation must inevitably result in impotence in relation to control or treatment. Thus Lady Wootton has argued that if science could establish the causes of crime "we should be well on the way to a world in which criminality and near-criminality behavior no longer presented any problem." But unfortunately it is not true that knowledge of causes invariably implies a corresponding ability to control or prevent. Moreover, there are a number of other reasons for thinking that to mount yet another costly safari to search for the source or sources of criminality would be a wasteful expenditure of scarce resources, and it may be well to enumerate these reasons.

In the first place, specifically criminological research into the causation of crime is unlikely to achieve significant results. This raises the question, Who is the criminologist? The answer is simple: He doesn't exist. Some day he may exist, but not yet; not until the disciplines of biology, neurology, psychiatry, psychology, anthropology, sociology, statistics, penology, and a group of attendant specialties are far more developed than they are today, and not until a catholic human mind emerges capable of synthesizing them sufficiently to focus them on the many problems of crime and its treatment. He will also have to be a competent criminal lawyer. For the time being the title "criminologist" is freely applied to one trained in any of the above disciplines who turns his attention toward the many problems of crime, its treatment and prevention, and who seeks to make use of some of the information and skills of any of the other disciplines. "Criminologist" thus encompasses persons of widely diverse training and interests, their only common denominator being an interest in acquiring understanding of various aspects of the phenomenon of crime.

There is no reason at all to think that criminologists will proceed more expeditiously than those disciplines on which they depend for an understanding of human behavior. Criminology is a dependent discipline, gaining its insights from other social and behavioral sciences and investigating one aspect of human behavior whose significant defining characteristic is the introjection of legal sanctions into the area of human behavior. It seems to us unlikely that the criminologist will gain psychological insights in advance of those developed by the discipline of psychology or that he will understand social developments or the role of the citizen in social processes better than the sociologist.

Second, such investigations as have been carried out have established that a variety of adverse background factors correlate positively with criminality. Such factors as unemployment, bad housing conditions, disrupted families, and lack of education have all been found to be correlated with delinquency rates. It seems abundantly well established, particularly by the Chicago ecological school of criminological research, the distinguished work of Shaw and McKay and their followers, that the inner city and the interstitial areas of the city which are changing their character from residential to industrial or maintaining an uneasy balance between the two are disproportionately productive of crime and delinquency. Likewise, it seems abundantly established by Bowlby and his many followers that children from affectionless and disrupted homes are disproportionately involved in crime and delinquency.

But here two observations are pertinent. In the first place Shaw and McKay did not assert that the slums were directly productive of delinquency, and the evidence of rehousing operations in postwar Britain does not bear out the assumption that the nature of the immediate environment is a major factor in promoting delinquency. Similarly, the conclusions of Bowlby's pioneer investigation, *Forty-four Juvenile Thieves,* have been enormously modified by subsequent research and no one believes that deficiencies in parental care necessarily lead to delinquency. Our second point is this. We have never regarded poor educational facilities, unemployment, broken homes, slums, poverty, or grossly adverse social conditions of any kind as desirable features of our society. We wish to get rid of slums, not particularly because they are productive of delinquency and crime, but because we think they are a despicable way for people to have to live. We wish to facilitate happy and stable family lives not because we wish to reduce delinquency but because, all in all, we think that is the better way for people to live. In brief, the insights that we have gained from criminological research into the causes of crime and delinquency have not led us to want to do anything that we wouldn't have wished to achieve without such insights.

A public health analogy is appropriate here. Just as the provision of pure water has proved to be the great public health measure, so the elimination of social adversities and handicaps is likely to prove preventive of at least some forms of crime and delinquency. But just as many persons have survived the hazard of drinking impure water, and some continue to fall sick despite its removal, so many persons have suffered adverse social conditions without becoming criminal, and crime will continue after the elimination of those conditions.

In the third place, just as the understanding of causation does not entail a corollary capacity for control, so the control of phenomena is not always dependent upon the prior understanding of causation. Treatment cannot wait on the identification of causes. It is a vulgar error to assume that one needs to understand the etiology of a social condition before it can be controlled. In the field of mental health, treatment skills have far outdistanced etiological understanding, and diagnosis is related more to the prediction of the course and the most effective treatment of a condition than to its causation. The history of medicine is full of instances of the successful development and utilization of treatment and preventive methods which worked (e.g., lime juice for scurvy, quinine for malaria) long before the real nature of the illness involved was understood.

Fourth — and underlying our whole approach to this topic — we are convinced that attempts to fit all the phenomena of crime into a Procrustean cause/effect framework are fundamentally misconceived. The use of the mechanical model derived from physical science in the behavioral and social sciences has in general proved notoriously unfruitful. We do not believe that this is because the type of causation involved is peculiarly complex (i.e., the multifactorial approach) but rather because the application of causal analysis in this field usually involves the same sort of logical error as the anthropocentric interpretation of animal behavior. The conceptual scheme does not fit the facts of experience. This is the basic reason for our refusal to commit scarce resources to this type of research.

A final point on etiology. It may be thought that this prejudice against etiological studies would also embrace opposition to an effort to understand the origins and precipitants of criminal or delinquent behavior in any individual case. This does not follow at all. It is perfectly rational to eschew overreaching etiological studies and yet to insist on the wisdom of the most careful efforts to understand the background of any individual example of criminal and delinquent behavior before seeking to react to that individual case. It should be manifestly clear from what has been said earlier in this chapter that our ukase against etiological research does not preclude support for other types of research in this area. As stated, we will enthusiastically support research studies evaluative of the effects of our prevention and control programs. Indeed, that is specifically provided for in the decree.

We will also support studies of individual cases with a view to deciding on their best disposition; and we will urge that the treasury give the most considerate attention to applications from departments of sociology, psychology, psychiatry, anthropology, and genetics when they are applying for research funds for studying human behavior other than specifically human criminal or delinquent behavior, so defined. The provision of funds or support of any kind for the pursuit of criminology's cherished ignis fatuus, "the causes of crime," will, however, be strictly proscribed.

3

From Murder and
from Violence,
Good Lord, Deliver Us

In a metaphorical sense all crimes are violent and all criminals are violent criminals. They do violence to our persons or our property, to our principles or our sense of propriety, or to peace and public order. There is an element of aggression in most criminal acts. But it is customary to regard certain offenses involving the exercise of physical force or the threat of physical force in order to intimidate as belonging to a special category of "crimes of violence." And, as the litany gracefully reveals, it is this sort of crime which is the most menacing element in the public's fear of crime and criminals. "The crimes that concern Americans the most," says the report of the President's Commission on Crime, "are those that affect their personal safety — at home, at work, or in the streets." It is those crimes with which we deal in this chapter.

We are not here directly concerned with the larger problem of collective violence — war, riots, disorderly demonstrations, and the like. It is true, of course, that insofar as riots are the sum of thousands of individual acts of murder, assault, arson, theft, and vandalism they represent a part of the crime problem. But they represent much more than that, as the report of the National Advisory Commission on Civil Disorders (the Kerner Commission) makes abundantly clear. And the sort of analysis and evaluation of the findings on riots which would be required for an adequate treatment of that problem would take us far beyond the scope of this book. We therefore draw a somewhat arbitrary distinction between political or ideological violence, as exemplified in war, social conflicts, labor riots, student unrest, lynch mobs, and other forms of collective violence, and individual forms of criminal violence, such as willful homicide, rape, aggravated assault, and armed robbery. It is the latter category with which we are here concerned, although we shall also refer to one other kind of criminal behavior which results in even greater carnage — drunken driving.

We should perhaps add here also that we do not intend to contribute to the discussion of the question whether there is in American society and culture a distinctive element of violence peculiar to this country. But we would like to cite without comment the answer that a recent young applicant for United States government employment, asked to fill out Form 57, reportedly gave to the question, "Do you favor the overthrow of the Government by force, subversion, or violence?" Thinking it a multiple-choice question, he wrote "violence."

Incidence of Crimes of Violence

Of the seven index crimes in the Uniform Crime Reports, four are crimes of personal violence — murder, aggravated assault, rape, and robbery. They account for about 13 percent of all the index crimes in the country. The remaining three index crimes are burglary, larceny of $50 or more, and auto theft; these crimes against property make up the remaining 87 percent of serious crime. Nevertheless, the former clearly occasion more fear and disquiet than the latter; they are a far greater threat to human well-being and to social stability. These figures do not sufficiently sketch the dimensions of the problem of murder, violence, and sudden death in this country; nor, as we saw in chapter 2, are these data easy to assess precisely; but let us reflect for a while on the dimensions of the problem before we offer our remedies for it.

Murder and Non-Negligent Manslaughter

In the Uniform Crime Reports the heading "Murder and Non-Negligent Manslaughter" covers all intentional criminal killings and refers to "crimes known to the police," not to the prosecutorial and judicial disposition of those cases. It was not until 1949 that data on these crimes were published in the UCRs; in that year the rate per 100,000 for 1948 was stated to be 5.2. The 1967 rate per 100,000 was 6.1, the 1968 rate 6.8. In the intervening years the figure dropped to 4.0 in 1957, the average rate over the whole period being 4.9 per 100,000.

Thus recent willful homicide figures show an upturn. What is not well known, is that they are appreciably lower than the figures for the mid-thirties. The President's Commission analyzed some of the earlier unpublished figures held by the UCR section of the FBI and concluded that "the wilful homicide rate has decreased somewhat to about 70 percent of its high in 1933." Looking further back to the 1870s and the late 1890s it seems clear that rates of murder, non-negligent homicide, rape, and assault have all appreciably declined with the passage of time.

The hysteria in the press and on television about murder rates is thus historically unfounded; but again, in order not to be misunderstood, we must add: There is far too much avoidable willful homicide — and we shall show how to reduce it.

Two other dimensions of the problems of willful homicide merit mention at this stage of assessing our task. First, studies here and in the United Kingdom reveal that most murders are committed by relatives by blood or marriage of the victim or by persons well-acquainted with the victim. Taken together, murders involving spouse killing spouse, parent killing child, other family killings, romantic triangles and lovers' quarrels, and arguments between those previously acquainted with one another account for about 80 percent of all homicides in America. You are safer on the streets than at home; safer with a stranger than with a friend or relative. More speculatively, the victims of homicide have more in common, are a more homogeneous group for study, than the killers. Murder is the most "normal" of crimes.

A second important dimension of murder in America is the fact that around 65 percent of these crimes result from the use of a firearm. A further 19 percent are the product of cutting and stabbing weapons. The remaining 16 percent are attributable to the use of hands, fists, feet, hammers, clubs, poison, fire, explosives, automobiles, and knitting needles. A comparison with the figures for the United Kingdom reveals an interesting contrast. There, murder by shooting accounts for only 9.8 percent of the total, and what are called "sharp instruments" were used in only 16.8 percent of cases. In the United Kingdom the commonest method is an attack either with a blunt instrument or without a weapon; shooting is the least common method. It should also be added that the homicide rates in the two countries differ considerably. Figures published by the United Nations reveal that the homicide rate in the United States is about seven or eight times that of the United Kingdom; and the United States far outpaces all other industrialized nations. Direct comparisons of this kind must of course be regarded with some reservations because of differences in the definition of crimes and in reporting practices, and differences in cultures. Nevertheless, the most recent reported comparison between countries in relation to rates of homicide by gunfire indicates that, out of the fifteen countries reporting, the United States ranked first. The present American gunfire homicide rate is 2.7 per 100,000; that of the Netherlands, 0.03; Japan, 0.04; West Germany, 0.12; Canada, 0.52; and the United Kingdom, 0.05. To the student of criminal statistics, the United States may or may not be the land of the free, but it is certainly the home of the brave.

Aggravated Assault

The line between willful homicide and aggravated assault is uncertain; other than in terms of the outcome of violence. The speed of the ambulance, the competence of the surgeon, and the fortuitous point of impact of the missile or weapon do more to distinguish between these crimes than does any analysis of states of mind of the assailants. As defined by the UCRs aggravated assault includes assault with intent to kill or to inflict serious bodily injury, whether or not a dangerous weapon is used. It includes all cases of attempted homicide but excludes cases in which bodily injury is inflicted in the course of robbery or rape, which have their own index crime rubrics. The offender-victim pattern of aggravated assaults closely resembles that of willful homicide; as the 1968 UCR states: "Most aggravated assaults occur within the family unit or among neighbors or acquaintances. The victim and offender relationship, as well as the very nature of the attack makes this crime similar to murder." Other similarities are the fact that for both crimes Negro males are disproportionately involved; summer months account for a greater proportion of both crimes; both occur most frequently in the late evening and early morning hours of Saturday. In both cases also the police clear-up rate is high. In 1968, 86 percent of criminal homicides were solved, as were 66 percent of aggravated assaults.

In contrast to the relative constancy of the homicide rate, the aggravated assault rate has increased from 84.7 per 100,000 in 1960 to 141 per 100,000 in 1968, an increase of 66 percent. (This, incidentally, is considerably less than the recorded increases in index property offenses which were, over the same period, larceny 151 percent and auto theft 139 percent.) In view of the similarity in the patterns of criminal homicide and aggravated assault the discrepancy in the trends between the two suggests that other factors besides a real growth in the amount of crime be responsible for the marked discrepancy. In this connection a recent analysis of the UCR data on aggressive crimes by Dr. R. H. Beattie and Dr. J. P. Kenney, a statistician and a political scientist respectively, states:

> Aggravated assault reports include a substantial
> number of instances in which a serious assault occurs,
> but in which the persons involved were members
> of the family, bar companions and the like. Such
> assaults are not indicative of a general danger to the
> public. It is suggested that the marked increase in
> the number of aggravated assaults is probably due
> more to greater coverage of the kind of instances

mentioned than to an increase in the number
of unprovoked assaults.

Also, these increases in the rate of aggravated assault may in part
reflect a more empathic approach to human suffering — a larger sense
of social responsibility may well have led to more frequent reporting
of serious assaults to the police, particularly in the depressed inner-
city areas. Other factors liable to give rise to increased recording of
this type of crime include increased reporting by doctors and hospitals,
the growth in medical and hospital treatment facilities, and the greater
population coverage by medical insurance plans such as Blue Cross
which would be likely to step up hospital admissions and recourse to
medical treatment. Still only a minority of such assaults, even with
knives, are reported; but the proportion may well be increasing.

Another respect in which there is considerable variance between
criminal homicide and aggravated assault relates to the weapons most
often used. Thus, in 1968 about one of each five, 23 percent to be precise, of the serious assaults were committed with the use of a firearm
as opposed to 65 percent in cases of homicide, whereas a knife or other
cutting instrument was used in 31 percent of these assaults as opposed
to 19 percent in homicide cases. Twenty-two percent of these assaults
were committed with hands, fists, and feet, as opposed to only 8 percent of the homicides. It seems likely, however, that these differences
largely reflect the differential lethal efficiency of the various modes of
attack and weapons employed, a point we shall return to later.

Robbery

By the UCR definition, robbery involves stealing or taking anything
of value from the person of another by the use or threat of force. The
figures include assaults to rob and attempts to rob, the breakdown
between completed and inchoate crimes not being given. Nor are
there data on the frequency of actual injury. Unlike murder and aggravated assault, robbery does not usually involve a prior victim-
offender relationship, though such relationships are not exceptional.
Thus an intensive study, titled *Robbery in London*, carried out by the
Cambridge Institute of Criminology reveals that approximately 20 percent of the robberies studied involved some prior relationship.

Robbery appears to have increased, absolutely and as a rate, in
recent years. The President's Crime Commission reported that "robbery has fluctuated from a high in 1933 and a low during World

War II to a point where it is now about 20 percent above the beginning of the postwar era." It should be noted, however, that the rate is still 30 percent below the 1933 peak — a fact which would not be apparent to any newspaper reader or to the most careful analyst of the published Uniform Crime Reports. A sense of proportion might be better preserved and a consequent reduction in exaggerated fears produced if figures such as these, revealing long-term perspectives, were given more publicity and if journalistic alarms over short-term increases were given less. It is not without significance that in the mass media presentation of crime news, crimes of personal violence which, as we have pointed out above, account for only 13 percent of the total index crime in the country, get 90 percent of the crime news space and time. Over half of all robberies reported are street robberies, and the highest robbery rates are in the large cities, where they are thirty times as high as in the rural sections of the country. For crime-reporting purposes, data on robbery are collected for armed robbery, where a weapon is used, and strong-arm robbery, where no weapon is employed. In 1967, as in 1966 and in 1965, of robbery offenses 58 percent were armed robberies; in 1968, armed robberies made up 60 percent of all robberies. Sixty-three percent of reported armed robberies were committed by means of firearms. Our ukases on guns will tend strongly to a reduction of this crime.

Forcible Rape

Forcible rape is the carnal knowledge of a female against her will, through force or the threat of force. A District of Columbia Crime Commission survey found that about 25 percent of all rape victims were attacked with dangerous weapons. It should be noted that the UCR total for this offense also includes attempted rapes, which make up about one-third of the total. Together, forcible rapes and attempted rapes account for less than 1 percent of all crime index offenses and a little over 5 percent of index crimes of violence. Forcible rape appears to have shown a steady increase year by year and the rate or number of offenses per 100,000 of population tripled during the 1933–65 period. During the period 1960–68 the rate increased 84 percent.

It is very difficult to know what significance to attach to these figures. Thus the victim survey conducted by the National Opinion Research Center of the University of Chicago for the President's Crime Commission shows the rate of forcible rape reported to the NORC to be three and a half times the UCR rate. And the 1968 UCR says that "of all the Crime Index offenses, law enforcement administrators recognize that this offense is probably the most underreported crime due primarily to fear and/or embarrassment on the part of the victims." Yet at the same time the UCR points out that "18 percent of all reported forcible rapes reported to police were determined by investigation to be unfounded." This somewhat discrepant finding suggests that "fear and/or embarrassment" about matters of this kind are by no means universal.

With forcible rape, as with murder, it is not the marauding stranger who poses the greatest threat. National statistics are not available on relationships between victims and offenders in regard to rape, but the District of Columbia Crime Commission conducted a survey which revealed that victim-offender relationships in forcible rape closely resemble those for murder:

> Almost two-thirds of the 151 [rape] victims surveyed were attacked by persons with whom they were at least casually acquainted. Only 36 percent of the 224 assailants about whom some identifying information was obtained were complete strangers to their victims; 16 (7 percent) of the attackers were known to the victim by sight, although there had been no previous contact. Thirty-one (14 percent) of the 224 assailants were relatives, family friends or boy friends of the victims, and 88 (39 percent) were either acquaintances or neighbors.

Violence and Index Crimes

In summing up the available evidence regarding the crimes of violence considered above, the President's Commission report says that "on the average the likelihood of a serious personal attack on any American in a given year is about 1 in 550." The risk of injury serious enough to require any hospitalization is about 1 in 3,000; the risk of death from willful homicide is 1 in 20,000. These risks are by no means uniform, being much greater for slum dwellers and much less in the middle-class suburbs and prosperous countryside. But perhaps the most striking overall finding is that the risk of serious attack from strangers on the street is only half as great as the risk of such attacks from spouses, family members, friends, or acquaintances; moreover, the closer the relationship the greater the hazard.

We now move to consider a crime inflicting death and injury where the class bias is reversed, where the privileged are disproportionately involved.

Drunken Driving

The totals for motor vehicle deaths and injuries involving criminal behavior greatly exceed the totals for murders and assaults. In 1968 there were nearly 53,000 traffic fatalities in the United States; negligent manslaughter, which is largely a traffic offense, accounted for more than 7,500 of these traffic deaths. But studies in Michigan, California, and elsewhere have found that 65 percent of those responsible for fatal motor vehicle accidents had been drinking shortly before the impact and as many as 40 percent could be diagnosed as drunk.

A recent report issued by the National Traffic Safety Bureau of the Department of Transportation attributes some 25,000 highway deaths a year to alcoholic imbibing by either the driver of a vehicle involved in a fatal accident or a pedestrian who was struck by a car. In addition, it is said that some 800,000 of the 14 million vehicular accidents large and small that occur annually are due in some measure to drinking. The report also emphasizes that a substantial proportion of the most serious accidents involved a disproportionately small number of drivers who also are alcoholics or problem drinkers.

At least half of all the single vehicle mishaps in which the driver died and almost half the fatal multiple vehicle accidents were found to be the responsibility of the 1 to 4 percent of American drivers who are heavy drinkers. In addition to the 25,000 highway deaths it has also been estimated by the National Safety Council that drinking is a factor in regard to some 266,000 nonfatal injuries sustained. These figures may be contrasted with the 1968 willful killing total of 13,650 and an aggravated assault total of 282,400. If these estimates are accurate, then the offenses of negligent manslaughter and driving under the influence are clearly grossly underreported, for in 1968 only 3,144 persons were arrested for the former and 307,231 for the latter offense.

An English criminologist, Nigel Walker, has observed that the "antisocial use of vehicles is a much more important source of death bereavement, physical suffering and disablement than any intentional forms of violence." Yet both in the United States and the United Kingdom the penal system treats dangerous motoring offenses far less seriously than other crimes of violence. Neither in respect of the degree of selfishness involved nor in terms of the amount of harm done can the former be regarded as morally less blameworthy than the latter. Moreover, insofar as we see it as one of the principal functions of the criminal law to protect citizens from wanton harm inflicted by others, we do not propose to adopt an oblique approach but to deal with this matter directly as one of prime and urgent social importance.

Murder, violence, and sudden death are not of transient significance. They are of substantial number and the cause of even more substantial fear. It is unlikely that we could offer a program to diminish man's aggressions, his jealousies, greed, and selfishness, which underlie violent crime. Nor shall we try. Our task is of lesser reach but of immediate promise in reducing the lethal impact of those motive forces. It strikes not at the reform of man but rather at a modification of his environment which will reduce the suffering he inflicts on his brother.

Here are our ukases:

Guns
1. All firearms — handguns, rifles, and shotguns — must be registered and all persons required to obtain a license to possess or carry any such weapon. The license will cover only a particular identified weapon; the license must be renewed annually. Other than in exceptional cases, a license to possesse a handgun will be restricted to the police and to authorized security agencies. Licenses for rifles and shotguns will also be restrictively granted. Gun clubs, hunting clubs, and similar sporting associations using firearms will be required to store the firearms used by their members on club premises and to maintain close security over them.

2. Mail-order sales of firearms other than to firearms dealers shall be prohibited. Firearms dealers and the manufacturers of all guns and ammunition must be licensed by the federal Department of Justice; their license fee shall be sufficient to exclude dealing or manufacture for personal use. Firearms dealers and manufacturers of arms and ammunition shall be required to keep detailed records of their sales and manufacturers, which shall be made available to police and security officers on demand.

3. Any person who uses or attempts to use a firearm or imitation firearm in order to resist arrest or the arrest of another shall be punishable with imprisonment of up to ten years in addition to the punishment imposed for the offense (if any) for which he was being arrested.

4. Any person who at the time of committing or being arrested for any criminal offense has in his possession a firearm

or imitation firearm shall be punishable with imprisonment of up to five years in addition to the punishment imposed for the offense committed or for which he was arrested, unless he can show that his possession of the weapon was for a lawful purpose.

5. The possession of military weapons — machine guns, mortars, siege guns, flamethrowers, mines, antitank guns, and similar hardware — other than by the armed forces of the government, shall be prohibited.

Knives and Offensive Weapons

6. The possession of switchblade or gravity knives (also known as "spring blades," "swing backs," "snap" and "flick" knives) shall be prohibited.

Drunken Driving

7. Any person driving or attempting to drive a motor vehicle on a road or other public place having consumed alcohol in such quantity that the proportion in his blood exceeds 80 mg per 100 ml (0.08 percent) will be liable to a maximum penalty, in respect of his first such offense, of twelve months' disqualification from driving; second and subsequent such offenses, five years. A police officer in uniform may require a driver to provide a specimen of breath for a "breathalyzer" test, if he has reasonable cause to believe (*a*) that the driver has alcohol in his body, or (*b*) that the driver has committed a moving traffic offense, or (*c*) that the driver has been involved in an accident. If the breathalyzer test indicates that the driver is probably above the legal limit of ingested alcohol, he may be arrested and taken to the police station where he may be required to provide a specimen of blood or urine for laboratory analysis.

Capital Punishment

8. Capital punishment for all crimes, civil and military, shall be abolished.

Guns

Our five ukases on guns are designed for domestic disarmament. The task is prodigious. It may take a decade. Hence the need for a prompt beginning. And our program is further designed to use the general deterrent force of severe penal sanctions to inhibit the use of a gun in resisting arrest or committing a crime.

The best estimate of the number of guns in private hands in this country is ninety million; but guesses supported by some data range from fifty million to two hundred million. Each year an additional three million guns are purchased, and very few older guns become unusable. Nor does this massive weaponry lie idle. In 1968, by means of guns there were committed 8,870 murders, 64,950 aggravated assaults, and 99,000 armed robberies. Guns were also used in that year in over 10,000 suicides and in over 2,500 "accidental" deaths. The estimated total of nonfatal gun injuries was 100,000. Guns were used as the murder weapon in 96 percent of the 475 killings of policemen during the period 1960–68. Moreover, since the beginning of this century some three-quarters of a million people have been killed in the United States by privately owned guns, 30 percent more than in all the wars in which this country has been involved in its entire history. In sum and in short, the populace is armed with a dangerous weapon.

Yet it is a curious paradox that while the possession of a relatively innocuous drug whose potential for harm, if it exists, is limited to those who take it voluntarily is a criminal offense subject to draconian penalties, the possession of guns is subject to scarcely any control in most states. At last the federal government has moved to restrict the mail order of handguns, and later of rifles and shotguns; at last, through the sacrifice of some of our best, there is some opposition to the lobbying power of the National Rifle Association, but it is an ambivalent and toothless legislative pattern to be observed at the federal, state, and local levels. Argument is pursued concerning the obvious — should a minor, a convicted criminal, one who is mentally ill, an alcoholic, or a drug addict have the right to possess a gun? Our edicts do not fuss with such trivialities. Negative licensing of guns without sporting purposes, excluding a few defined categories from the right to possess a firearm, is an excessively cautious, only marginally useful mechanism, other than as a wedge to more rational legislation. We seek a disarmed populace. We are confident this offends no constitutional sanctity; we do not oppose a militia whose right to bear arms is guaranteed by the Constitution. Disarmament of the rest of us, unless we can show good cause to have a gun, must rest on positive or inclusive licensing. To say, all may have a gun except . . . , misses the point. What must be legislatively said is, none may have a gun unless . . .

Our ukases rest on the belief, for which there is strong empirical evidence, that the fewer death-dealing weapons there are in the community the fewer deaths will be dealt. Homicide or the killing of one human being by another, aggravated assault or "attempted murder" or "assault with intent to do great bodily harm," like many other human activities, would be likely to be less thoroughly and extensively pursued to the degree that the availability of the more potent and effective means of carrying them out is restricted.

Some have suggested that reducing the number of available guns would not reduce the rate of criminal homicide or the nature or amount of bodily harm done. They argue, if a gun were not available the aggressor would select another weapon to achieve his destructive or injurious goal. Guns don't kill, men do. And they add, potential criminals will not comply with gun regulations; you will disarm the virtuous and leave them prey to the armed criminal.

These arguments, wrongheaded though they may be, resound so freely that they must be manifestly repudiated if our legislative edicts are to be accepted. They rest on assumptions about the dangerousness of firearms as contrasted with other weapons and about the nature of "aggressors" and "potential criminals" in cases of homicide and aggravated assault which are denied by the available evidence. These assumptions are that equally dangerous alternative weapons are readily available, and that potential criminals in these cases are the sort of persons who would either avail themselves of the alternative weapons and kill with them or would not comply with whatever regulations were enacted, and therefore their homicidal or assaultive intentions and actions would not be affected.

In fact the most frequently used alternative weapon to a firearm in assault situations is a "knife or other cutting instrument," which was in 1968 employed in 19 percent of all homicides and 31 percent of all aggravated assaults. Yet if we compare fatality rates for firearms and knives in serious assault situations on the basis of the UCR figures we find that whereas 13 percent of assaults with firearms were fatal, only 3 percent of knife assaults resulted in the death of the victim. For the next most frequent type of serious assault after knife assaults, that involving the use of hands, fists, and feet, the fatality rate is only 1.7 percent.

These figures bear out what might be expected in the light of the greater range, potency, and functionality of firearms in conflict situations. The use of a gun does not require physical contact with the victim and therefore provides less opportunity for self-defense than the alternatives. Moreover, the use of a gun requires considerably less strength, agility, and skill than does the use of a knife.

It might be argued that such facts as these suggest that a gun would be more likely to be selected as a weapon in cases where an attack was seriously intended to produce death or great bodily harm. Hence, the differential fatality rates are in part due to the fact that more gun attacks are seriously intended than is the case with knives or hands, fists, and feet. But the available evidence shows that there is great homogeneity in the pattern of most homicide and aggravated assault cases in respect of such variables as time of occurrence, location, situational context, offender-victim relationship, and prior arrest records. The major difference between the two lies in the fact that a firearm is more common in homicides while a knife is more common in assaults; this fact, in the absence of evidence that firearm attacks are generally more seriously intended than knife or other types of attacks, may be attributed to the greater lethal potential of the gun. Moreover, with regard to the relative seriousness or earnestness of gun and knife attacks respectively, a recent investigation of physical patterns of knife and gun wounding in Chicago suggests that roughly the same proportion of each is seriously intended, and so the differential fatality rates cannot be attributed to variance of intent.

As to the nature of the aggressors or potential criminals in homicide or aggressive assault cases, the evidence indicates that they are usually not persons engaged in predetermined homicidal attacks but rather participants in family quarrels, domestic disputes, arguments between acquaintances, altercations, brawls, clashes of personality. While these disturbances precipitate violence, they neither require a death for their resolution nor usually result in fatal consequences for those involved. Even in known felony murders (killings resulting from robberies, murders of police, official gangland slayings, and other felonious activities), which average only around 13 or 14 percent of all murders, it cannot be assumed that a desire to kill was present in all or even a majority of cases.

And it is most implausible to assume that the individuals involved in the majority of murder cases are persons so determined to kill that in the absence of guns they will either seek to achieve that purpose with any available alternative or deliberately evade whatever restrictive gun legislation may be enacted. The truth seems to be as Marvin Wolfgang and Franco Ferracuti put it in *The Subculture of Violence* that "the handy gun has usually become the method of impulse, the vehicle of violence." Without the vehicle there is every reason to expect the violence to be both less lethal and less injurious. Wolfgang and

Ferracuti cite in this connection an article by Robert Coles which appeared in the *New Republic* in 1966:

> Every psychiatrist has treated patients who were thankful that guns were not around at one time or another in their lives. Temper tantrums, fits, seizures, hysterical episodes all make the presence of guns an additional and possibly mortal danger. . . . We cannot prevent insanity in adults or violent and delinquent urges in many children by curbing guns, but we can certainly make the translation of crazy or vicious impulses into pulled triggers less likely and less possible.

It was the view of the President's Crime Commission that within this country "a higher proportion of homicides are committed with firearms in those areas where firearms regulations are lax than in those areas where there are more stringent controls." This is so, despite the great difficulty of controlling the massive interstate flow of guns. And international comparisons support this correlation. Though Manhattan, under the Sullivan Law, has the strictest gun controls in the United States, London's licensing system, not frustrated by its neighbors, works better and is very much more restrictive. Of every 100 murders in the two cities, 36 victims die by gunfire in Manhattan as compared to 5 in London. It must be stressed that these figures compare the proportionate use of guns in murders, not the rates of murder, since Manhattan enjoys more murders per year than all of England and Wales.

In summary, the available evidence strongly suggests that effective control of firearms, by reducing the probability that potential criminal offenders will acquire and use them, could substantially reduce the incidence of criminal homicide and serious injury due to criminal assault. It is not irrelevant to mention here that there is widespread public support for much stricter firearms control. A Gallup Poll taken in 1964 showed that 71 percent of the men and 85 percent of the women in this country felt that no one should be permitted to own a gun without a police permit. Both violence and the fear of violence will be reduced by the implementation of that unequivocally expressed demand.

Our ukases on guns would achieve this in regard to new sales of guns. The legislation could also seek to reduce the existing huge stock of firearms in private hands; but it must be recognized that such retroactive disarmament is no light task. There must be regular opportunities for voluntary surrender of firearms, free of the threat of criminal sanction. Consideration should be given to governmental purchase of privately owned guns at prices slightly in excess of the market rate. Gun smuggling would present no serious threat under this plan, and there is merit in allowing those who surrender their guns to avoid financial loss and, indeed, to profit. It would be a great expense, true; but so is the gun slaughter. We do not offer this as a ukase since, as you will recall, we are bound by a self-denying treasury proscription. But the plan merits close attention.

Linking the gun with its owner in future sales of firearms can be achieved by ingraining serial numbers into the guns and recording the rifling traces of those that are rifled. At present, there are technical difficulties in the computerization of rifling traces; but these are not difficult in themselves to record and a few years will suffice to overcome the technical computer programming problem.

Another technical issue of firearms control deserves legislative attention. At present, metal detection machines are bulky and tend to lack discrimination, giving warning of tobacco tins, bunches of keys, and the metal frames on ladies' handbags. We require portable and discriminatory monitors capable of secretly searching anyone passing through a door or along a footpath to ascertain if he carries a concealed gun. There are surely no 1984 fears in this. There can be no right of privacy in regard to armament.

Just as transponders have been developed for use in airplanes, large and small, to facilitate their swift and certain identification on the radar screen of the Federal Aviation Administration's traffic controller in the airport tower, so we are informed, it is technically feasible to require a "trace element" to be built into the metal of all guns hereafter manufactured, to so treat all those hereafter sold, and to so treat all that are licensed. Again, our self-denying treasury ordinance leads us to limit ourselves to a mention of this scheme. Its implications for effective gun control are obvious.

Sometimes our ukases may have to be rejected as politically unwise even from our authoritarian position; dictators, too, are to a degree limited by public opinion. Already, for his lengthy and balanced evidence to the President's Commission on Violence one of the authors has been described in a magazine called *Guns* as "a real corker," which is, we suspect, more pejorative than laudatory. Guns may provide an example of such a frustration of our benevolence. It may be that lesser steps toward social wisdom are all that can be tolerated. If this be so, that hand guns are more dangerous and less useful than other guns may provide a basis for acceptable social control.

As a ukase: None other than a policeman or trained security officer should be permitted to own, possess or carry a hand gun. The hand gun as distinguished from the long gun, rifle, or shotgun is used neither for hunting nor for sport (apart from by a very few exotic afficionados who can still be allowed their ornate armaments for sporting and target practice under an arsenal principle). A hand gun — pistol or revolver — is used to threaten, wound or kill only people; other animals are not its customary objective. It is disproportionately, grossly disproportionately, the weapon of homicide, of suicide, and of severe and fatal accidents. Further, it is a most ineffective instrument of self-defense. As a proposition of fact, for each innocent life the hand gun saves through self-defense, it sacrifices several family members on the evil altars of homicide, suicide, and fatal accident.

The hand gun is susceptible of legal definition and control; further, most types of ammunition for pistols and revolvers are not used in long guns, a fact which provides a further useful mechanism of inhibiting the use of hand guns.

The position of the President's Commission on Violence, recommending much more far-reaching governmental control of the hand gun than of the rifle and shotgun, makes exceedingly good sense for a community politically disinclined to reduce violence by the more complete legislative program we have propounded.

The President's Commission on Violence apparently believes that the benefits of ownership and sporting use of long guns outweigh the collateral social costs; we disagree, but nevertheless support their program as a first step. A resolute attack on the private ownership of hand guns is a century overdue. If all this means we are unacceptable to the National Rifle Association or unwelcome in Texas, we shall bear those adversities with courage.

In conclusion on firearms. Our five ukases on guns will disarm the populace and yet allow the target shooters and the hunters to have their guns — under reasonable controls. In fairness we should confess our disapproval of the hunter's use of a gun; we see hunting as did Oscar Wilde — the unspeakable in pursuit of the uneatable. But if hunters must kill in this way, it is no present business of ours unless their "sport" increases the level of homicide and suicide (and of accidental death) which indeed it does and will continue to do unless controls of the type we have suggested are imposed on the use and storage of their guns. And, particularly from these "sportsmen," we must never tolerate the argument that if the murderer lacked a gun he would kill in some other way. If they believe that, they should, on grounds of sportsmanship, throw away their guns and club the deer to death, knife the bears, and poison the ducks.

Knives

Our ukase against switchblades and gravity knives is directed at the next most deadly weapon actually used in homicide and serious assaults. Though guns are more lethal, knives are more frequently criminally used. In 1968, knives accounted for 22 percent more attacks than guns: 90,096 knife assaults as opposed to 74,161 gun assaults. And those figures underestimate the disproportion, since gun assaults are more likely to be reported to the police than knife assaults, as victim studies repeatedly demonstrate.

No one needs such weapons; they are designed for violence; they are not tools of trade; no one would suffer, except their manufacturers and distributors, from their total prohibition. It is unlikely that a serious black market in these weapons would develop. The desire to own them is not sufficiently compelling to push the price to a level that would support the smuggler and the black marketeer.

Since 1958, the interstate shipment of switchblade knives has been prohibited but, according to the Justice Department, there have been only eight convictions for this offense in the past five years. In at least twelve states these knives are specifically prohibited and in some others there are laws relating to "possession" and "carrying." But in general the penalties are inadequate, the laws remain unenforced, and very few localities have taken effective action. Knives are on the list of forbidden imports at the moment, but domestic switchblade production reported at one million knives a year is presently unhindered. The enactment of a total federal prohibition will facilitate enforcement in an area where enormous variations in state laws and enforcement policies render knives easily accessible almost everywhere at prices ranging from as low as eighty-eight cents. It is of course true that a great variety of potentially lethal instruments such as hammers, scissors, and baseball bats (and for that matter hands and feet) are readily available and not susceptible to control. This, however, is no reason for not controlling weapons which serve no socially useful purpose and are used almost exclusively to threaten or inflict physical injury. We should not overlook the fact that easy access to weapons of this kind may not merely facilitate violence but may also stimulate, inspire, and provoke it.

Drunken Driving

We have absolute confidence that our edict on drunken driving will, when it is applied, prevent more deaths and avoid more grievous injuries than flow from the combined consequences of all homicides and assaults in this country. It is a predominantly middle-class offense we now strike at; it is tolerated because it is thought to lack those qualities of immoral and intentful wrongdoing that are supposedly characteristic of other criminal injuries to the person. This is not so. Drunken driving has a quality of reckless indifference to a known risk to the life and safety of others for a selfish and transient pleasure and is therefore criminal in our eyes. It is only because so many of us can identify so easily with the drunken driver that our critical judgment is stayed. This is precisely the situation where the criminal law can effectively operate as a generally deterrent force for social welfare, by the threat of punishment and by a clear affirmation of minimum standards of behavior that will have an educative effect on us all.

The evidence of the effectiveness of such a ukase as we offer is very strong. In March 1967, the European Council of Ministers of Transport adopted a draft resolution based on the report of a working party which had been studying the relationship between drinking and road accidents since 1961. The resolution adopted included recommendations that member countries should:

a) Take the necessary steps to ensure that not only drunken drivers but those under the influence of drink may be more easily traced.

b) Perfect and simplify the detection of drivers whose ability is impaired by quick trace tests (e.g., the breath test).

c) Ensure legal provision for a blood test in appropriate cases.

d) Prescribe a legal limit of blood alcohol concentration for drivers (80 mg per 100 ml was the recommended maximum figure).

Studies in this country, in Europe, in Australia, and elsewhere establish both that the ingestion of alcohol, above very small quantities to reduce the hesitancies of a few nervous drivers, impairs driving ability and that it is a major cause of traffic accidents and fatalities. Studies of the records of fatal road accidents, controlled laboratory tests, and experiments with experienced drivers in actual driving situations all confirm the deleterious effects of alcohol on driving. The largest and most thorough of recent studies carried out under the direction of Professor Borkenstein at Indiana University reveals that drivers with a blood alcohol level of 160 mg per 100 ml are twenty times more likely to be involved in accidents than if they had not been drinking. At 80 mg per 100 ml they are twice as likely to be involved in an accident as the nondrinker. Furthermore, when drivers with blood alcohol levels over 80 mg per 100 ml have accidents, these tend to be more severe than the average accident. In Britain, where legislation along the lines of our ukase was enacted in October 1967, a careful assessment of the effects of the new policy has revealed that a dramatic decrease in road traffic accidents, serious accidents in particular, took place after the new law came into effect. In the last three months of 1967 road deaths were reduced by 23 percent and casualties by 16 percent as compared with the previous year. There were 36 percent fewer road deaths at Christmas and 30 percent fewer serious injuries than in 1966.

It might be argued that the publicity campaign accompanying the introduction of this legislation explains these reductions of mortality and morbidity on the roads. And it is true that it is not easy to distinguish the generally deterrent threat component of such legislation from its educative and habituative effects. Nor, other than to the scholar, does it much matter; lives will be saved and crippling injuries avoided without sacrifice of any important countervailing social values. The figures do, however, reveal more than a general decline in death and injury on the roads; the timing of the saving of lives and avoiding of injury is of significance. In the mornings, the predrinking period, the change is not dramatic; but between 8:00 P.M. and 4:00 A.M. fatal and serious injuries fell by 41 percent and in the late night period after 10:00 P.M. casualties fell by nearly 50 percent.

In Austria, where a similar law was introduced in 1960, accidents involving drink fell by more than 25 percent in the first full year and demonstrated a similar pattern of time distribution of lives saved and injuries avoided.

It should be recognized that our edicts on drunken driving are modestly phrased; many countries have much stricter controls than we have proclaimed. Czechoslovakia, Bulgaria, and the German Democratic Republic set the alcohol limit at 30 mg per 100 ml and Poland, Norway, and Sweden have a limit of 50 mg per 100 ml. Our limit of 80 mg per 100 ml is shared by the United Kingdom, Switzerland, and Austria. In Norway and Sweden it is the policy of the courts to impose prison sentences, in addition to the loss of the driver's license for at least a year. In Denmark fines are exceptional and the usual punishment is fourteen days' imprisonment for a first offense. In Bulgaria drivers who have been drinking and cause death on the road are subject to a *minimum* sentence of ten years' imprisonment.

It may be, of course, that although the immediate impact of the British legislation has been substantial, the reduction in the casualty rates may not be subsequently sustained. Nevertheless, in the Scandinavian countries which have for a long time had strict legislation against driving under the influence of alcohol, alcohol is responsible for only a very slight proportion of road traffic accidents and there seems to be no doubt that the severity of the legislation has considerably limited the incidence of driving after drinking. In the circumstances, with the United States death rate for motor vehicle accidents at five times that for willful homicide, and with driving while intoxicated "probably involved in more than one-half of all motor vehicle deaths" (i.e., more than 26,000 deaths per year) according to the President's Crime Commission, there can be no justification for failing to provide such protection as the law can give. On present figures, the United Kingdom legislation is saving one thousand lives a year. Our edicts, on this experience, would certainly save four thousand American lives each year — and that is being conservative.

We are not disinclined to alcohol, particularly as an aid to social intercourse. We avoid inflicting clichés on you, the reader, concerning drinking and driving, volatile mixtures and so on; we simply urge you, assuming you share our propensities for both drinking and driving, that a hedonistic calculus should lead you to keep them segregated. Taxis are not that expensive. Alternative sober driving arrangements can often be made with sometimes surprisingly gratifying results.

Finally, we shall not allow our ukase on drunken driving to be rendered nugatory by legalistic quibbles about self-incrimination and the Fifth Amendment. It shall be provided that licenses to drive a motor vehicle will be issued only upon the signed consent of the licensee to the administration of the breathalyzer test whenever a police officer in uniform, seeing him driving or attempting to drive a motor vehicle, believes him to have been drinking, to have committed a moving traffic offense, or to have been involved in an accident. It shall be provided that breach of this condition of the license will be grounds for its immediate forfeiture for twelve months. The driver who has been convicted of the offense of drunken driving and is subsequently licensed to drive a motor vehicle shall likewise when licensed consent to the breathalyzer test condition, but this time upon pain of forfeiture of the license for five years. Such "conditional consent" provisions have been held to be constitutional; and they make good sense.

Capital Punishment

The final ukase in our program to help the good Lord deliver us from murder, violence, and sudden death is of a different character. By reducing the gun and knife population we shall reduce death and injury, and the fear of death and injury; by reducing drunken driving we shall save even more lives and avoid even more injuries, though, surprisingly, these deaths and injuries are not of a type which are greatly feared. If they were, few would even enter a car, drunk or sober. But our final ukase will save very few lives indeed; in 1966 one murderer was executed in the United States; in 1967, only two; in 1968, none. Nor are these particularly valuable lives to save; and the alternative pattern of their existence, if kept alive, is not peculiarly attractive. Nevertheless, we regard the total abolition of capital punishment for all crimes, civil and military, as an important plank in our legislative program. The state must eschew unnecessary violence.

One of us has spent too much of his life on this topic — including a period as chairman of a commission of inquiry appointed by the government of Ceylon to study the consequences of its abolition of capital punishment shortly after independence, and a recent period, on behalf of the Department of Economic and Social Affairs of the United Nations, studying the worldwide developments in capital punishment from 1961 through 1965. The conclusion which emerges from such studies and from all the literature and research reports on the death penalty is, to the point of monotony: the existence or nonexistence of capital punishment is irrelevant to the murder, or attempted murder, rate. This is as well established as any other proposition in social science. If, therefore, we are to be sincere in our efforts to reduce violence, there is one type of violence that we can with complete certainty eliminate. That is the killing of criminals by the state.

The question is, Will people learn to respect life better by threat or by example? And the uniform answer of history, comparative studies, and experience is that man is an emulative animal. It is, therefore, no search for the unexpected or the aphoristic that leads us to propound, as an important edict in the reduction of violence, the total abolition of capital punishment.

Excursus on Violence

The fear of criminal violence in our community is very great. In some respects it is greater than it need be. We think very few citizens realize that the willful homicide rate is substantially lower than it was in 1933 or that the robbery rate is also well below the 1933 figure. Before 1933 there was no estimated national rate for any offenses, but such evidence as is available indicates that rates for violent crimes especially in the large cities were even higher then. We believe also that the increased figures for forcible rape and aggravated assault reflect not so much a real increase in crime as a greater willingness to report to the police and a stronger demand for police protection. As the President's Crime Commission states:

> One change of importance in the amount of crime that is reported in our society is the change in the expectations of the poor and members of minority groups about civil rights and social protection. Not long ago there was a tendency to dismiss reports of all but the most serious offenses in slum areas and segregated minority group districts. The poor and the segregated minority groups were left to take care of their own problems. Commission studies indicate that whatever the past pattern was these areas now have a strong feeling of need for adequate police protection. Crimes that were once unknown to the police, or ignored when complaints were received, are now much more likely to be reported and recorded as part of the regular statistical procedure.

Insofar as this is an accurate assessment of recent trends in reported crime it indicates a development which can only be welcomed — not an increase in violence but a growing refusal to accept violence as a normal feature of ordinary life in our cities. Yet there is, as there has always been, far too much violent crime. Man is a violent animal, given as is no other mammal to killing within his species. His intraspecies violence grows proportionally as the territory in which he moves alone or with his family engenders more intraspecific conflicts than his precipitate temper can tolerate. Our program is designed to hasten the domestication of man; the restrictions we impose are a small price that must be paid.

Man is peculiarly perceptive of his environment and competent in adjusting it to what he believes is his welfare; but these very competencies threaten his extinction, for they are not balanced by sufficient understanding of himself. His skill in postponing death via public health and disease prevention and treatment methods has produced an excess of population, thus generating more intraspecies tension, which seriously imperils his continued existence. Konrad Lorenz's *On Aggression* and Anthony Storr's *Human Aggression* raise this and other issues (with which we do not deal) central to any program to reduce violence.

Reluctantly we have confined our brief on violence to the role of the criminal justice system and have denied ourselves the speculative delight of remaking man to a peaceful image on evidence we but dimly comprehend. There remain, however, two much discussed techniques of reducing criminal violence which have not been included in our program and whose exclusion demands justification: predicting who among us are prone to violent crime and doing something about them; and a censorship system to reduce the display of violence in "the media" as a method of reducing criminal violence.

Preselecting the Violent

In chapter 7, on psychiatry and crime, we discuss problems in predicting human behavior and in assessing its responsiveness to treatment modalities, including the fashionable question of the violent psychopath. Here, we wish merely to explain why our ukases on violence do not include provisions for the preselection and preventive treatment of those who are prone to violence. It is an attractive idea and it has generated a substantial literature. The theme goes: let us select the likely violent criminals and train them to less damaging resolutions of their aggressions. We have excluded this seductive notion from our edicts for the compelling reason that we lack, and so does everyone else, sufficient capacity to predict who will be violent, unless we so "overpredict" as to do gross injustice to many people who will never inflict violent injury on anyone.

A technical issue in prediction is essential to the discussion. It must be recognized that prediction may fail in two ways, not only in one. We preselect 30 of a given 100 as likely violent criminals. Assume that 20 of those 100 do in fact later commit a crime of violence, and that our 30 includes 15 of those who do and 15 of those who do not. This would be excellent prediction, and its advocates would say: "We have successfully preselected 15 out of 20, or 75 percent, of those who commit crimes of violence." But note that we have selected 15 "false positives," those alleged to be likely to commit crimes of violence but who do not, and we have also selected 5 "false negatives," those 5 among the remaining 70 who were predicted as safe but proved to be violent. Of course, by overpredicting violence we could reduce the false negatives, but only at the cost of greatly increasing the false positives. If, as is usually the case, those predicted as violent will suffer for the prediction, it is clear that problems of justice quickly and forcefully intrude into our mathematics.

Two target populations have been suggested for the prediction of violence and for preventive intervention: the unconvicted and the convicted. Among the former, the literature has concentrated on serious delinquency of children and youth; among the latter, on those already convicted of crimes of violence. Sheldon and Eleanor Glueck of Harvard, important contributors to knowledge of delinquency, have in recent years developed prediction tables designed to select the future serious delinquents while they are still in the early school grades. Regrettably, their tables overpredict to an unacceptable level and would, if official intervention were based on them, stigmatize too many false positives. Further, it has not been established that intervention, voluntary or compulsory, in the lives of those children predicted as likely to be seriously delinquent minimizes their future delinquency rates. Only irresponsible scholarship would now argue for the application of prediction tables to the unconvicted, children or adult, as a basis for official intervention under the criminal law to prevent crimes of violence; and, in fairness to the Gluecks, it must be added that they have never suggested that such an intervention would be justified. No ukase can thus be directed to the preselection and preventive treatment of those among the population at large thought prone to violence.

The second possible target population raises more difficulty. In sentencing convicted criminals courts properly take into account their past and likely future violence. They bear these facts and these predictions in mind in setting the punishment or in defining its upper and lower limits. Parole boards properly do the same. These are predictions of violence influencing discretions exercised under the criminal law. Even if they include many false positives, as they surely do, that is what sentencing and paroling is. Later, we shall offer a ukase requiring the more scientific assessment of these present guesses, so that sentencing and paroling will better protect the community as well as more justly treat the individual offender. But these guesses remain an unavoidable part of our punishing and releasing processes.

Within existing upper limits of power under the criminal law we have to do our best to protect the community from those who seem to us likely to commit crimes of violence. Whenever we go further and seek to increase those limits of punishing powers to extend our penal control over offenders because of our expectations of their violence, we lapse into injustice. The leading example is the sexual psychopath laws which have spread like a rash over this country. These laws, based upon a series of pertinaciously held false premises, define a category of criminals as highly dangerous and provide for their incarceration until they are "cured." Serious sexual offenders do not, as is assumed, have a high rate of recidivism; very few relapse into serious sexual crime. It is true that the peepers and flashers (voyeurs and exhibitionists) do commonly relapse, but they present less likelihood of violence than a random sample of males on the streets. Further, assumptions to the contrary notwithstanding, minor sex offenders very rarely gravitate to serious sexual offenses or to crimes of violence. The whole miserable legislative structure is an ill-concealed expression of punitive emotion masquerading as medical treatment.

It comes to this. In sentencing and paroling, our insecure predictions of risk of violence appropriately function within existing powers of punishment; to go further, to seek to increase these powers on unproved claims of predictive ability, is unjust. We must develop prediction tables of the type described in chapter 7, and we must critically test them. For the present, in the light of our insufficient competence in predicting violence there is no justification for interfering with the lives of those preselected as violent.

We must stress that we refer only to the police power under the criminal law. We are not discussing the mental health or welfare powers of the state. We are not denying that in some few cases commitment to a mental hospital may be necessary and appropriate on the basis that the patient is a danger to himself or to others — which is a prediction. There are many problems in our civil commitment laws, but we are not disposed to join Dr. Szasz and to repudiate prediction, root and branch. Likewise, the welfare authorities, when they predict that the family environment of a child may make him likely to become ill or delinquent, and therefore offer the child, the mother, or the family further assistance designed to minimize these risks, behave entirely properly. But the criminal law speaks with compulsion; it is not optional and facultative; unvalidated predictions of violent criminality are inapt foundations for its coercions.

Violence and the Media

An uncharacteristic modesty overcomes us; we do not include edicts limiting the depiction of violence on motion picture and television screens, in the press, in books, magazines, and the comics. We recognize limits to our knowledge and do not seek to censor man's rich fantasy life, nor to limit the vicarious satisfaction of aggression by children or adults by proscribing certain stimuli for the jungle of his conscious and subconscious life.

There are two themes which explain our restraint: our view that aggression must not be seen as an entirely negative social force and that one must therefore be cautious in seeking to limit its portrayal; and second, the ambiguity of evidence concerning the consequences of censorship. These two themes are, of course, closely related. In developing them we shall allow ourselves some collateral reflections on violence and the media, germane for consideration by anyone who seeks to censor media violence.

Civilization provides socially acceptable means for channeling and expressing man's aggressive instincts, for turning them from individual brutalities to social virtues. This channeling of human aggression is much needed, given man's propensity to intraspecies killing. His aggressions threaten his extinction. But again we must put aside the temptation to remake society and must concentrate on our present concern, the limitation of crimes of violence.

The portly and unathletic sit in the seats of power. They may have their strong and sometimes paranoid aggressions, but they have directed them into socially acceptable and, indeed, eulogized channels. Much the same obtains in the demimonde: who has the larger biceps, the bouncer or the proprietor? Few are so stupid as to see violence and brutality as the path to success, even in crime. It is well to remember that we live in a world in which, other than in those societal writhings called revolutions, the violent, by and large, do not prosper.

It is also necessary to bear in mind the sharp differences in class attitudes to violence. Middle-class children are advised, if conflict threatens on the street, to disengage and to return home unblemished by bruise, sore knuckle, or stiffened sinew. By contrast, the children of some other classes of society are expected, if they are male, to express their manhood by giving as good or better than they receive or are threatened with. Let us not assume a morally neutral posture; it seems to us that the progress of civilization, and the confirmation of the values we regard as worthwhile, requires the diminution of the violent expression of man's aggression. The patina of civilization is thin indeed, as the history of this century stunningly relates, and every element that can strengthen it, that can diminish man's affinity for violence, is a worthy contribution to social welfare.

Hence we seek substitutes for the violent release of aggression. We recognize the many beneficent effects of aggression — that productivity, creativity, and happiness flow from the aggressive and competitive drives in man. Yet from the same pressures there flows much suffering in the form of brutal and violent crime. Can propaganda or the censor reduce these injurious outbursts of aggression?

Propaganda has long seemed to us a much overrated weapon. Perhaps the most massive campaign ever mounted, and under the highest auspices, started nearly two thousand years ago and has been steadily pursued, with its powerful slogan, "Love Thy Neighbor," possessing a Madison Avenue brevity and punch. A glance at the world suggests that substantial consumer resistance is still being encountered, despite the energy and intelligence of its proponents and the vast funds they have dedicated to the campaign. Similarly, at a substantially lower level, during World War II both of us, though on different continents, were subjected to intense propaganda appeals directed to accepting our allies as comrades and friends; yet we felt more in danger from our brothers in arms in the rest camps and watering places of North Africa and the South Pacific than when we approached action against the enemy. We might add that the army VD films designed to discourage "fraternization" were, despite their shock value, singularly ineffective either in doing that or in preventing venereal disease rates from exceeding those for battle casualties.

On the other hand, there are certainly areas of human behavior where propaganda powerfully and successfully influences human behavior, where the media are highly effective. What was the last brand of toothpaste you purchased? And why?

It may be that propaganda could influence those interested in violence and habituated to it toward a diversity of modes of expression. Assume that the world is divided into those who enjoy violence, and who will in their spare time seek out situations in which violence is displayed or in which they may be involved, and those who eschew such situations. The division is of course arbitrary and unreal, but indulge it for a moment. If we could mount television programs and spot advertisements that demonstrated knuckle-dusters, ornate knives, handsome guns, and their various means of use, we could sell them to the former group; we would hardly influence the latter. The same is true in sex. Assume an arbitrary division between homosexuals and heterosexuals; intrasex stories and advertising interest the former; they do not divert heterosexuals. We are equally unlikely to persuade the violent to nonviolence, though we may influence the means they select to express aggression.

We thus doubt that adjurations to nonviolence in the media are likely to win an audience, or that they would be effective. We do not imagine that the exigencies of crime control will inspire such a campaign for gentleness, though we regard that quality as the very stuff of a decent society. Hence we turn to censorship, the other side of the coin of propaganda, where it may be possible to limit stimuli for the violence prone — which may be a substantial group — and thus diminish criminal violence.

A quite fundamental point about the depiction of violence in the media is a necessary prelude to the explanation of our reluctance to advocate a censorship system. In an important sense, the reality of violence is not depicted on motion picture or television screens, in the newspapers, in the magazines, on the radio, and so far as we know, in the comics. What is shown is an idealization of violence. Violence is idealized in two ways. First, the hero achieves ultimate happiness by violence despite the fact that everything which has justified that benign state is antipathetic to violence. Consider many novels you have read and films you have seen. Normally the hero has a generous allowance of admirable qualities, well meriting the love of a good woman and the approval of his peer group. These qualities do not usually include an affinity for violence. His triumph, however, requires a penultimate scene in which he unexpectedly demonstrates his prodigious capacity for effective violence as a prelude to the purified contentment of the concluding scene. Now, in our experience, heroes with these qualities are very likely to get their teeth kicked in rather than to do the kicking. They seem to us quite unlikely to possess, beyond their other fine qualities, a capacity for controlled and Bond-like violence. Idealized violence succeeds where worthy qualities have failed. Much of the folklore and fiction of our society, depicted for the mass media audience, resolves plots by violence in which virtues triumph through the addition of this unattractive component.

The second way in which violence is idealized is this: In our experience, when a man is shot and dies, he does not die aseptically. When a man is knifed and falls to his death agonies, he does not fall neatly with clean steel quivering above him. The sphincter loosens, the bladder opens, the intestines spill out in most unattractive ways, and the death agony is not a transient process. The media do not depict violence; they depict a bowdlerized version of violence. It is strange that when films do seek for reality, they have a high likelihood of being banned, but when they idealize violence the risk of such a consequence is slight. The excellent English film, Peter Watkins's *The War Game*, was widely banned for its realism.

We are not advocating that this idealization of violence should be changed. We are not suggesting that every hero should have his teeth kicked in, or that every film with violence in it should struggle to surpass *Bonnie and Clyde* and move toward clinical realism. We are merely noting the point that we are not talking about the depiction of violence when we discuss the censorship of "violence" in the media; we are in fact talking about limiting their idealized and aseptic presentation of violence.

The portrayal of idealized violence on the media could have two broad effects on different categories of viewers. It could be cathartic;

Feshbach's "substitution hypothesis," could apply, by which the release of impulse through fantasy tends temporarily to reduce the strength of the impulse. For some, it is highly likely that the portrayal of violence allows safe release of their more violent aggressive drives — a vicarious satisfaction. The other possibility is that it may act as a stimulus to emulation, an instruction in the worth and pleasures of violence, a guide to technique, a preachment of "heroic" virtues. The question: How many in each group, and do age differences function so that we might have an age-selective censorship? And the answer: We don't know, and you don't know, and neither do those who have researched these questions.

There have been two major, long-term, intensive studies of the impact of television on children: that by Himmelweit, Oppenheim, and Vince, published in London in 1958; and the Stanford University study published in 1961. They agree in their findings, English children matching American and Canadian children in their reactions to television. Consider the caution of this finding of the Stanford study:

> Under at least some conditions a fantasy experience
> on television will reduce aggressive tendencies. . . .
> there is no definite pattern: sometimes aggression
> seems to be reduced, sometimes increased.

And its resounding conclusion:

> For *some* children, under *some* conditions, *some*
> television is harmful. For *other* children under the
> same conditions, or for the same children under *other*
> conditions it may be beneficial. For *most* children
> under *most* conditions *most* television is probably
> neither particularly harmful nor particularly
> beneficial.

Could caution exceed this? Perhaps it can. Bernard Berelson risked even less when he concluded his study *Communications and Public Opinion* with the dogmatic assertion that "some kinds of communication on some kinds of issues, brought to the attention of some kinds of people under some kinds of conditions, have some kinds of effects." Who can doubt it?

It may be thought that since the portrayal of violence has no redeeming social value its censorship in the media is justified. But even here, like Dr. Berelson, we are full of uncertainty. Clearly fantasies of violence have great attraction to children, as all fairy tales and children's fiction demonstrates. As Dr. Lawrence Freedman phrased it, "the day-dreams of most children would make the fiercest television show seem tame; its most erotic productions would appear vague by comparison; the cupidity of its give-aways would be dwarfed by their massive acquisitiveness." And we return to the difficult inner question: Are portrayals, idealized portrayals, of violence a catharsis or a lesson? And the answer: Nobody knows.

We do, however, have some experience of the adverse consequences of banning that which people seem strongly to desire; and this leads us to an uneasy posture of caution in relation to the censorship of violence. It is clear that given a choice we would censor the portrayal of violence long before we would censor the portrayal of sex, but this is really only avoiding the question. So we take a hands-off attitude. It may be weak, but at least it is honest. There exists in the community a difference of opinion about the censorship of sex and violence in the media. We think that the criminologist should not interfere qua criminologist in that dispute but that he is bound to point out the lack of evidence to indicate any influence on the levels of criminal violence in the community by the resolution of the dispute one way or the other. Hence our ukases are silent on this subject. We impose no prohibition, however, on your formulation of your own edict, but we urge you anxiously to consider the adequacy of the evidence for inter-ference in the fantasy life of man.

4

The Police
and the Citizen

The police have such a poor image of themselves. They see themselves as the menial retainers of an authoritarian system, the paramilitary enforcers of an immutable criminal law. They talk as if they lack discretion; in fact, they have larger discretion than prosecutors, judges, and legislators. They see themselves as relatively powerless; yet the rawest police recruit when first on the beat disposes of a larger, immediate power than is accorded any other citizen. They allow themselves to become pawns in political and racial clashes; they fail to see that they are the community's most important social workers. They apparently accept a situation where there are not two pigmentations in this country; there are three — white, black, and blue.

We, too, have a dream. It is that the social conscience of the current generation of young people which has led them to Peace Corps and protest will learn to express itself in police service. The college student today, could he but disabuse himself of his prejudice toward "the fuzz," would find in police service the most promising prospects of serious contribution to social welfare. But before this can happen, the police will have to rid themselves of what so many of their critics not inaccurately describe as a paranoid reaction to the world.

They huddle together, an anxious ingroup, battling the forces of wickedness, political corruption, citizen irresponsibility, and declining morals, particularly the immorality of youth. Their extra-corps contacts are cautious in the extreme. They are, they believe, insufficiently esteemed, inadequately rewarded, but gallantly carrying the burdens of society for a parsimonious and misguided citizenry.

Even the most authoritative text on the police in America, Bruce Smith's *Police Systems in the United States*, speaks of "the widely held belief . . . that our entire police organism is rotten from top to bottom, and from periphery to core . . . that American police systems are beyond all hope of reconstruction, and that in the future, as in the past, they will merit little of public esteem." Professor Smith is of the opinion that "perhaps a majority of Americans share that belief." In fact, he and the police both miss the interesting ambivalence in the community's attitude to the police.

A survey conducted by the National Opinion Research Center for the President's Crime Commission and numerous recent public opinion polls indicate that the overwhelming majority of the public has a high opinion of the work of the police. This is true, though to a lesser extent, even in those inner-city depressed ghetto areas where the policeman is seen as an enemy, the representative of an unjust society. The majority of the inhabitants of the ghetto see the police as the protectors of their persons and property and solicit more intensive police patrol and protection. There is no lack of logic in the ghetto dweller's statement: "I hate the police and we need more police here." The police-community relations problem in such a territory is complex and important. In this chapter we shall offer a concrete proposal on this subject.

For the rest, we limit our consideration of police problems to two main issues: the organization and training of the police; and technical ways in which functional efficiency can be improved, mainly by bringing the citizen into closer and more efficient relations with the police power. The prevention of crime and the apprehension of criminals are by no means the only functions of the police; but it is this aspect of their work which is our present concern. And it is one, among the heterogeneous tasks we expect the police to perform, which sometimes seems to be almost lost sight of, receiving only cursory attention in much writing about the police.

The Police Role

As we have already said, in this country we have one of the most moralistic criminal law systems that the world has yet produced. It is enforceable only in a sporadic, uneven, and discriminatory fashion. We have the most severe drug laws and the largest number of addicts. We have highly restrictive sex laws in a society that can hardly be regarded as dedicated either to monogamy or the missionary position in copulation, and in which sexual stimuli are ubiquitous. In relation to these laws the police have ritual, sacerdotal functions to perform, like a secular priesthood. And they have also to handle our drunks and alcoholics, our snarled and feverish traffic, our vagrants, our treed cats, our parading dignitaries, some of our gamblers, our burgeoning riots, and in the remainder of their time to protect us from serious crime.

Why are there no strong police voices for a retrenchment of our moralistic criminal law? Why do the police not argue: let us protect you, not coddle your spurious virtue? Why are they not dedicated to achieving a more modestly phrased but socially effective criminal law, aiming to protect us as far as it can from physical violence and certain serious property depradations — and little else? They do not hesitate to object to the Supreme Court's decisions on arrest, search, and interrogative procedures. But they seem to want to have it both ways. They want to be the accepting, uninquiring enforcers of morals laws, because they are the law, and the critical repudiator of judicial interpretation of other laws. Both are law: what the legislator says about sex, narcotics, drunks, and gambling, and what the Supreme Court says about individual liberty. In the morals area they so readily put on the priestly garb. They say they have a duty to "uphold the community morals and enforce its system of morality" and they must not "abandon this responsibility." Yet the community and the politicians are so irresponsibly ambivalent in what they expect of the police in the violent, mobile, anonymous, race-conscious, crowded swirl of urban existence. In many of our cities we pay the police less than the garbage collectors, overload them with a morally pretentious law, and require them to demonstrate wisdom and skill higher than that expected of any of the established professions. The policeman is required to be an expert on the law, a psychologist, a strategist, on occasion a midwife, a protector of public safety, a ruthless prosecutor of crime, and at the same time a guardian of civil liberty.

This, of course, is not a fresh insight. Forty years ago August Vollmer, the former police chief who in 1929 became America's first full professor of police administration at the University of Chicago put it pungently:

> The policeman is denounced by the public, criticized
> by preachers, ridiculed in the movies, berated by
> the newspapers and unsupported by prosecuting
> officers and judges. He is shunned by the respectables,
> hated by criminals, deceived by everyone, kicked
> around like a football by brainless or crooked
> politicians. He is exposed to countless temptations
> and dangers, condemned when he enforces the law
> and dismissed when he doesn't. He is supposed to
> possess the qualifications of a soldier, doctor, lawyer,
> diplomat and educator, with remuneration less than
> that of a daily laborer.

Nor is this situation peculiar to America. More recently Ben Whitaker, an English barrister who made a detailed study of the British police, wrote:

> The public use the police as a scapegoat for its
> neurotic attitude towards crime. Janus-like we have

always turned two faces toward a policeman. We expect him to be human and yet inhuman. We employ him to administer the law, and yet ask him to waive it. We resent him when he enforces the law in our own case, yet demand his dismissal when he does not elsewhere. We offer him bribes, yet denounce his corruption. We expect him to be a member of society, yet not to share its values. We admire violence, even against society itself, but condemn force by the police on our behalf. We tell the police that they are entitled to information from the public, yet we ostracize informers. We ask for crime to be eradicated, but only by the use of "sporting" methods.

How many of us would succeed in meeting the demands of this superhuman role? Who is to blame if the policeman occasionally fails in the performance of some aspects of his multivariant function? Quite clearly the fault is ours. Adequate pay, status, and training, and an achievable role in society are all denied the police. They have become pathetically accepting of those denials and we seem lamentably willing to suffer the consequences. It is no longer possible to be blind to the nature of those consequences. Unless we are prepared to act, we shall pay for our neglect not merely in dollars but in the harder coinage of human suffering, fear, and social disorder.

One of the most valuable features of the President's Crime Commission report is that, in it, the criminal justice system is seen for the first time as a single system, not as a group of discordant governmental processes. Previously, students have been content to do studies and make recommendations in relation to the police function, the prosecutorial function, the defense function, the courts, the corrections, as if they were separate and discrete processes having no interrelationships. This report recognizes that, in technical jargon, disturbing the parameters of a subsystem has consequences throughout the system. Or, put more vulgarly, if you press something here, something else is likely to pop out quite unexpectedly over there. Or, put more concretely, police do prosecutorial work, defense work, judicial work, and correctional work. Or, put even more aggressively, a policeman exercises a larger judicial discretion than a judge, and if you are to understand police work you have to recognize the great range of discretions that he has to apply.

Let us provide a concrete illustration of this point. The Center for

Studies in Criminal Justice at the University of Chicago ran a service called Legal Services to Youth, providing legal assistance to children and youths arrested in a ghetto area northwest of the university. It is an area with the highest or second highest delinquency rate in Chicago. We found that of every hundred youths arrested, only forty reached the court intake processes. Of those forty, only twenty actually reached the court. Those figures are accurate; the next figure is a guess, but we think it is a reasonably informed guess. We believe, and the police in the area share this view, that the hundred they arrested represented five hundred "probable cause" arrest situations.

So five hundred arrest situations on the streets were reduced to one hundred arrests, reduced to forty court intakes, reduced to twenty in court, and then of those twenty a very few found themselves in the correctional system. Thus, the police decided more often than the judges whether the criminal justice system should be invoked. Of the five hundred arrest situations, police and the court intake personnel exercised judicial discretions and prosecutorial discretions in relation to four hundred and eighty youths and the courts exercised those discretions in relation to twenty. To analyze our system of criminal justice under the mythology that the police make an arrest when they see what they think is a properly arrestable criminal and that they then pass him on to others in the system to handle is wild nonsense. It is impossible to think rationally about the crime problem without constantly bearing in mind the interdependence of the subsystems that make up the criminal justice system. This may sound like an obvious insight; but its implications for the recruitment, training, and salary structure of police forces have long gone unrecognized.

Let us turn from these larger considerations of the police role in society to the details of our program for the police. We here put aside a number of issues which have been the subject of fierce public discussion and controversy in recent years. Such topics as police corruption and police brutality are not dealt with at length. Nor do we go into the influence on police administration of party politics which in America sometimes appears to be a dominant one, although no unitary pattern is discernible among the 40,000 state, county, and city police forces with widely diverse characteristics scattered across this country. Let us define our program and then defend it.

> **1.** Police salaries must be raised to provide adequate starting stipends and appreciable increments for each promotion. At

the top, the salaries of police inspectors should be equivalent to those of circuit court judges while a chief inspector should receive the same remuneration as a Supreme Court justice. Police salaries must be sufficient to recruit and retain college graduates.

2. Police recruitment standards must be raised in respect of education, intelligence, and personality characteristics and relaxed in respect of height, weight, visual acuity, and residential qualifications.

3. Police will be recruited at three levels: Police agents (college graduates), police officers (high school graduates), and community service officers (on an aptitude and intelligence test basis). In-service training will be organized to avoid inequities arising from lateral entry. All recruits will serve at least one year's probation.

4. Police academies, national and regional, must be established to provide basic training for all recruits and in-service training at all levels. In addition, all police must be given incentives and aid to continue their general education or to acquire special skills.

5. Every jurisdiction shall provide adequate procedures, independent of police departments themselves, for processing citizen grievances and complaints. If this is not done through the agency of an ombudsman handling complaints against all state employees, a civilian review board concentrating on the police must be established.

6. Traffic warden corps shall be established to relieve the police of routine traffic law enforcement.

7. Portable transceivers shall be carried by all police on patrol so that they may be in immediate contact with police headquarters without being tied to a patrol vehicle.

8. The established technology of crime prevention must be applied and its newer developments tested. Primitive protective devices and halting communications must be replaced by a sophisticated technology and swift communications.

a) Automobiles must be equipped with antitheft devices such as ignition locks, alarms, and steering-wheel locks.

b) A single emergency police number shall be introduced for the entire United States. All public telephones shall be adapted so that emergency calls to the police can be made directly without using money. Police call boxes shall be left open and designated "public emergency call boxes."

c) In selected cities on an experimental basis and, if successful, more generally, pocket radio alarm signal transmitters on the police wavelength shall be available to citizens.

d) Home protection systems using available technology — telephone and silent alarm systems — shall be tested in selected areas.

Police Salaries

The deleterious effects of years of parsimonious police salaries are two-fold. In the first place, the failure to pay adequate salaries has a direct effect on recruitment in that police forces cannot attract (or cannot hold after recruitment) men of the caliber required to perform one of the most sensitive and important functions in our society. Second, as Professor James Q. Wilson of Harvard has pointed out, low salaries and allowances "are interpreted by policemen as palpable evidence of the contempt in which the police are held by the public and the politicians." Yet, although the cost of policing, like that of other services, has considerably increased — the present average increase in expenditures is almost 10 percent per year — the percentage of governmental allotments to law enforcement has declined and continues to decline. Thus, in 1902 police agencies were allotted 4.9 percent of total governmental fiscal outlay. In 1962 this figure had declined to 3.5 percent. And this decline continues.

At present 65.5 percent of police departments are below authorized strength. The average large-city force is 10 percent below standard capacity. Turnover in personnel is an even greater problem than recruitment. Not only does 5 percent of the police departments' force leave the service every year but the mass of police officers recruited just after World War II will reach retirement age within the next decade. By way of example, 41 percent of the Los Angeles Police Department became eligible to retire in 1967.

In order to meet this problem alone, there is need to raise police salary scales, which are below those for most skilled occupations. In 1960 the median salary for professional and technical workers was $7,124; for craftsmen and foremen, $5,699; and for police, $5,321. In small cities the median annual pay for a patrolman is $4,600. In general, the maximum patrolman's salary is less than $1,000 above his starting salary.

Our self-denying treasury ordinance must, on this occasion, be waived. The entire criminal justice system turns on the quality of the police; the funds involved are small and we have saved them elsewhere; police salaries must be competitive and progressive with salaries offered in other professions which seek to employ and retain men of the same age, ability, education, and experience. Penny-pinching here is dangerous and expensive.

Recruitment Standards

It would be naïve to imagine that the police problem will be solved merely by devoting increased revenues to the police and providing higher salaries on the levels suggested by our ukase. It is equally important that the rigid and pointless standards regarding height, weight, visual acuity, and prior residence which act as deterrents to the recruitment of able personnel should be relaxed. As the President's Crime Commission report says, "successful athletes come in all sizes." And Ben Whitaker notes that criminals (themselves subjected to no physical requirements for recruitment) are often able to recognize British detectives by their height. "Some of the most brilliant French detectives," he says, "who are selected for their ability separately from the police, are not only tiny but also have glasses and flat feet." Moreover, the arbitrary height and weight restrictions generally imposed on the police emphasize an aspect of police work which is by no means the most important in modern society. Tact, emotional stability, balanced social attitudes, and intelligence are infinitely more vital to the successful performance of the police role in our society than pounds of flesh, of which, our admittedly unsystematic observation suggests, there may well be a present surplus in our police forces.

Recruitment Levels

Attracting the talented to the police requires lateral entry, different levels of recruitment. That is unarguable; there is, however, ample room for disagreement on the structure of these levels. We have adopted the structure recommended by the President's Crime Commission, made after consultation with police practitioners at all departmental levels and other experts from across the country. The underlying idea is that police work would be more efficiently performed and made a more attractive career for the better qualified if a differential classification of officers were introduced with different levels of education, skill, and ability laid down for each category.

The *police agent* should have at least two years of college and preferably a baccalaureate degree in either the arts or the sciences. He would perform many of the tasks currently performed by detectives but, in addition, would be required to handle all the more serious police tasks calling for a large degree of judgment, intelligence, education, and initiative. It would, of course, be necessary that the agent position be open to officers already serving who do not have the necessary academic qualifications, and furthermore all officers should be not only encouraged but assisted to qualify for the position by being granted academic leaves of absence and funds for the payment of tuition. The *police officer* would perform the duties of general enforcement including routine patrol and emergency services. The educational requirement for entry at this level would be a high school diploma and passing college aptitude tests. In view of the fact that over 55 percent of all high school graduates enroll in college it is not unreasonable to demand this. As a matter of fact at least twenty-two police departments have already established requirements above this level, varying from one semester of college education to, in one instance, a four-year college degree.

The *community service officer* (CSO) would be an apprentice policeman — a new type of police cadet — recruited between the age of seventeen and twenty-one without the requirement of a high school diploma but with the intelligence and capacity to advance his education up to and beyond that level. The community service officer would work under the supervision and in close cooperation with police officers and agents. The President's Crime Commission task force report on the police succinctly defines the purposes of creating the position of community service officer:

1. To improve police service in high crime rate areas.
2. To enable police to hire persons who can provide a greater understanding of minority group problems.
3. To relieve police agents and officers of lesser police duties.
4. To tap a new reservoir of manpower by helping talented young men who have not been able as yet to complete their education to qualify for police work.

The provision of a rational career structure of this kind, both by making it possible for the college graduate to assume the position of agent (after a period of probation and in-service training) and by enabling officers and CSOs to become agents as they qualify, would not only increase the attractiveness of police work but would also equip the police to deal more effectively with current law enforcement needs.

In relation to lateral entry we would like to make the point that as long as the police see themselves as predominantly human garbage collectors it is entirely right for them to oppose lateral entry and to insist on promotion by effluxion of time and the avoidance of scandal. If, however, they see themselves as the pivotal points of social stability and community decency, and truly recognize the challenge and promise of their work, they must yield a larger role in promotion to knowledge, skill, and differentials of efficiency and range. Once it be ceded that an inspector of police should be paid the same salary as a circuit court judge and that a chief inspector should receive the same remuneration as a Supreme Court justice, and we become sincere in our protestations that police work must become a profession, then the case for lateral entry and merit promotion becomes compelling. Always, of course, we must allow room for the lowest level of recruit at the CSO stage to progress, if he has the capacity, to the most senior stage. And always we must provide adequate in-service training opportunities and scholarships for higher education so that opportunity for advancement from the bottom to the top of the system genuinely does exist. At the same time the chief of police must have much greater freedom to promote in accordance with his assessed views of capacity and ability. It may be necessary to build some controls by way of examination or other success ratings into this process so that caprice will not rule, but at least some freedom to allow relatively rapid movement through the ranks to executive and near policy-making positions is essential.

Police Training

Some years ago the British police historian Charles Reith wrote, in regard to police training in the United States: "It can be said of police training schools that the recruit is taught everything except the essential requirements of his calling, which is how to secure and maintain the approval and respect of the public whom he encounters daily in the course of his duties." This assessment remains applicable today, if on the generous side, since in the average police department, serving communities with less than a quarter of a million people, the police recruit now receives less than three weeks' training.

Both recruit training and in-service training have in the past been neglected in this country for a variety of reasons. Training programs are expensive; a chronic manpower shortage restricts time and resources for training; and, in any event, such programs are too often seen by senior police administrators as mere window dressing for that earthy common sense which recruits either already have or may develop by working with experienced officers.

In the British Isles all probationary police constables attend district training centers for three months after joining and subsequently for two fortnight-long refresher courses during their probation. Our ukase concerning the establishment of regional police academies is designed to provide similar facilities in the United States. We would still fall short of the more protracted police training in Scandinavia and Holland, but it would be a substantial forward step. With regard to the content of training both in Britain and throughout the United States the emphasis is still largely on the technical and mechanical aspects of police work, with little attention paid to such vital matters as the need for exercise of discretion in law enforcement, police–minority group relations, the police role in the community, and the kind of basic psychology and sociology which would aid the recruit to understand and perform the highly sensitive and complex functions involved in the law enforcement task. Regional police academies could employ professional educators and civilian experts to teach specialized courses which at present cannot be taught at all because in nearly every training program not only the administrative but also the teaching staff is composed only of regular police officers assigned on a full- or part-time basis. As far as recruits are concerned, a minimum of four hundred hours of classroom work should be combined with supervised field experience and spread over a six-month period. At present less than one-third of police departments have probationary periods over six months and few use the probationary process effectively. All recruits should serve at least one year's probation and be carefully observed during that period. The police academies could in part be staffed by instructors drawn from big-city recruit programs which already approximate the plan here outlined; indeed, in some cases the existing large police department training schools might well become regional academies by expanding to make room for trainees from smaller departments.

It would also be the function of the academies to provide at least one week of intensive in-service training a year for all police agents and officers. We have added to our ukase a requirement that all police departments should actively encourage their personnel to continue their education. This could be done by helping to pay tuition bills, granting study leave, making educational achievement a prerequisite for promotion or an aid to it and so on. At the present moment very few police departments do anything of this kind.

Complaints against the Police

It might seem at first sight that in a book primarily concerned with crime control any discussion of the contentious and controversial subject of citizen complaints against the police would be out of place and moreover that whatever is done about this problem is hardly likely to help reduce crime rates. But as the President's Crime Commission task force report on the police rightly observed, "no lasting improvement in law enforcement is likely in this country unless police-community relations are substantially improved." At the same time they found that their "studies of police-community relations in 11 localities throughout this country showed serious problems of Negro hostility to the police in virtually all medium and large cities." Nor were Negroes the only minority group to express hostility toward the police; Latin Americans, Puerto Ricans, Mexican Americans, and even "youth generally" showed significant degrees of alienation. Such hostility can, and not infrequently does, lead to attacks on police officers, refusal to cooperate with the police, interference with arrests, and sometimes disturbances and riots; it therefore constitutes a formidable obstacle to effective law enforcement. It is significant too that charges of police brutality and misconduct figured prominently in the commission's survey findings.

Because of the fundamental importance of establishing good relations between the police and the community, the way in which complaints made against the police by private individuals are handled cannot be ignored here. At present 75 percent of police departments have no formal complaint requirements at all and in many places where procedures are laid down there is a deliberate policy of discouraging complaints against police officers. As a result the police are unable to clear themselves of what are frequently quite unfounded charges against them and at the same time public suspicion and antagonism to the police is encouraged because both real and imaginary grievances are placed on an equal footing.

There are a number of reasons why police internal review procedures are an unsatisfactory means for dealing with citizen complaints. The principal one is that no government authority should be a judge in its own cause and that a complainant should have the opportunity to bring his case before an impartial tribunal. The principle involved was expressed by Lord Campbell in 1852: "It is of the last importance that the maxim that no man is to be a judge in his own cause should be held sacred. *And that is not to be confined to a cause in which he is a party, but applies to a cause in which he has an interest.*" The passage in italics is the relevant one here. But it is no less important for the police themselves that every allegation should be properly investigated and cleared up. At present, the President's Crime Commission found, there is widespread and justified dissatisfaction with police internal review procedures. As the deputy chief of the Cincinnati police said with refreshing candor: "The thing that bothers me is that police continue to receive huge numbers of complaints but there are only a few instances where the complaint is upheld. They can't be wrong that much — and we can't be right that much." The deputy chief's disquiet is shared by large numbers of private citizens, although other senior police officers sometimes take a different view. Thus Chief Edward S. Kreins of California recently remarked with pride that "only one fourth of one percent of all complaints of this nature [i.e., police brutality and corruption] are ever shown to be valid." But this evades the critics' point that it may be precisely the absence of independent scrutiny that is the reason for the apparently impressive figure.

Chief Kreins has also objected to independent civilian review boards on the grounds that "review board procedures would deprive officers of such criminal safeguards as the right to confront their accusers, or protection against double jeopardy, of representation by an attorney and the right to remain silent." But there is no reason at all why the rights to confront accusers, to be represented by counsel, and to remain silent should be abrogated. As for double jeopardy, Ben Whitaker says very aptly: "Those who argue that these inquiries would place men in jeopardy twice over forget that members of other professions, such as journalists, doctors, lawyers, and dentists, already face complaints before similar tribunals, sometimes with a layman as chairman." The police cannot expect to have the advantages of professionalization without paying at least some price for it.

If it is argued (as it is in the President's Crime Commission task force report on the police) that it is "unreasonable to single out the police as the only agency which should be subject to special scrutiny from the outside," we would give two answers. First, we agree: the ombudsman inquiring into the citizens' complaints of excess or abuse of power by *all* state authorities, covering the police as well as other officials, works well in the countries where such a system now exists. There is practically unanimous agreement that both citizens and government officials including the police are well satisfied ("generally enthusiastic" according to the task force report on the police) with the work of the ombudsmen. We do not doubt that the ombudsman system would work well here, and that it is needed. Second, if the ombudsman is not accepted: it *is* wise now to single out the police for civilian review board control, for the compelling reason that they wield the greatest power that the state has over the individual citizen. Their actions are of singular importance to all of us. They have such far-reaching and exceptional power that we must have effective and exceptional processes to complain about those rare occasions when that power is abused.

That is why we take the view that in the absence of an effective ombudsman covering the operation of the state police power as well as other state powers over the citizen, it is essential that there be a civilian review board dealing with the abuse of police power over the citizen.

Before we leave this subject there is one other topic which deserves mention. In the task force report on the police, "court exclusion of evidence" is cited as one example of the way in which the public is protected against police abuses. It is true that it is possible to view the Supreme Court rules regarding illegally obtained evidence in this way. Indeed, there is no doubt that the American due process exclusionary rules are the product of the failure of police disciplinary processes. The early development of due process rules excluding coerced confessions, however, has a different origin: coerced confessions were first excluded because of their inherent unreliability. Later coerced confessions were excluded even if there was collateral corroborative evidence that they were reliable. If you beat hell out of a man and in the process of the beating he reveals something about the murder weapon that only the murderer could have known, then there is no reason to doubt the validity of his confession even though it was the product of coercion. Nevertheless, in the second stage of the development of the rule we exclude the confession not because of its unreliability but because it reveals improper police practices. This is true also at all stages of development in relation to the rule excluding from evidence the products of illegal search and seizure. Why should we exclude such evidence? It is, in fact, peculiarly inculpating. It seems to us, looking at the development of the American due process exclusionary rules, that the only compelling answer to this question is that the courts ultimately faced the fact that all other means of disciplinary control over police practices had failed. The English and Australian position in relation to the fruits of illegal searches and seizures is plainly more reasonable than the American position. We should at once admit the illegally seized evidence on the question of the accused's guilt and later and quite separately pursue diligent disciplinary processes against the policeman who conducted the search. Why is that not true here? The answer must surely lie in the protracted and widespread failure of police disciplinary processes to operate at all. Thus, *faut de mieux*, the Supreme Court is forced to move and to exercise its only weapon against improper police practices. We would suggest as ombudsman or the civilian review board better and more effectively develop their processes there would be strong grounds for the relaxation of the American exclusionary rule.

Technology and the Police

Very little progress has been made in introducing technology into the police world. As Thomas Reddin, the distinguished chief of the Los Angeles police, said before retiring to the larger prosperity of being a television announcer: "This nation's 'knowledge explosion' has so far left law enforcement untouched." In the present context it is not possible to consider all the ways in which there might be promise of significant scientific contributions to law enforcement. We are here concerned only with specific proposals capable of immediate implementation designed to prevent or control crime, increase public safety, and diminish fear. Some of these proposals are designed directly to obstruct or prevent the commission of crimes. Others are based on the assumption that to increase the threat of apprehension raises the risk in committing crime and therefore reduces the likelihood of crime being committed. By improving the possibility of apprehension the threat of apprehension is more effectively projected.

Auto Theft

Let us begin with auto theft. According to the FBI figures the key had been left in the ignition or the ignition had been left unlocked in 42 percent of all stolen car cases. In those cases where the ignition was locked at least 20 percent were stolen simply by shorting the ignition by such simple methods as the use of paper clips or tinfoil. It is reported that in one city the elimination of the unlocked "off" position on the 1965 Chevrolet resulted in 50 percent fewer of those models being stolen than were stolen in 1964. It seems clear, on this evidence, that a substantial reduction in auto theft could be achieved simply by installing, in all cars, an ignition system that automatically ejects the key when the engine is turned off so that keys are not left in cars when they are not in use. The addition of devices making ignition jumping impossible, locks on steering wheels, and alarms would together substantially reduce car stealing — by 75 percent at least. This can be asserted confidently because UCR data indicate that the majority (about 75 percent) of cars are taken for joyriding and about 55 percent are recovered within forty-eight hours, 86 percent being eventually recovered. Only 25 percent are stolen for such criminal purposes as stripping for parts, resale, or use in connection with crime.

Antitheft devices could be expected drastically to curtail if not abolish the joyriding category of theft and effectively to reduce the latter category. By making these devices compulsory throughout the automobile industry no individual manufacturer would suffer a competitive disadvantage. The cost to the consumer would be small compared with the direct financial loss of the $140 million which the Department of Justice attributed in 1967 as due to auto theft, including automobiles never recovered and damages to recovered automobiles. In addition to the saving to automobile owners and the enormous reduction in law enforcement costs in this area (auto theft makes up 17 percent of the crime index offenses) it is important to take into account that car stealing is predominantly a youthful crime and is frequently the act which starts a youth on a career of lawbreaking. If we also take into account insurance costs and the fact that, as the UCR put it, "auto theft activity, regardless of the theft purpose, frequently results in injury or death to the perpetrators, innocent bystanders and police officers," it is evident that the implementation of our ukase will in this case impressively diminish a serious and very expensive crime problem.

Emergency Telephone Communications

Studies by the President's Crime Commission demonstrated the importance of reducing police response time as a means of increasing the ability of the police to detect and apprehend criminals. Moreover, not only is there a correlation between response time and arrests but also rapid response has the collateral advantage that it creates an impression of effective police presence. Our ukases here are in the main adapted from the Crime Commission's recommendations and are designed both to facilitate and speed police response and also to act as a deterrent to criminals. The opening of police call boxes to the public, the institution of a universal emergency police telephone number, and the direct free emergency line to the police on all public telephones are relatively simple and inexpensive methods of improving emergency communication facilities. Police call boxes were in fact opened to the public in Washington, D.C., during World War II. The other two suggestions are already in operation in England.

Pedestrian Protection Systems

In urban areas the problem of crime in the streets, ranging from assault to robbery, rape, and murder is one which concerns the public more than other aspects of the crime problem. It is notable too that the UCRs indicate that the urban rate for aggravated assault is double that for rural areas, and that the urban rate for robbery is nearly nine times the rural rate. Police patrols can never be sufficiently intensive to eliminate street crime, for saturation patrolling is inordinately expensive. The pedestrian protection system we propose to institute has been reviewed and investigated for technical feasibility by the Electronics Group in the Fermi Institute at the University of Chicago. The essence of the scheme is that individual radio transmitters which can be carried in the hand or pocket and at the push of a button relay a call for help to the local police station should be made available on a rental basis in selected areas to those who request them. Not all potential victims in the area to be protected by these devices need to have them. If only a fraction of the population are carrying them, this would have a substantial deterrent effect on potential criminals. The system involves the provision of transmitters (at an estimated cost of $30 to $50), electronic relay stations at the corners of blocks (at an estimated cost of $5,000 each), a rather simple computer system to determine the location of the call and the identity of the caller, and simple direction finders for police cars. The cost of the computer system and direction finders would be small and the system would require no substantial change in routine police operation and methods — at the most, one man to watch the output of the computer. It has been estimated that direct protection might be provided for 40,000 people at a capital cost of $2 million, or $50 per head; and of course indirect protection for a number vastly in excess of that would be included. The fact that each transmitter would be identified with one individual would prevent any significant incidence of false alarms, which has always been regarded as a major problem of proposed citizen alarm systems.

Home Protection Systems

Home protection systems designed to provide protection against burglary on a similar selective basis but with the same wide general preventive implications are equally necessary. Like robbery, the prevalence of burglary is probably a principal source of American alarm about crime. It is the most frequent kind of stealing and is the crime with the highest volume among those offenses known to police and reported in the Crime Index. The President's Crime Commission report states:

> 1,173,201 burglaries were reported to the FBI in 1965 [the figure for 1967 was 1,605,700]. . . . Burglary is expensive; the FBI calculates that the worth of property stolen by burglars in 1965 was some $284 million [the figure for 1967 was $438 million]. Burglary is frightening; having one's home broken into and ransacked is an experience that unnerves almost anyone. Finally, burglars are seldom caught; only 25 percent of the burglaries known to the police in 1965 were solved [the figure for 1967 was 20 percent], and many burglaries were not reported to the police.

It is estimated that burglaries occur about three times more often than they are reported, which would mean a real clearance rate of only 8 percent. Because burglary is, in the words of the report, "so frequent, so costly, so upsetting and so difficult to control," it should be one of the principal objectives of any crime control program to provide protection for the public from this sort of offense. In this instance possibly the cheapest and most effective system might be a concealed push button alarm on the ordinary home telephone giving direct contact with the local police station which would dispatch a patrol car immediately.

Mobile Radio Equipment

In the United Kingdom the Lancashire County Police have supplied all foot patrolmen on the beat with pocket transceiver radio sets developed in the police department's own workshops. Police forces serving Oakland and Berkeley, California; Meriden, Connecticut; and Kalamazoo, Michigan, have been similarly equipped. It has been estimated that in Lancashire "a policeman on the beat who has one can do the work of one and a half men without." The task force report on the police estimates that large-scale production economies could produce a miniaturized set at a low cost (perhaps $150). Since one patrolman, at current rates, costs $4,600, this would constitute a sound investment. Such miniaturized transceivers would enable motor patrol officers to maintain communications when they leave their cars and permit them to engage in foot patrol well away from their vehicles without losing contact with headquarters. They would not only enable patrolmen to call for assistance in emergencies but would also keep supervisors in closer contact with officers and permit a more effective use of manpower. They would also facilitate the use of a maximum number of one-man cars which are generally regarded as providing more economical, intensive, and effective patrol of a city than two-man patrol cars.

Traffic Wardens

The enforcement of the traffic laws is a major police responsibility and one which is growing constantly. In this area there is a great deal of routine work which consumes enormous amounts of police time and resources. There is no reason why the police should not be relieved of some of the less important tasks and thus freed to attend to their primary criminal and preventive functions. The establishment in every state, for work in all large cities, of a corps of traffic wardens whose duties would include the enforcement of the law with regard to the parking of automobiles, the supervision of pedestrian crossings, and general traffic duties would meet this need and might help to relieve some of the ordinary citizens' hostility toward the police, which has universally been found to arise out of police dealings with the public in minor traffic matters. Another advantage of recruiting a special corps for these duties would be that the personnel appointed need not be subject to such strict physical, educational, and age requirements as the police and moreover could be paid considerably less. In the United Kingdom traffic wardens' salaries are more than 40 percent lower than those of police constables. In some parts of the United Kingdom women have been employed as traffic wardens, and it is reported that their activities are much less resented than are those of male wardens.

Police Uniforms

Before concluding we may deal with one matter which although it may not be of such importance as to call for a ukase, is, we believe, a matter of substance. Police uniforms in this country vary from the paramilitary to that of the concentration camp guard. The jackboots are occasionally to be seen and the gun or guns, gas canister, metal cuffs, and sundry other implements of war stick out for all to see like genitals of the short-coated street dog. The style of the uniform is not irrelevant to its occupant's behavior. We are not saying "clothes maketh the cop" but we believe that there is a significant relationship. Which comes first, the behavior or the uniform? The dynamics of this relationship are unimportant; the point is that if one of the variables to it is changed it will have consequent effects upon the other. The writings on the psychopathology of clothes are extensive and not confined to fashion magazines; that the style and form of the uniform can influence human behavior is beyond argument.

Although this theme may not justify a ukase, it certainly merits testing in our scheme for the reduction of crime and the fear of crime in this country. We recommend experimentation with the consequences of a nonmilitary uniform for the uniformed police. They must remain readily and distinctly identifiable as police; the uniform must be capable of adjustment to side arms, night stick, and other frequently carried police equipment; but it must divorce the uniformed policeman from his present appearance of a highly armed invader from Mars.

We suggest gray slacks, white or blue shirt, dark single colored tie (with colors possibly identifying different units in the police), black shoes, and a dark blazer edged and pocketed in a sharply contrasted color and design which will be widely publicized as that of the police. The blazer should be cut sufficiently loosely to help to conceal side arms. Headware should be of the type customary to other men in the community, but also distinctively edged and badged.

One police uniform, of somewhat different design to our sporting style, which largely achieves the purposes we pursue, is that of the "bobby." The English policeman's uniform is readily identifiable, particularly the distinctive hat; but for the rest, from heavy black shoes to the top of his dark blue, neatly belted, English air force officer's type uniform, the trappings of the soldier in action are quite absent. It is nonmilitary yet it is very recognizable and distinctive.

There would, of course, be resistance by some policemen to such refashioning. And the satirists and cartoonists of the press would delight in the arrangement. Mockery would come easy. Dinner table chatter would be enlivened by much badinage insinuating a decadent adherence to the glass of fashion by the police, an effete clothes-consciousness. We do not think such superficiality should stand in the way of our experiment.

It is easier to talk rationally to and have a proper respect for and collaboration with someone who is not dressed as a foreign invader, and this is particularly important where police relations are of sensitive significance, as in the inner-city ghetto areas. Police really are there seen by some as foreign invaders, as well as foreign protectors, and it would be desirable to use the uniform to improve relationships. Also, it is easier for the policeman to behave thoughtfully and according to the exigencies of the moment when he is not under the necessity firmly to fit the jackboot.

At all events, such a scheme of "redressing" the police has a substantial advantage in that it is testable in a small town or in one police district or with a few units. Police resentment could be overcome by a generous uniform allowance for this experiment and by its introjection into a training program as an experiment. The Hawthorne Effect, by which the fact of experimenting itself influences consequences, would need watching, but this would give an opportunity to teach the police in the experiment, and a control group, also in the experiment, about such basic research methodological processes which are today far removed from police training programs — and should not be.

It is true of course that some police uniforms in this country are reasonably nonmilitary in their design and look quite neat. Moreover such recently adopted changes in police uniforms as the check headband in Chicago achieve the objective of easy recognition without military influence. We may say at this point that, whatever the uniform, the police should receive an adequate uniform allowance. In some police forces salaries are intended to cover uniforms; this practice makes for a threadbare quality which is best avoided. There should be an adequate clothing allowance and it should be mandatory that the money be spent on uniforms.

As stated above we have not seen fit to include a ukase on this subject in our program. What we have proposed is rather the first experimental step toward what may well be a very important ukase when the experiment has been completed.

Conclusion

It may reasonably be asked if any discussion of crime prevention and the police function which deals principally with organizational and technical matters and at the same time ignores such fundamental questions as, for example, police corruption can be anything but superficial. In reply to this objection we would make two points.

In the first place it is certainly arguable that, as James Q. Wilson puts it, "crime prevention . . . cannot be attained by listing gadgets that might be built. . . . basically crime can only be reduced by fundamental social changes." But even if it is true, and there is certainly some truth in the contention, fundamental social changes cannot be introduced overnight, and loss due to crime continues. The fact that we are to move into a new house someday soon (How soon? is an interesting question) does not mean that we must ignore the leaky roof and blocked drains of our present domicile. Moreover, not all the changes necessary to reduce crime involve fundamental social reconstruction. Much can be done, or so we would argue, by the application of intelligence and a rational approach to matters which for too long have been governed by emotion and unreason.

The question of police corruption, as it happens, provides an excellent example. For in that connection, as Albert Deutsch says in *The Trouble with Cops*, the "key to the whole picture is the question of the unenforceable and unpopular vice laws we pile up on our statute books in haste and violate at leisure. We are still possessed by the impulse to solve complex moral problems by the simple passage of repressive laws."

For Deutsch, in the 1950s, found, as did Lincoln Steffens in his *Shame of the Cities* at the turn of the century, that "nearly all police graft is derived from illicit vice operations." August Vollmer was equally convinced that the "unwillingness of people to face the facts about vice and their faithful and reverential devotion to the idea that the problem can be solved with the passing of repressive laws" was the root problem.

We do not suggest that the implementation of the program outlined in chapter 1 and the removal from the statute books of the overload of restrictive morals and vice legislation will end all police corruption. But the kind of systematic corruption associated with organized crime, illegal businesses, and commercialized vice will be largely eradicated. For the rest the professionalization of the police on the lines indicated in this chapter will do much to diminish petty corruption. And, pending the millennium when no citizen will ever offer and no policeman will ever accept or seek a bribe, we shall have to recognize that no police force, however recruited, trained, or supervised, can ever be completely immune to what a nineteenth-century divine called "the corruptibility incident to ordinary human nature."

5

Rehabilitation — Rhetoric and Reality

> There are in America as well as in Europe estimable
> men whose minds feed upon philosophical
> reveries. . . . They hope for an epoch when all
> criminals may be radically reformed, the prisons be
> entirely empty, and justice find no crimes to punish.

Thus wrote Alexis de Tocqueville, who not only incisively analyzed democracy in America but also cast a cool but not unsympathetic eye on her penal system. Today, well over a century later, the sanguine expectations that Tocqueville encountered have been repeatedly and consistently disappointed.

The American correctional system handles about 1.3 million offenders on an average day; it has 2.5 million admissions in the course of a year; its annual budget is over a billion dollars. The facilities, programs, and personnel of the correctional system are badly overtaxed. Moreover, assuming that present trends in courts and convictions continue, the system will in the future, unless policies are radically changed, have to face even more extreme pressures. On the basis of a national survey conducted by the National Council on Crime and Delinquency, it is estimated that the total number of individuals in the United States under some sort of correctional supervision will reach 1.8 million by 1975.

Of the one billion dollars spent annually on corrections, well over half goes to feed, clothe, and guard adult criminals in prisons and jails. For prison is, in the United States as in the rest of the world, the core of the penal system. Excluding those sentenced to fines, about two-thirds of all offenders are committed to institutions. If one includes juvenile institutions, approximately four-fifths of the correctional system budget and nine-tenths of the correctional employees are devoted to institutional programs. Imprisonment today remains the major sanction and chief penalty of our criminal law as it has been for over a century. Indeed, one criminologist with experience of running prisons, Hans Mattick, has said that "the genius of American penology lies in the fact that we have demonstrated that eighteenth- and nineteenth-century methods can be forced to work in the middle of the twentieth century."

There are twenty-five prisons in the United States over a hundred years old. Sixty-one prisons opened before 1900 are still in use. Inside these fortress structures only a small fraction of those confined are exposed to any kind of correctional service other than restraint. The

President's Crime Commission report speaks of conditions which "are often a positive detriment to rehabilitation" and of life in many penal institutions as "at best barren and futile, at worst unspeakably brutal and degrading." The task force on corrections summed up its findings regarding the four hundred institutions for adult felons in this country as follows: "Some are grossly understaffed and underequipped — conspicuous products of public indifference. Overcrowding and idleness are the salient features of some, brutality and corruption of a few others. Far too few are well organized and adequately funded." As for the local jails which handle misdemeanants, these are described by the task force as "generally the most inadequate in every way. . . . Not only are the great majority of these facilities old but many do not even meet the minimum standards in sanitation, living space, and segregation of different ages and types of offenders that have obtained generally in the rest of corrections for several decades."

Our program thus addresses an antique, overloaded, neglected, expensive, cruel, and inefficient "correctional" system. Hence our ukases:

1. The money bail system shall be abolished. All but the small number of offenders who present high risk of flight or criminal acts prior to trial shall be granted pretrial release upon such conditions and restrictions as the court may think necessary and with stringent penalties for failure to appear.

2. Unless cause to the contrary can be shown, the treatment of offenders shall be community based.

3. For a felony no term of imprisonment of less than one year shall be imposed by the courts.

4. All correctional authorities shall develop community treatment programs for offenders, providing special intensive treatment as an alternative to institutionalization.

5. All correctional authorities shall make an immediate start on prison plans designed to reduce the size of penal institutions, develop modern industrial programs, and expand work-release, graduated release, and furloughs for prisoners.

6. All state and federal laws restricting the sale of prison-made products shall be repealed.

7. All local jails and other correctional facilities including probation and parole services shall be integrated within unitary state correctional systems.

8. All correctional authorities shall recruit additional probation and parole officers as needed for an average ratio of thirty-five offenders per officer.

9. Parole and probation services shall be made available in all jurisdictions for felons, juveniles, and such adult misdemeanants as need or can profit from them.

10. Every release from a penal institution for felons and for such categories of misdemeanants as the correctional authorities see fit shall be on parole for a fixed period of between one and five years.

The Custodial Function: Bail

One of the functions of the jail remains, as it has always been — at one time it was indeed almost the sole function — the custody of persons pending trial. It has been estimated that 40 percent or more of the jail population is made up of unconvicted defendants. A large proportion of these, from 40 to 60 percent, will later be released without being convicted. The conditions under which these persons, who have not yet been convicted of a crime and are legally innocent, are detained have been described in a legislative report on one jurisdiction: "The indignities of repeated physical search, regimental living, crowded living, crowded cells, utter isolation from the outside world, unsympathetic surveillance, outrageous visitors' facilities, Fort Knox-like security measures, are surely so searing that one unwarranted day in jail in itself can be a major social injustice." The task force report on corrections comments on this that "it is doubtful that the situation in this State is much worse than in most others and it may be superior to many." It should also be noted that in addition to those found not guilty and released there are large numbers who on conviction are given shorter terms than they have already served while awaiting trial or are placed on probation rather than imprisoned. The majority of the persons thus detained are there because they cannot afford to pay bail. Thus a survey in 1963 found that 84 percent of the detainees awaiting trial in the District of Columbia jail were eligible for release on bond but could not raise it. As President Johnson said when signing the 1966 Bail Reform Act: "He does not stay in jail because he is guilty. He does not stay in jail because any sentence has been passed. He does not stay in jail because he is any more likely to flee before trial. He stays in jail for one reason only — because he is poor."

It should be obvious that both justice and economy demand that there should be a substantial increase in the numbers of persons for whom detention is unnecessary, who should be released pending trial. Quite apart from the costs in terms of human suffering and the wastage of human resources involved in needless pretrial detention, the cost in terms of money is enormous. The task force on corrections estimated that for the nation as a whole "pretrial detention expenses probably exceed $100 million per year." Clearly, pretrial detention should be reduced to the minimum possible — that is, to "the relatively small percent of defendants who present a significant risk of flight or criminal conduct before trial" (President's Crime Commission report). This can be achieved by the abolition of money bail and the release of all defendants save the few for whom detention is essential in the interests of the community.

It has been argued against our plan for the abolition of money bail that it would be improper to empower magistrates and judges to jail defendants they believe to be dangerous on the ground that methods and data for predicting dangerousness have not been developed. But judges at present commonly set high money bail as a means of keeping in jail persons they fear will commit crimes if released before trial, although the only recognized purpose of the bail system is ensuring appearance at trial. That they are able to judge when this is necessary has been challenged on occasion but a more cogent objection would be that setting money bail is an inadequate measure both against flight and against criminal conduct pending trial. The task force on corrections reported: "Dangerous persons with sufficient funds to post bail or pay a bondsman go free: in fact, a Commission study indicated that some professional criminals appear to consider the cost of bail bonds a routine expense of doing business. . . . Moreover the need to raise funds for a bond premium may have the unintended effect of leading the defendant to commit criminal acts."

It is also pertinent to remark that judges are no better qualified to predict nonappearance than to predict dangerousness although the whole bail system postulates their ability to do so. In our view it is essential that research which has already begun on identifying the factors relevant to the risk of flight before trial be continued and intensified. Further research is necessary to discover the factors bearing on the likelihood of persons' committing various offenses while released pending trial. This does not mean, however, that we can afford to preserve the present largely ineffective, highly inequitable, and almost criminally wasteful system until those researches have been completed.

As the task force report on the courts put it, "Society has an important interest in securing protection from dangerous offenders who may commit crimes if released before trial." But the VERA Foundation Manhattan Bail Bond Project in New York City and similar programs in other places have demonstrated that for the rest "vast numbers of releases, few defaulters, and scarcely any commissions of crime by parolees in the interim between release and trial" are possible. The essence of these programs is that where defendants can establish a "credit rating" in terms of such factors as job stability and family ties the defendants' promise to appear for trial is accepted in lieu of the usual cash bail or bond. The proportion of those currently detained who can meet the requisite criteria for release has been estimated at between 50 and 60 percent. The yearly cost of unnecessarily detaining such persons: $50 million.

The Correctional Function

There is a marked tendency for some of the experts in the field of corrections to declare flatly that imprisonment has failed. Penal administrators, research workers, and others currently working in or observing prison systems quite commonly assert that all prison programs have proved ineffective. Some years ago John Bartlow Martin in his widely acclaimed *Break Down the Walls* (1951) wrote:

> The American prison system makes no sense. Prisons
> have failed as deterrents to crime. They have failed as
> rehabilitative institutions. What then shall we do? Let
> us face it: Prisons should be abolished. The prison
> cannot be reformed. It rests upon false premises.
> Nothing can improve it. It will never be anything but
> a graveyard of good intentions. Prison is not just the
> enemy of the prisoners. It is the enemy of society.
> This behemoth, this monster error, has nullified every
> good work. It must be done away with.

Others have been more cautiously agnostic and have said merely that we know nothing about the effectiveness of imprisonment. It is necessary therefore, first of all, to say something about this prevailing pessimism or skepticism, to consider how far it is rationally justified or to what extent it may be due to the demise of exaggerated hopes and the frustration of ideals. One source of disaffection is easy to identify. The President's Commission task force report on corrections states: "The ultimate goal of corrections under any theory is to make the community safer by reducing the incidence of crime." But at a time when the incidence of crime does not appear to have been reduced — rather the reverse — and the community certainly doesn't *feel* safer, this "ultimate goal" seems to be receding rather than coming closer. So, not surprisingly, some persons have assumed that all our correctional programs have failed. Indeed, some critics have directly attributed increased crime to the fact that in recent years such programs have become less deliberately punitive and more rehabilitative in intent.

About this two things need to be said. In the first place the incidence of crime is not simply a function of penal practice. There is no evidence that the volume or rate of crime is so related to penal policy that it is dependent upon and varies with changes in correctional programs and practices. But there is considerable evidence that the amount and rates of crime are related to such factors as the density and size of the community population; the age, sex, and race composition of the population; the economic status and relative stability of the population; the strength and efficiency of the police force; and even seasonal weather conditions. All these things are outside and beyond the control of penal administration. To attribute an increase in crime to penal policy is therefore like holding an umbrella responsible for the rainfall.

The analogy, however, is not exact and could be misleading. Certainly the penal system is supposed to exercise a preventive effect on the potential offender at large. But although we know very little about the extent to which our past or present sanctions have achieved general deterrent effects, we do know that crime rates frequently vary quite independently of penal policy. Few people today believe that by devising deliberately punitive measures for the individuals incarcerated in prison we can achieve any very significant general preventive effect. As Sir Lionel Fox, who controlled the English prison system for a quarter of a century, put it: "Contemporary thought relies not on the punitive treatment of the individual offender but on 'the totality of the consequences of being found out' — general prevention is inherent in the whole action of the penal system." Nevertheless the principal function of the prison is the treatment of convicted offenders, the declared purpose of that treatment being to prevent the offender from offending again. Since the late eighteenth century when the prison system as we know it was devised by the ingenious Quakers of the Pennsylvania Prison Society, it has been the recognized task of that system to treat the convicted offender in such a fashion that he will eschew crime in the future. And this means that in one respect at least it is possible to talk meaningfully about the effectiveness of imprisonment. For the effectiveness of the prison system as a crime control agency in relation to the offenders who have been processed through it is — to a degree — measurable.

Here too it is frequently and quite confidently asserted that we have failed. "Between 60 percent and 70 percent of the men who leave prison come back for new crimes," says John Bartlow Martin. Where what Daniel Glaser in *The Effectiveness of a Prison and Parole System* (1964) calls "the legend that two-thirds return to prison" originated is not known. Possibly it started in this methodologically confused way. Most prison populations include about two-thirds who have been in prison before. It is easy but wrong to conclude that prisons therefore have a 60 to 70 percent failure rate. The prison is a sample grossly skewed by recidivists. Much lower failure rates can produce a prison population where two-thirds are ex-prisoners; prison is in large part a collection of its own failures.

The kind of rigorous studies necessary to determine the extent to which released prisoners in the United States return to prison have not been done. Those studies which have attempted to follow releases suggest on the contrary that about two-thirds do *not* return. One of the principal conclusions of Glaser's study is that "in the first two to five years after their release, only about a third of all the men released from an entire prison system are returned to prison." In view of the fact that many studies have shown that a three-year follow-up provides about 90 percent of the probable future returns to prison, Glaser's finding suggests that it is unwise to dismiss prisons as complete failures.

On the other hand neither can one say that their effectiveness has been demonstrated. The two-thirds "success" rate, a figure which incidentally also holds for the English prison system, no doubt masks a great deal of "spontaneous remission" in cases where the experience of imprisonment was irrelevant to later lawful behavior and conceivably more rigorous follow-up studies would uncover a good deal more post-release criminality than the rather crude methods so far employed. Moreover Glaser's study revealed that the economic difficulties of men released from confinement are an important factor in relation to recidivism and that it is possible to demonstrate statistically a close relationship between economic hardship and crime for certain types of offenders. This suggests that the situation in which the prisoner finds himself on release may be the principal determinant of post-release behavior rather than the experience of imprisonment.

However that may be, it leads us to consider a deeper source of disquiet and cynicism — the fact that there is some evidence to support what Nigel Walker calls "the hypothesis of the interchangeability of penal measures." This is the hypothesis that of the offenders who do not repeat their offenses after a given type of sentence all but a very few would have refrained similarly after most other kinds of sentence — in other words, that for most offenders penal measures are interchangeable. Perhaps the most sriking support for this hypothesis comes from an English study made by Leslie Wilkins comparing the results of probation with the results of other penal measures (prison, reformatory, or fine) for groups of offenders matched in respect of such variables as the offenders' sex, age, previous criminal career, number of charges and offenses taken into consideration, and type of offense. He found that no significant difference in reconviction rates was detectable.

There are a number of other studies comparing reconviction rates for different methods of disposal of offenders which suggest that it makes no appreciable difference to reconvictions what sentence the courts decide upon, for all sentences appear to produce roughly similar results. Thus Dr. Roger Hood, summarizing the conclusions of comparative studies of treatment results in a report to the Council of Europe in 1964, stated: "Overall results are not much different as between different treatments." Not surprisingly a number of workers in the correctional field have regarded these findings as disappointing because they have interpreted them to indicate that all penal measures are equally futile and ineffective. There is no reason, however, why these findings should be regarded as depressing or should give rise to cynicism.

The similarity between the reconviction rates of offenders despite differences in their sentences is not really very surprising. "Treatment" in penal institutions generally consists of little more than variations in the conditions of custody, and probation rarely involves more than cursory supervision. It would be surprising if either proved a significant influence on conduct. It would mean that, in the absence of any prior research whatever, we had fortuitously stumbled upon methods of changing human beings powerful enough to counteract all the other social and psychological pressures to which they are subject and radically to affect their behavior.

It is of course understandable that anyone committed to belief in the superiority of a particular penal method should feel some chagrin. But for an objective observer there are positive inferences to be drawn for social policy which to a large extent counterbalance any negative implications. For the interchangeability hypothesis indicates that one of the major penological problems of our time — overcrowding, shortages of adequate staff and equipment, and all the social and economic costs of maintaining penal institutions — can be drastically reduced, without any increase in reconviction rates simply by sentencing fewer offenders to imprisonment.

The General Deterrent Function

It will no doubt be suggested that a substantial abatement of imprisonment might well lead to a derogation of the *general deterrent* efficacy of the penal system. At this point therefore we shall deal briefly with the time-honored debate concerning the conflict between the principles of deterrence and reform. Professor Elmer K. Nelson, who was head of the President's Crime Commission's task force on corrections, stated: "The dilemma posed by the societal need to achieve a general deterrent effect through the operations of correctional agencies, while those same agencies are also committed to a goal of treating and helping offenders is indeed severe." But what is the precise nature of the dilemma?

Discussions of this ancient antinomy which have consumed gallons of jurisprudential ink turn out on examination to resemble nothing so much as boxing matches between blindfolded contestants.

How are general preventive effects estimated? In practice, as Professor Johannes Andenaes has aptly put it: "On the basis of rather cloudy notions of human nature and social conditions, law committees and judges sometimes try to predict how a certain innovation is likely to function in a particular situation in a given society." Nor is this fog of uncertainty due to juridical myopia. The fact is we do not know the conditions under which or the degree to which the general deterrent effects of criminal sanctions occur.

The position is little better in relation to the treatment of offenders. Professor Walter C. Bailey of the University of California, Los Angeles, recently carried out an investigation of one hundred reports of empirical evaluations of correctional treatment. This study, sponsored by the United States Department of Health, Education, and Welfare, examined reports systematically selected primarily from correctional outcome studies published between 1940 and 1960. The main question considered was, "How effective is correctional treatment?" The answer, "Evidence of the effectiveness of correctional treatment is inconsistent, contradictory and of questionable reliability." On the evidence provided by Professor Bailey it is perfectly reasonable to conclude that most correctional treatment programs do more harm than good. The best recent summary account of the state of knowledge of this topic can be found in Leslie Wilkins's excellent "A Survey of the Field from the Standpoint of Facts and Figures" in the 1967 Council of Europe report entitled *The Effectiveness of Punishment and Other Measures of Treatment*: "The major achievement of research in the field of social pathology and treatment has been negative, resulting in the undermining of nearly all the current mythology regarding the effectiveness of treatment in any form." Yet it is widely felt that we have somehow to hold a balance between what is necessary from the point of view of general deterrence and what can be conceded consistently with this in the way of rehabilitation or reform measures. In what sort of balance can these unknown quantities be weighed?

The real dilemma that we have to face is surely not that of achieving some sort of metaphysical equipoise between imponderables but rather the fact that our knowledge of both the preventive and the treatment dimensions has scarcely advanced since the days of Cesare Beccaria and Jeremy Bentham. The quality of the discussion, incidentally, has if anything deteriorated.

Community Treatment

In the light of our phenomenal ignorance, what rational strategy is possible? The first point to note is that our ignorance is not total. Leslie Wilkins, in the paper referred to above, states that while "there is much that is unknown," at the same time "much is known," and he provides "a selected sample" of the knowledge we do possess about the treatment of offenders. Three propositions which he puts forward are directly relevant to policy making in this field:

1. Humanitarian systems of treatment (e.g., probation) are no less effective in reducing the probability of recidivism than severe forms of punishment.
2. Money (if not souls) can be saved by revised treatment systems. The cheaper systems are more often than not also more humanitarian.
3. Much money is wasted in many countries by the provision of unnecessary security precautions. The public pays very heavily for the marginal gains that may be provided by repressive custodial apparatus and systems.

One of the most striking pieces of evidence which would support these propositions is an impressive attempt at controlled experimentation in the correctional field: the California Youth Authority's Community Treatment Project, now in its seventh year. There, after initial screening which excludes some 25 percent of the males and 5 to 10 percent of the girls because of the serious nature of their offenses, mental abnormality, or strenuous community objections to direct release, convicted juvenile delinquents have been assigned on a random basis to either an experimental group or a control group. Those in the experimental group are returned to the community and receive either singly or in combination such treatments as intensive individual counseling, group counseling, group therapy, family counseling, school tutoring services, and involvement in various other group activities. Each delinquent in this group is treated according to a custom-tailored plan implemented at a level of high intensity with a ratio of one staff member to twelve youths. The youths in the control group are assigned to California's regular institutional treatment program. The findings of this research so far reveal that only 28 percent of the experimental group have had their paroles revoked as compared with 52 percent in the control group which was institutionalized and then returned to the community under regular parole supervision.

The results of this experiment have somewhat more positive implications than the comparative studies we have referred to above. Even those studies suggested, as Dr. Roger Hood stated in the report to the Council of Europe cited earlier, that "some offenders can be dealt with in a manner that both avoids institutional contamination for the offender, offers equal protection to the public, saves the time of those engaged in treatment so that they can concentrate on more difficult cases, and saves public money." The California experiment, which incidentally is unusually rigorous in its evaluative design, goes much further.

The saving in public money is certainly substantial. The cost of the California Community Treatment Project per youth is less than half the average cost of institutionalizing an offender. Moreover the program is now handling a group larger than the population of one of the new juvenile institutions that the California Youth Authority is building. An investment of some $6 to $8 million is thus obviated. At the same time the program offers not merely "equal protection to the public" but, at less than half the price, much more effective protection than the traditional methods.

It is true that there are always likely to be offenders who because of the nature of their offenses (e.g., gross cruelty, violence, or sexual molestation) will have to be imprisoned if only because the community would not accept their release. And in some cases involving multiple offenses or serious, persistent recidivism institutionalization may offer the only effective protection for society. But, as the President's Crime Commission reported, *"for the large bulk of offenders . . .* institutional commitments can cause more problems than they solve." It is scarcely more than a tautology to say that the incarceration of offenders by isolating them from the community raises difficulties regarding reintegration on release. And there is a considerable literature dealing with the work of prison aftercare which indicates that this is itself a formidable social problem.

Our ukase dealing with the development of community treatment programs reflects our judgment that, in regard to the general deterrence question, it is better in the present state of knowledge for the penal system to concentrate on the task of making the community safer by preventing the actual offender's return to crime upon his release than to pursue the problematic preclusion of offenses by others. This does not mean that the general preventive aspect of penal policy is to be disregarded. But over a wide area it is likely that the shame, hardship, and stigma involved in arrest, public trial, and conviction are the principal elements in both individual and general deterrence rather than the nature of the sentence or the disposition of offenders. It would seem, moreover, on the available evidence that the deterrent influence of punishment is in inverse ratio to the gravity of the offense. We must not habitually and thoughtlessly override the immediate object of preventing the offender from repeating his offense by assumptions of the efficacy of punishments on deterring potential imitators. Sometimes, of course, general deterrence must be given primary emphasis; but not often. There is no universal formula. As H. L. A. Hart pointed out some years ago, in discussing punishment, "we should bear in mind that in this, as in most other social institutions, the pursuit of one aim may be qualified by . . . the pursuit of others." Penal policy always represents a choice among a plurality of aims and objections and every decision we reach may be attended by some disadvantages.

Institutional Treatment

We have argued that one of the principal practical implications of our discussion is that the enormously expensive and clumsy machinery of imprisonment is today relied on excessively and that its use could be drastically curtailed with great advantage in terms of financial, social, and human costs. This is not a revolutionary theory. Indeed today it would be widely accepted as a truism of sound sentencing practice that a prison sentence should be imposed only when no alternative punishment is reasonably appropriate. This approach to sentencing has received a most interesting formulation in the sentencing provisions of the American Law Institute's Model Penal Code. The code specifically directs the court not to impose a sentence of imprisonment unless it is of the view that such a sentence is necessary for the protection of the public. The code further provides that for a felony no term of imprisonment of less than one year shall be imposed by the court. This is, of course, not a technique for increasing the duration of prison sentences, though it may in occasional cases have that effect; the theory is that if a court does not think the crime or the criminal merit or require a prison sentence of at least a year's duration then punishment other than imprisonment should be imposed. In England, and the story is substantially the same in most countries, only about one in every thirty of those convicted by the criminal courts is sentenced to prison; if only indictable offenses are considered, less than one in every five so convicted is imprisoned. As the excellent sentencing handbook prepared by the Home Office for the use of the courts put it: "Imprisonment is thus increasingly coming to be regarded as the sentence to be imposed only where other methods of treatment have failed or are considered inappropriate."

Nevertheless the fact remains that although the prison or penitentiary as we know it will almost certainly have followed the death penalty, banishment, and transportation into desuetude before the end of the century, institutional confinement in some form will remain necessary for some offenders. The kinds of diversification and modification in the prison system which will develop cannot be planned in detail or predicted with certainty. In a dynamic situation it is unwise to attempt to impose final lines of development, but some forms of innovation and variation are already in evidence. Moreover, change is essential. There is no evidence that imprisonment as a penal method is any more effective today than it was a century ago. If the figures relating to recidivism are taken as a test of effectiveness, there has apparently been no significant change throughout the period for which records are available. It is today generally recognized that institutional incarceration, far from being necessarily beneficial, is in fact usually deleterious to human beings. Worldwide experience with all "total institutions," prisons and mental hospitals alike, reveals their adverse effects on the later behavior of their inmates. This is true even for groups such as prisoners of war who have been imprisoned without any antecedent crime or other behavioral difficulty. For some time, therefore, experimental development has been taking place, tending toward the eventual elimination of prison in the form we now know it.

That form is, in outline: a walled institution where adult criminals in large numbers are held for protracted periods, with economically meaningless and insufficient employment, with vocational training or education for a few, with rare contacts with the outside world, in cellular conditions varying from the decent to those which a zoo would not tolerate, the purposes being to lead the prisoners to eschew crime in the future and to deter others of like mind from running the risk of sharing their incarceration. It is confidently predicted that, before the end of this century, prison in that form will become extinct, though the word may live on to cover quite different social organizations.

This is not, of course, advocacy of a general "gaol delivery." Prison, the basic sanction of criminal justice, must be preserved until its alternatives and its modifications are demonstrably of greater social utility. In our present ignorance of the effectiveness of our armory of punishments against criminals and of their educative and deterrent effects on the community, experimentation cannot be precipitate, and penal reforms within the walls remain an important aim. What is suggested is that the variations and modifications of prison are already at a stage where their recognition as such is necessary and that we deal here with selected aspects of that experimentation which merit further development.

The open institution plays an increasingly important part in the prison systems of the world. In its origins the emphasis was on the younger offender and on the prisoner approaching the end of his sentence. But the categories have widened dramatically, and now the concept of the open institution covers a whole group of different types of institution having in common only the absence of a security achieved by bolts and bars and armed guards. There are open camps or farms attached administratively to security prisons, holding prisoners at the last part or for most of their sentences; there are open camps for re-forestation, land reclamation, and farming, independent of any parent institution; open camps are also applicable to urban industrial activity — Japan, among other countries, has experimented with open institutions where the "prisoners" work daily at shipbuilding side by side with free labor. The open institution holds long-termers and short-termers; in Israel (and soon it will be so elsewhere) it holds the unconvicted awaiting trial. We have not yet come near to exhausting the possibilities of experiment; only a very few prisoners require cells and walls to keep them in, and cells and walls grossly increase the social isolation of the prison, impede reeducation, and inhibit the preservation of those ties which so often contribute to social conformity. The open institution is a most promising diversification of the prison.

At our present level of knowledge crime cannot be regarded as one aspect or symptom of mental illness. It would be unwise to turn our prisons into mental hospitals. There is, however, a proportion of prisoners for whom effective treatment can be given, and therefore effective community protection provided, only in an institution which in its routine, purposes, and techniques is closer to the mental hospital than to the prison. The proportion is a matter for argument; but something of the order of 10 percent of the prisoners in most security institutions of the world would be better held and treated in institutions run by psychiatrists and providing a therapeutic community life within them. In England, the "prison" at Grendon Underwood represents a long overdue acceptance of the advice in the government paper by doctors Norwood East and W. H. de B. Hubert written just before World War II that a special institution for the non-sane–non-insane criminal should be built. This institution and others like it in Denmark, Holland, Sweden, the United States, and elsewhere are hybrids of the prison and the mental hospital. That they are a most promising strain is already apparent, particularly from the work of the Danish institution at Herstedvester, near Copenhagen, excellently described in G. K. Stürup's *Treating the "Untreatable"* (1969). And there is a portent of significance for the future evolution of prison in the name of that institution.

Herstedvester started as a "prison for psychopaths"; Herstedvester and its sister institution in Denmark now repudiate that appellation and are run excellently for those prisoners regarded by the courts, guided by a presentence investigation, as unlikely to benefit from ordinary imprisonment or other sanction. The change from "psychopaths" to "those who are unlikely to benefit from traditional punishment" is not only a reflection of dissatisfaction with the clinical and semantic validity of the term "psychopath"; it also reveals a change from a primarily psychiatric classification of the inmates of that institution, by which they are regarded as half-mad, half-bad, and certainly psychologically disturbed beyond other prisoners, to an appreciation that the people who should be sent to Herstedvester are simply the most difficult and most intractable criminals — without making any particular psychiatric classificatory statements about them.

One aspect of the work at Herstedvester leads helpfully to a further variation or mutation on prison. The period that criminals actually spend in Herstedvester has been steadily reduced over the years until now the norm is two years. At a rough estimate, the norm of "time in" for similar criminals in England and Australia would be four years, and in America seven years. The period and intensity of supervision is, however, much greater after the prisoner leaves Herstedvester than is the aftercare supervision following imprisonment in most other countries, and there is a much higher likelihood of the criminal's return to Herstedvester for misbehavior or difficulty in social adaptation short of crime. If necessary, those paroled from Herstedvester are helped and supported in the community, supervised and controlled, for many years; the period in the institution is merely a part of the overall correctional effort, institutional and in the community, and in duration it is often the lesser part.

A similar idea is to be seen also in the reorganization of the Swedish correctional system, with the administrative consolidation of probation, prison, and aftercare services, regionalization, flexibility of release and transfer procedures, and a deliberate plan to make the prison term merely a part of the correctional plan and to reduce the period of imprisonment. Such plans are creating, in effect, a new short-term imprisonment, with surveillance and support in the community thereafter, instead of the former protracted prison sentences.

Special institutions for addicts — alcoholic and narcotic, where the latter are a serious social problem — are variations on the traditional prison which are emerging in many countries. We have already made it clear that we do not think addiction should be treated as criminal. Nevertheless when alcoholism is at the root of a prisoner's criminality, or when he is imprisoned because of a combination of drunkenness and offensive behavior, or some other socially prohibited conduct, it is cruel and futile to look to the traditional prison for his reclamation and for society's protection from him, except during the time of his incarceration. The realization of this futility has led to widespread experimentation, varying from institutions akin to mental hospitals to the encouragement of the grouping of alcoholics or narcotic addicts in probation hostels. Alcoholics Anonymous, the development of the Nalline test for heroin addiction as a strong weapon of probation supervision, a gradual understanding of the physiological and psychological pressures toward addiction, combined with the manifest failure of the traditional prison as a means of treating these problems, have led to a situation where, though our methods of treatment and control are unsure, institutions such as hostels and other outpatient facilities in the community are supplanting the traditional prison for this group.

A distinction must be drawn between the amelioration of prison conditions and the diminution of the social isolation of prison. The amelioration of living conditions in prison — the elimination of needless humiliations and indignities, the provision of a reasonable day's work instead of the damaging degradation of enforced idleness, the availability of educational and vocational training programs — and similar developments are to be seen at different stages throughout the world. It would be wrong to minimize their social and human value; but they bear only lightly on that to which all else in prison is accessory — the loss of freedom.

Prison is expulsion from the group; it is banishment to a country worse than that existing outside the prison. And it is a strange and inefficient banishment because there is normally a return; a new and meaningful life is not possible in the country to which the criminal is banished, and life there tends to sever his cultural roots and to cripple him socially and sometimes psychologically for his return.

Other modifications of the prison are also taking place, however, and these have as their purpose the elimination of banishment, the diminution of the social isolation of prison, and the preservation of the familial and social ties which are so important to a law-abiding life. Some of these modifications are home leave, working out, day leave, furloughs to find employment, unrestricted correspondence, frequent visits by family and approved friends, halfway hostels as release procedures, and the creation of elements of a therapeutic community within the walls.

There is a conflict inherent in our prison purposes. As a deterrent punishment we impose social isolation and at the same time we aspire to influence the prisoner to reformation; yet experience, and such evidence as we have, leads inexorably to the view that in the preservation and strengthening of the prisoner's familial ties, and the preservation and creation of other social links with the community, lies our best hope for his avoiding crime on release. We must, in our own interests, preserve and nourish his family and community relationships.

Letters to and from family and friends have been treated as rare privileges; the advanced correctional administrators of the world now regard letters as necessities of rehabilitation, and pathetic arguments about the administrative problems of censoring so many letters are quickly met. Likewise, visits are moving from rare privileges to essential and reasonably frequent therapeutic opportunities.

It is a truism of prison reform that "aftercare" starts on the day the criminal is admitted to prison, that his mind should be then turned toward a meaningful training program leading to an attainable goal for residential and vocational opportunities after release. So the social worker, stressing and aiming to strengthen community ties, trying to deny the consequences of the banishment of prison, comes early into the life of the prisoner.

Some countries develop systems of home leave, allowing all but a few prisoners regular home leave after part of their sentence has been served. Such systems start as a release procedure but work their way back into the prison regime; they start as a privilege allowed to the younger prisoners and develop into a wise rehabilitative process applicable to most prisoners. Home leave must be used in our penal system, not for reasons of sentimentality but because it better protects the community and maximizes the chances of reform by preserving the prisoner's familial and desirable community relationships. When allied with some indefiniteness in the duration of the sentence, the regular testing of fitness for release by a home-leave program is obviously sound community protection.

Similiar pressures lie behind "day leave" in the Scandinavian systems and behind "working out" as it gradually develops in several regions of the world. Part-time imprisonment thus stands both as an alternative to prison and as a modification of prison. Toward the end of a sentence it seems rational and safe to let selected prisoners reestablish their working lives by going on furlough, assisted and supervised by a social worker or aftercare officer, to find a job, and then to let them go daily to that job from prison. Again, what starts as a privilege for a few toward the end of their sentences may, with successful application, be spread to wider groups of prisoners and come to be applied earlier in their sentences.

The hostel scheme, as a release procedure, is a similar step in this process of lessening the social isolation of prison. Hostels within the prison walls started in England for habitual criminals; they proved surprisingly successful and were extended to apply to prisoners with sentences of four years and over. Hostels for young offenders as a halfway house instead of, or as providing a path out of, borstal or other reformatory institutions, are, of course, widely established. Here we see a development from both ends of the correctional spectrum. Hostels as a release procedure aiming at lessening the effects of the social isolation of prison and as a means of curtailing the time spent in prison are used for the least promising, the habitual, criminals and the long-termers, and also for the most promising, the young offenders. It is clear that the hostel, for these twin purposes, will become an accepted part of the penal program — and prison will become but one element of the correctional plan in which a halfway release hostel (when appropriate) and supervised aftercare will normally play equally significant roles.

Yet even when reduction of the social isolation is achieved there are a number of features of the prison system which demand urgent attention; the problem of providing effective prison industries is one of them. In the vast majority of correctional institutions penal work programs are small and inefficient and involve repetitious drudgery with outdated equipment. The President's Crime Commission found that idleness was the "prevailing characteristic of most American prisons and jails." A number of state and federal laws restricting the sale of prison-made products have helped to ensure the continuance of this situation.

Such legislation represents a pernicious perversion of public policy. It is based on the unacceptable premise that when a person is convicted of a crime and sent to prison he ceases to be a citizen. The threat to organized labor or business interests in the community by prison industry is minuscule. The extent of the demoralization entailed in keeping prisoners in a state of workless, infantile dependency is incalculable. The development of prison industries can not only provide for the habilitation of inmates to constructive and rewarding employment but also provide opportunities for training in vocational skills. That effective prison industries can be developed has been demonstrated by the success of Federal Prison Industries, Inc., where the industrial plant, equipment employed, production design services, production management, and quality control are comparable to that found in outside industry. The Federal system provides a model for all states in this respect.

A better model for state systems possibly, because of the scale of operations, might be the Swedish work program where the penal administration slogan is: "First build a factory, then add a prison to it." Prisoners work a forty-five-hour, five-day week from seven in the morning to five in the evening with one and a half hours for lunch; the able-bodied idle prisoner is rare in Sweden. A few inmates, of course, are employed on maintenance work, but the atmosphere of all the industrial prisons is close to that of a factory. And even many of the very small open institutions are also industrial. One finds institutions of forty inmates living in lightly built and unlocked and unfenced facilities in which about half the inmates are engaged in farm work and half are running a small lumberyard or carpentry workshop. The industries range from small, almost village industries, to substantial mass-production factories. The machine shop industry provides 500 jobs, the wood industry 850, and the garment industry 850. These are the major products, but there are also large laundries and substantial boat-building and prefabricated house building activities (200). Indeed, for the 5,000 prisoners, 2,500 jobs are available in various types of industry, while roughly 1,000 are employed in farming and forestry activities.

The correctional administration is one of Sweden's largest rural landowners, with 6,500 acres of farm land. The building industry is of importance, prison labor having recently been used to build several open institutions. There still remain tensions between employers and trade union organizations over the extent to which prison building should be done by prison inmates for the larger closed and complex institution, but for the smaller open institutions the battle is won and they are largely the products of inmate labor.

The value of the produce of the Swedish correctional system per annum is 60 million kroner ($12 million). The average wage of the prisoner in industries, farming, and maintenance in Sweden is one dollar per day. The institution of Tillberga, however, in the eastern institutional group, is the first of a series of six institutions of a new character. It is the largest open institution in Sweden, with a population of 120; but unlike most open institutions it is not organized even in part as a farming or forestry camp, but rather entirely as a factory. It consists of three "houses" proximate to a large factory for the manufacture of prefabricated houses and also for a certain amount of machine shop work. It has a staff of 44, of which 18 are guards while 13 work in the factory and 13 in administration. Most of the 120 inmates are short-term prisoners who come direct to the institution without escort from the courts. Many of them are sentenced for drunken driving and, as is the Swedish practice, have been committed to prison for a short term. Most are under twenty-five years of age. At Tillberga prisoners are paid the ordinary ruling wage in the community for the type of work they do. They pay for their room and board, the remainder of the funds being their own, as if they were working at large in the community. They do not pay for the guards. This is surely proper; like other people they pay income tax and as citizens they must make a contribution, as we all do, to the costs of prisons. It would be improper, simply because they are prisoners, that a larger cost for prisons should fall upon them than on the rest of us. Prisons exist for us quite as much as they do for the prisoners.

It will be years, we suspect, before we will be experimenting with the full wages prison in this country; but the logic behind it is compelling and it is only a question of time surely before the advantages to the community and to the prisoners that such a system offers for certain classifications of prisoners bring it into existence. The experiment at Tillberga is an important pathfinder.

Another respect in which American prisons are deficient and indeed represent dangerous anachronisms is in their size. Forty years ago the American Prison Association warned that no prison should contain more than 1,200 inmates. Today not only do some forty-five American penal institutions contain more than that number but there are also a number of prisons such as the State Prison of Southern Michigan at Jackson, San Quentin in California, and the Ohio Penitentiary at Columbus which hold more than three times that number. Yet even 1,200 inmates would be regarded as far too many by most penologists today. The British Howard League for Penal Reform has stated that 150 is the optimum size and the energetic and imaginative Swedish director-general of prisons, Torsten Eriksson, regards 60 inmates as the maximum desirable population for a penal institution.

Eriksson has not yet succeeded in putting his ideal into practice. But for the 5,000 prisoners in Sweden there are eighty-eight prisons. With a range and diversity of small prisons and with more than one institutional staff member for every two prisoners, it has proved possible to set up a correctional system which avoids the mass anonymity characteristic of the penal system in the United States, and which largely avoids the hot-house growth of the evil subculture which has characterized our correctional efforts. Our institutions are grossly too large. Sweden has avoided the mega-institution; we should abandon it. There is little point in arguing the merits of this; few will disagree. It is a question of ignorance and tradition masquerading as political and social priorities. With small institutions, much else that we all seek to achieve in our correctional work is possible; with the mega-institution, little is possible. Discussing the number of staff and prisoners with a warden of a small jail in Georgia recently, one of the authors asked, "What is your inmate-staff ratio?" and received the comforting reply, "Some like it, some don't."

Another lesson to be learned from the Swedish correctional system relates to the use of female staff in penal institutions. Women are found to be working not only in institutions for younger offenders in Sweden but also throughout their adult correctional system. They work not only in the front offices outside the security perimeter but within the walls and within the cell blocks. And there are women governors of prisons for male prisoners. Only in Langholmen, the central prison of Stockholm, is there an exclusively male society. Monasticism is avoided even in the main long-term institution of Hall, the central prison for the internment group who are the persistent and professional criminals; it is likewise avoided for the eighteen-to-twenty-one-year-old group of vigorous males. Indeed, at the institution of Mariefred, holding such offenders, the warden is a woman. The advantages of our learning this lesson from Sweden are obvious: women bring a softening influence to the prison society, assisting men to strengthen their inner controls through a variety of deeply entrenched processes of psychosocial growth.

What are the disadvantages or risks involved in emulating this sensible plan, which would be sensible even did we not face chronic staff shortages? We suppose the risks or disadvantages are fourfold: loss of discipline, a barrage of obscenity, sexual assault, and successful courtship by those we too often regard as pariahs. The first we doubt, the second is a matter of staff training, the third is not a serious threat, and the fourth is to be occasionally expected and welcomed. We would not isolate a woman or women members of staff among a large number of recalcitrant, hostile male prisoners; the main custodial staff should remain male as it is in Sweden. The lesson is clear and is that women should be employed within the correctional institution for those skills in psychology, casework, administration, and counseling which they can offer as well as men, and nothing but advantages to the entire correctional system will ensue.

One final development of great importance to the modification of prison merits attention. Through group counseling, group therapy, guided group interaction, unstructured group discussions — whatever the nomenclature — groups of prisoners in many correctional systems are being brought together in relatively free verbal association to discuss their adjustment to society. This topic is not forced upon them; it is what invariably emerges after the settling-down period of complaints about the prison, its administration, and its staff. It is being found that from such peer clashes, from the interaction between the group and the individual, some prisoners are being led to sufficient insight and motivation to avoid crime in the future. Reform and rehabilitation cannot be imposed; it is universally agreed that an inner and anxious desire for change is a prerequisite; and such a desire is rarely the product of contemplation, exhortation, or severe punishment.

It comes more readily from a larger understanding of oneself and one's relationship to society which, in turn, often emerges from interaction in free verbal association with others who have lived and suffered in similar ways — hence Alcoholics Anonymous and many other group associations where the similarly troubled support one another. In the adoption of such methods on a large scale in California, New Jersey, the United Kingdom, the Scandinavian countries, and to an extent in Australia, New Zealand, and elsewhere, we see an effort to abate some consequences of the social isolation of prison. The prisoner and the prison authorities look to the prison community itself — the prisoners and the staff — to provide a group, wise in the ways of punishment and reform, who will assist the prisoner to self-understanding and to a motivation to acceptable social life. The prison group is for the first time mobilized for correctional rehabilitation. This is a very different situation from imprisonment in social isolation — as punishment, for repentance, even for reformation.

Parole and Probation

Although, as we have said, four-fifths of the correctional budget is spent and nine-tenths of correctional employees work in penal institutions, only one-third of all offenders are confined in them; the remaining two-thirds are under supervision in the community. We have already indicated that, for the great majority of those confined, special community programs must be developed as alternatives to institutionalization. It remains to deal with the two-thirds of offenders already being supervised outside the walls on parole or probation.

More than 60 percent of adult felons in the nation as a whole are released on parole before the expiration of the maximum terms of their sentences. But there are sharp variations in the extent of parole use in different states, from one in which only 9 percent of prisoners are paroled to some where virtually all are. Most juveniles are released on parole but supervision is commonly inadequate. Most misdemeanants are not paroled. Nearly two-thirds of the local jails have no parole procedures and those that do release only 8 percent of inmates in this way. Slightly more than half of all offenders sentenced to correctional treatment are placed on probation. Yet there are still many jurisdictions which lack any probation facilities for misdemeanant offenders. Of 250 counties studied by the President's Crime Commission survey of corrections one-third provided no probation service at all.

Many small juvenile courts rely almost entirely on suspended sentences in lieu of probation supervision.

Various studies have attempted to measure the success of parole and probation. As far as parole is concerned, authoritative estimates indicate that among adult offenders 55 to 65 percent of those released are not subsequently returned to prison. And only about one-third of those that are returned have been convicted of new felonies; the remainder are returned for parole violations. Success rates for probation are generally considerably higher than for parole. In an analysis of fifteen different studies of probation Ralph W. England found that from 60 to 90 percent of probationers complete their probation terms without revocation. An exhaustive survey of probation in California covering 11,638 adult probationers granted probation during the period 1956–58 found that about 72 percent were successful in terms of not having their probation revoked.

Yet these successes in both parole and probation have been achieved by services for the most part grossly understaffed, almost always underpaid, and too often undertrained. The best estimate available from current research indicates that an average of thirty-five cases per officer is about the highest likely to permit effective supervision and assistance in either service. Of course, no case-load standard can be applied to all types of offender. The optimum overall case load of thirty-five is based on a determination of what an average case load would be when different types of offender were given the appropriate kinds and degrees of supervision. Up to twenty persons in a case load of thirty-five could receive close intensive supervision; if none required such supervision, the case load could be larger.

Current average case loads vastly exceed the optimum level. Over 76 percent of all misdemeanants and 67 percent of all felons on probation are in case loads of one hundred or more. Less than 4 percent of the probation officers in the nation carry case loads of forty or fewer. Adults released on parole are supervised in case loads averaging sixty-eight; and over 22 percent of adult parolees are being supervised in case loads of more than eighty. The average case load for juveniles is about sixty-four.

It is clear that there is considerable need for additional probation and parole officers. In the juvenile field nearly double the present 7,706 parole and probation officers are required to reduce the average case load to thirty-five. For adult felons almost three times the number of officers currently employed are needed. It must be remembered, however, that offenders are kept under supervision at much less cost than in institutions. The national survey of corrections done for the President's Crime Commission found for example that to keep a juvenile offender on probation costs only one-tenth of the amount required to keep him in a state training school. Similar 1-to-10 cost ratios prevail in regard to both felons and misdemeanants. It is true that this difference arises in part because expenditures for probation and parole are currently inadequate but, as the President's Crime Commission points out, probation and parole expenditures "can clearly be increased several fold and still remain less expensive than institutional programs." When one takes into account also capital costs (up to and beyond $20,000 per bed in a correctional institution), the cost of welfare assistance for prisoners' families, and the loss in production and taxable income involved in imprisonment, the 1-to-10 ratio is clearly a considerable underestimate of the real cost differential. In these circumstances the failure to provide adequate probation and parole facilities for misdemeanants, who make up more than two-thirds of the nearly two million commitments to all correctional facilities and programs in a year, is extremely costly as well as unsound penal practice.

Integrated and Regional State Correctional Systems

One of the currently contentious issues in the organization of corrections in the federal system in the United States is whether the federal probation and parole services should be joined with the Federal Bureau of Prisons and the Federal Parole Board in a single department administratively responsible to the Department of Justice. Unification and regionalization at the federal level, and in a country the size of the United States, raise problems of great complexity, with political and jurisprudential penumbrae which at present we would prefer to avoid; let us therefore suggest only some of the advantages of a unified and regionalized structure for a state as distinct from a federal correctional system.

Such an integrated, regional correctional system is, of course, not unknown in this country. The Wisconsin system is so organized. The advantage of unifying institutional and extra-institutional processes, of some coherent single administrative structure of probation, prison, and parole, flows essentially from the fact that the connection between institutional and noninstitutional correctional processes is growing closer and requires overall planning. The prison is now rarely thought to provide an independent, self-contained correctional process. All who hope to rehabilitate offenders see the process as involving a gradual release procedure and an effective aftercare program linked in a single plan. And effective probation is coming to be seen as requiring some institutional support in an appreciable proportion of cases. The probation hostel may be necessary for some cases; institutional control of leisure in community treatment centers may be needed for others.

And so prison, probation, and parole grow closer together and structurally intertwine. The prison may be required as a base from which the prisoner goes out to work; a halfway house may be used as a release procedure; and aftercare will always be closed linked with the prison program and should provide the last stage in the execution of the prisoner's rehabilitative plan. It is hard to provide such continuous institutional and postinstitutional correctional processes, and such institutional and contemporaneously noninstitutional processes (halfway house, working out, community treatment center, probation hostel) unless there is the closest of ties between those responsible for the various services.

Continuity of treatment plan and execution is necessary to the release procedure; it also proves necessary when we apply more effective control mechanisms in our aftercare processes, for this reason: At present when a prisoner on parole breaks a condition of his release, the choice facing the correctional authorities is too limited. He can be warned, or he can be taken back into custody. Just as we are developing "halfway-out" houses as release procedures so should we develop "halfway-in" houses to provide for those released prisoners who require a period of closer control than can be given when they are relatively free on parole but who do not need to be sent back to prison. This group may not be large, but it is appreciable, and again there is a happy confluence between better rehabilitative processes and less cost.

Another advantage of unification of correctional service should be mentioned. It has long seemed to us that the prison warden, to be entirely effective in his job, should not only be informed concerning probation and parole work but also should have had a period of active involvement in casework in the community. Likewise, the senior probation or parole officer should have had institutional experience if he is to be most effective. Within the correctional system, no one should reach a high position without a variety of work experiences both inside and outside the walls. Thus the theme of continuity of treatment would be maintained by the very structure of the services involved.

So much for the value of unification in a state system. Regionalization needs little justification. It carries forward the theme of avoiding enterprises too large for any single man to have reasonably close and detailed acquaintance with their workings. And there is also the advantage of linking the correctional system, in each of the regions, close to the needs, opportunities, and social attitudes of the particular social group in which the offender lived and will live; regional differences require appropriate differences in correctional systems. Finally and obviously, regionalization greatly facilitates maintaining closer ties between the prisoner and his family, by visits and furloughs, than is possible where correctional administration is not regionalized.

Sentencing

To Blackstone the judicial function of sentencing the convicted criminal presented no trace of intellectual challenge, the judge acting merely as a channel through which the law expressed its predetermined and impartial decision. For such a purpose the classic figure of Justitia was an apt symbol, with her covered eyes, her scales to weigh the moral and social gravity of the crime, and her sword swift to execute the customary capital punishment. Time has not dealt kindly with her. Though excellently symbolizing impartial, even-handed, and effective justice generally, Justitia is ill-equipped to meet our current demands from penal sentences — her scales are incapable of weighing the criminal and his crime in the balance of the community's needs; her sword cannot fulfill our range of punishments; and the bandage, hiding from her eyes the developments in the social sciences, is an anachronism.

For the particular task of sentencing convicted criminals Justitia would be well advised to change her equipment. From her left hand she should drop the scales and put in its place the case history, the symbol of the full psychological, sociological, and criminological investigation of the individual criminal. Her right hand will find very little use for a sword in the modern penal system; she needs to have at the fingertips of that hand a grasp of the increasing range of penal techniques. Around her knees she would be well advised to gather the adolescent social sciences, who though they have not her tradition or established place in the community are vigorous and rapidly growing children of some ability. Finally, it is essential that she remove that anachronistic bandage from her eyes and look about at the developments in society generally and the demands on her for the imposition of rational sentences on those aberrant members of the community who break the rules of the criminal law.

It is necessary to draw a distinction between the guilt-finding function of the criminal court and its sentence-imposing function. Were the decision as to the guilt or innocence of the accused the only duty of the criminal courts there would be less room for criticism. For there is no doubt that the criminal court achieves greater success in its fact-finding and law-applying than in its sentence-inflicting. It is probable that its relative success in the former function springs largely from its unemotional, painstaking, and objective approach and that its relative failure in choosing appropriate punishments arises from its emotional, expeditious, and subjective reaction to the established offense and to the convicted criminal. Until the unemotional, painstaking, and objective approach is extended from the proof of the crime to the analysis of the criminal and his environment, it is unlikely that we will develop a rational sentencing policy.

We expect more from our criminal sanctions than we did in Blackstone's day, but we have neither developed techniques nor fashioned principles to meet our expectations. Over twenty years ago Mr. Justice Frankfurter said that "the inadequacy of our traditional methods for determining the appropriate treatment for offenders, once wrongdoing is established, can no longer be disregarded." But in the intervening years there has been little change, although about half the states are now undertaking projects to revise their penal laws and sentencing codes. The President's Crime Commission report contains a passage which illustrates admirably the anomalies and inconsistencies which currently exist:

> The Oregon Penal Code contains 466 penalties
> that can be imposed for one or more of 1,413 offenses.
> A recent study of the Colorado statutes disclosed that
> a person convicted of first-degree murder must serve
> 10 years before becoming eligible for parole, while
> a person convicted of a lesser degree of the same
> offense must serve 15 or more years; stealing a dog is
> punishable by 10 years' imprisonment, while killing a
> dog carries a maximum of 6 months. Under Federal

Law, armed bank robbery is punishable by fine,
probation, or any prison term up to 25 years, but
in cases involving armed robbery of a post office, the
judge is limited to granting probation or imposing
a 25-year prison sentence.

It is not surprising, as Herbert Wechsler has said, that no branch
of the criminal law is "more unprincipled or more anarchical." Yet, as
he eloquently expressed it:

This is the law on which men place their ultimate
reliance for protection against all the deepest injuries
that human conduct can inflict on individuals and
institutions. By the same token, penal law governs
the strongest force that we permit official agencies
to bring to bear on individuals. Its promise as an
instrument of safety is matched only by its power to
destroy. Nowhere in the entire legal field is more at
stake for the community or for the individual.

We do not propose in this book to deal at length with the operation
and procedures of the criminal courts. There are already available and
easily accessible many works in which the criminal court process as it
exists in this country has been imaginatively and constructively discussed. But insofar as the work of the correctional system is largely
determined by the court's sentence, it is necessary to say something
about sentencing policies and procedures. In this we are broadly in
agreement with the approach taken by the American Law Institute
in its Model Penal Code; and this agreement is reflected in several of
the ukases in this chapter.

We have referred briefly above to one of the code's sentencing provisions: its direction that the court not impose a sentence of imprisonment unless it is necessary for the protection of the public and that
for a felony the minimum term of imprisonment must be for at least
a year. The code further provides, and we agree, that for all but the
most serious offenses the minimum should not exceed three years. In
addition to minimum sentences the code also prescribes maximum
terms ranging from life imprisonment for such offenses as murder and
rape accompanied by serious bodily injury to five years for such
offenses as theft in excess of $500, perjury, and forgery of a check.
Eligibility for parole arises upon expiration of the minimum.

We are not here concerned to deal with the precise number of punishment categories required or the penalities to be attached to each category. The important points are that there should be what Wechsler calls "discipline in legislative use of penal sanctions" and that within the limits set by prescribed maximum and minimum the correctional administration should be free to decide how long the prisoners ought to be held beyond the minimum. The correctional administration is in the best position to judge when the release of the prisoner will be safe, and here it can take advantage of any improved methods developed by the behavioral sciences for predicting behavior and identifying dangerous offenders. The adoption of the Model Penal Code will involve the abrogation of mandatory sentencing provisions, such as in the federal narcotics laws prescribing mandatory ten- and twenty-year prison sentences. These are commonly nullified in practice anyway — empty threats achieving nothing.

The code also embodies statutory criteria and separate sentencing provisions to discriminate between offenders requiring lengthy imprisonment and others. Thus courts are allowed to impose extended terms of imprisonment — beyond the ordinary maximum — in cases where the defendant is a persistent offender, a professional criminal, a dangerous, mentally abnormal person, or a multiple offender whose criminality is particularly extensive. The provision of statutory criteria of this kind to guide courts in the exercise of their discretion is an important move in the direction of rational sentencing policy.

No less important are the code's provisions regarding statutory standards governing the granting of probation. In almost every jurisdiction in America legislatures have restricted the power of the courts to grant probation. These arbitrary denials of discretion to the courts, like mandatory prison sentences, are met with evasion in many cases but they represent an improper obstruction to the course of justice. At the same time, the statutory provisions authorizing the use of probation are commonly couched in such vague and general terms that, as the President's Crime Commission puts it, "each judge is left virtually unrestrained in applying his own theories of probation to individual cases."

The Model Penal Code directs the court to suspend sentences or grant probation unless it finds that imprisonment is necessary for the protection of the public because (a) there is undue risk that during the period of a suspended sentence or probation the defendant will commit another crime; or (b) the defendant is in need of correctional treatment that can be provided most effectively by his commitment to an institution; or (c) a lesser sentence will depreciate the seriousness of the defendant's crime. These standards too are general but they clearly accord a priority to dispositions which avoid institutionalization. And at the same time, the code provides a lengthy list of grounds which "shall be accorded weight in favor of withholding a sentence of imprisonment."

We are also in agreement with the provisions of the Model Penal Code regarding parole. Our ukase to the effect that every release be upon parole for a fixed period of between one and five years is derived from the code. It is based on the theory that parole should be seen as an essential part of every institutional sentence and not as an act of benign clemency on the part of the authorities. The parole period is a period of supervised conditional release required for community protection which starts when parole release occurs. At present the period of parole is measured by the length of the unexpired portion of the prison sentence, which is dangerously irrational. It means that those who are the worst risks and therefore are held longest in institutions have the shortest period under supervision, whereas the best risks, released early, have the longest terms under supervision.

Another respect in which sentencing practices are deficient at present relates to the imposition of fines. An inordinate number of offenders are imprisoned for failure to pay fines. For some states as many as 60 percent of jail inmates have been imprisoned for default in payment of fines. Sentences which offer the choice of paying a fine or going to prison are discriminatory in that those unable to pay are punished more severely. A substantial reduction in needless imprisonment can be achieved by allowing time to pay fines and by the use of civil attachment and execution for the collection of unpaid fines. In England the number of committals in default of payment of fines was reduced from 85,000 in 1910 to less than 3,000 in 1947 by these methods; and today less than 1 percent of fines lead to imprisonment for default.

It is worth mentioning at this point that although the majority of convicted persons are punished by fining, the fine is rarely mentioned in books dealing with the punishment and treatment of offenders. Yet as Nigel Walker has pointed out, "although fines are the least spectacular of penal measures, they are numerically the most important, certainly the cheapest and by no means the least effective." Walker cites the dramatic fall in convictions for soliciting by prostitutes in England from about 11,000 per year to less than 2,000 after the passage of the Street Offences Act, 1959, which sharply increased the maximum fines for this offense. Today the amounts of fines for many offenses are limited by statutes in a way which is wholly unrealistic because of the decrease in the value of money since the statutes were enacted. A wholesale revision of those statutes is long overdue. By increasing the amounts of fines and providing for time to pay, we can both maximize their general and individual deterrent efficacy and reduce the jail population.

Correctional Services for Juveniles

Insofar as our discussion has been concerned with general principles it applies to juveniles as much as to adults. The two major principles which are generally accepted by authorities in correctional services for juveniles are that traditional methods of incarceration in institutions should be avoided as far as possible and that we should develop a wide range of alternative treatment procedures designed for different types of juvenile delinquents. These principles apply equally to the adult offender and we have no specific to offer for the juvenile. And those who pretend to do so are being less than honest.

The truth of the matter is put clearly in the excellent paper, "Juvenile Delinquency — Its Prevention and Control," by Stanton Wheeler, Leonard S. Cottrell, Jr., and Anne Romasco which is published as an appendix to the President's Crime Commission task force report, *Juvenile Delinquency and Youth Crime.* "As of now," the authors say, "there are no demonstrable and proven methods for reducing the incidence of serious delinquent acts through preventive or rehabilitative procedures. Either the descriptive knowledge has not been translated into feasible action programs, or the programs have not been successfully implemented; or if implemented, they have lacked evaluation; or if evaluated, the results have usually been negative; and in the few cases of reported positive results, replications have been lacking."

To this it is necessary to add two points. In the first place our ignorance is in the main the result of failure to attempt to acquire knowledge. To quote the task force appendix again: "We spend millions of dollars a year in preventive and corrective efforts with little other than guesswork to tell us whether we are getting the desired effects." To this point we shall return in our chapter on research. The other point is this. We can distinguish between programs for the prevention of delinquency and those for the correction and rehabilitation of delinquents. It would not be right to leave the impression that our ignorance is equally abysmal in both areas. In regard to the latter we are beginning in some places — e.g., in the Research Division of California Youth Authority — to obtain some information about program effectiveness. The California Youth Authority Community Treatment Project, discussed in this chapter, provides an example of this. There are other examples of forms of treatment short of incarceration which are at least as successful as institutional confinement. In these circumstances we believe that with juveniles as with adults we should use institutional confinement only when necessary for the safety of the community.

Conclusion

The implementation of the part of our program dealing with corrections may only marginally reduce the incidence of crime. The President's Crime Commission task force on the assessment of crime in its review of the available evidence regarding high crime areas indicates that crime rates in general and property offense rates in particular are highest in central urban areas characterized by physical deterioration, high rates of economic dependency, poverty, transiency, broken families, high concentrations of depressed minority groups, poor educational facilities, minimal community organization, and the like.

The fact that studies undertaken in different cities, with different populations, in different parts of the country, with different cultural traditions in different periods have consistently shown the coincidence of high crime rates with these social, economic, and demographic features suggests, as the President's Crime Commission indicated, that "a broad attack on the underlying social and economic conditions which produce such heavy concentrations of both offenses and offenders" is necessary. But it is no argument for preserving a correctional system which is irrational, uneconomic, and ineffective.

The program outlined here will provide both cheaper and more effective protection. At the same time it will in the main be less afflictive and involve less disruption of family life and less suffering on the part of innocent dependents. No doubt those who still subscribe to the curious notion that by hurting, humiliating, and harassing offenders we can somehow morally improve them will see this as a defect in our approach. But until some evidence is adduced in support of this idea we are not disposed to take it seriously.

6

Juvenile Delinquency

> Juvenile delinquency is not a simple term. It means
> different things to different individuals, and it
> means different things to different groups. It has meant
> different things in the same group at different
> times. . . . In popular usage, the term juvenile
> delinquency is used to describe a large number of
> disapproved behaviors of children and youth. In this
> sense, almost anything that the youth does that
> others do not like is called juvenile delinquency.

This excerpt from the opening paragraph of the United States Department of Health, Education, and Welfare's *Report to the Congress on Juvenile Delinquency* (1960) pinpoints a crucial difficulty. It has been said that among the many problems confronting the student of juvenile delinquency probably none is as perplexing and elusive as the designation "juvenile delinquency" itself. This is no exaggeration. In the ever growing literature on the subject and in the enormous variety of statutes dealing with it, one finds widely divergent patterns and types of behavior subsumed under the heading of juvenile delinquency. The truth of the matter could be put paradoxically by saying that, although juvenile delinquency exists, there is no such thing as juvenile delinquency. Or, to put it more explicitly: although the multifarious types of behavior designated by the expression undoubtedly occur, they do not constitute a homogeneous group.

Defining juvenile delinquency is, of course, essential to any useful assessment of its extent or of its causes. Some higher order of precision in these matters than our present wild guesses is essential to designing a rational program to deal with juvenile delinquency. Our ukases will be offered after the phenomenon of juvenile delinquency, its definition, extent, and causes, have been assessed.

Definition

Conditions included in the various statutory descriptions of delinquent behavior comprise a medley consisting of anything from smoking cigarettes, truancy, sleeping in alleys, and using vulgar language to major felonies such as rape and homicide. Moreover, such vague, imprecise, and subjective terms as idleness, loitering, waywardness, stubbornness, incorrigibility, and immoral conduct are commonly employed; concepts so loose that, as Paul Tappan has observed, "to many they may appear to describe the normal behavior of the little-inhibited and non-neurotic child." Indeed, there must be few children who do not at one time or another engage in behavior that is somewhere defined as delinquent; and much of the conduct for which children are referred to juvenile courts in some jurisdictions is of a kind which could well be — and often is — dealt with by parents themselves or by school authorities. It should be recognized that a certain amount of misconduct and some behavior problems are to be expected in all children as a part of the process of growing up. There is nothing novel about this. Twenty-five hundred years ago Socrates complained that the youth of his day were contemptuous of authority, disrespectful to their parents and elders, and tyrannical to their teachers. There is no doubt that much of what is officially defined by law as delinquent represents no more than the perennial nonconformity of youth. If we find this intolerable, we will have to prohibit procreation.

Juvenile delinquency, moreover, is defined not only in terms of types of conduct, but also by the fact that only those within certain age limits are regarded as eligible for this category. Here again we find immense diversity, for there is no consensus regarding either the age floor or the age ceiling for juvenile delinquency. The common-law rule and the most common statutory rule is that a child under the age of seven is presumed to be incapable of committing crime, and in some countries juvenile courts provide that children under this age cannot be delinquent. In others, although they may not be convicted of crime, they may be found delinquent. In perhaps the majority of jurisdictions no lower age limit is fixed. A similar lack of uniformity exists in regard to the upper age limit. It may be as low as sixteen or as high as twenty-five. These various age limits are important for they determine whether the offender is recognized as a juvenile delinquent and placed in the jurisdiction of the juvenile courts, subjected to processes other than those of the criminal law, or whether he faces the public rigors of the adult courts.

The indiscriminate and uncoordinate type of classification involved in current usage of the label "juvenile delinquency" makes the evaluation and comparison of statistical records extremely difficult; but it has other unfortunate consequences also. Because the label is used to refer to almost any unconventional or disapproved behavior of children and youths, the anxiety and hostility generated by the more serious offenses attaches itself sometimes to all youthful delinquency and leads to a blanket condemnation of youth. Thus in the words of the report to the Congress cited above,

Some people develop a suspicious and accusing set of attitudes towards youth and view with some alarm the never-ending variety of transient inventions of youth in the field of social behaviour, dress, and even patterns of language. Such anxiety certainly is not helpful with respect to handling the problem of delinquency. . . . Indeed, it may aggravate the situation.

It is not possible to say how widespread are the adult community's attitudes of anxiety, resentment, and mistrust toward youth; but that they exist is undeniable. Nor is there any doubt that their existence provokes a reciprocal reaction of hostility and defiance, thus initiating a pernicious circle of reaction which progressively intensifies the difficulty. Popular talk and publicity regarding juvenile delinquency both reflect and help to perpetuate the situation. Inevitably these emotional reactions militate against the achievement of any clear understanding of the nature and dimensions of delinquency, which is an essential preliminary to any rational attempt to deal with it.

Nature and Extent

It follows from the confusion of definitions that accurate and reliable measures of the volume and rates of juvenile delinquency are difficult to obtain. It is not possible to enumerate all the obstacles involved, but among them one can mention the frequently meager and inconsistent records kept by courts and other agencies; the fact that many states specifically exclude their juvenile courts from jurisdiction in cases of felony; and the incidence of hidden delinquencies which never come to official notice. Moreover, in the absence of accepted standardized definitions, meaningful international comparisons are difficult to make and of dubious validity when made.

In these circumstances one of the most remarkable features of the situation is the frequency with which quite confident pronouncements on the amount and seriousness of juvenile delinquency are made. One thing is certain: such confidence is rarely, if ever, justified. Most generalizations are either meaningless or invalid and are achieved only by disregarding the complexity of the evidence. Yet on television and radio, in newspapers, magazines, and books, it is constantly suggested that throughout the world we are faced with an unprecedented wave of juvenile delinquency which threatens to overwhelm us. The Teddy

Boys, the Ton-up Boys, the Bodgies and Mods and Rockers of the English, American, and Australian communities are paralleled, it is said, by the exotic armies of Halbstarken (the half-strong) in Germany, Skinnknutte (leather jackets) in Sweden, Taiyozoku (children of the sun) in Japan, Silyagi (style boys) in Russia, Blousons noirs (black jackets) in France, and many more. Yet it is questionable whether this proliferation of new soubriquets reflects any novel development.

Despite the lack of reliable statistics the available evidence suggests that juvenile crime was far more persistent, widespread, and serious in the nineteenth and early twentieth centuries than it is today. In 1816 "the lamentable depravity . . . amongst the young, of both sexes" in London resulted in the formation of a society to investigate it and the publication of a report of the Committee for Investigating the Causes of the Alarming Increase of Juvenile Delinquency. Certainly the much publicized and romanticized activities of today's street gangs seem a pale shadow of the battles waged by similar gangs in the past. A passage from Harrison Salisbury's *The Shook up Generation* may help to put the matter in perspective:

> A hundred years ago whole areas of New York were held in the grip of street gangs like the Hudson Dusters, the Forty Thieves, the Dead Rabbits, the Pug Uglies, the Swamp Angels and the Slaughter Houses. These gangs fought savage battles in the streets. A death toll of 15 or 20 was not uncommon. Even the police feared to enter some neighborhoods.

Yet today "a death toll" of one or two provokes nationwide alarm and prolonged and agonized debate. It is pertinent to ask whether there is any solid basis of fact for the widespread agreement that in the years since World War II there has been considerable increase in juvenile delinquency.

In this connection a number of points must be made. In the first place it is important to remember that there is nothing new in the precocity of criminals, for as we pointed out earlier a large proportion of serious crime has always been committed by the young. No doubt this reflects the fact that, as Winifred Elkin has suggested, "people find it easier to accept the demands of society as they grow older."

In our time, however, the amount of attention devoted to juvenile crime has vastly increased. It seems likely that a large part of the explanation for this lies in the fact that since the war "teenagers" (a term unknown before 1946) have almost everywhere obtained a greatly increased share of the national income. Moreover the bulk of that money is available for free spending; and teenagers represent a substantial market. As a result they attract attention — not only as the objects of advertising campaigns but also as the subjects of news stories. Not surprisingly, on the "man-bites-dog" principle, the small antisocial minority of this age group receives more than its share of publicity. Before long, the image of the juvenile delinquent or the teenage hoodlum, a somewhat amorphous stereotype, becomes a permanent and pervasive feature of popular thought and opinion. It is commonly forgotten that not more than 3 percent of the entire juvenile population under eighteen is processed by the police and juvenile courts in any one year.

In these circumstances it is probable that some increases in juvenile crime rates do not represent real increases but rather reflect the fact that the police, consciously or unconsciously influenced by the disproportionate publicity, tend to regard disruptive behavior by young people more intolerantly, view juvenile offenses more seriously, step up law enforcement, and even initiate "drives" against juvenile delinquency. At the same time widespread developments in reporting procedures and recording systems have commonly resulted in apparent increases in both adult and juvenile crime. There is also the fact, noted by the President's Crime Commission, that "over the years there has been a tendency toward more formal records and actions, particularly in the treatment of juveniles."

A concrete illustration of what this means is provided by Marvin Wolfgang in his admirable paper "The Culture of Youth," which is printed as an appendix to the presidential task force report *Juvenile Delinquency and Youth Crime*: "Typical in the files of a recent study were cases involving two 9-year old boys, one of whom twisted the arm of the other on the school yard to obtain 25 cents of the latter's lunch money. This act was recorded and counted as 'highway robbery.'" In another case, a nine-year-old boy engaged in exploratory sexual activity with an eight-year-old girl on a play lot. The girl's mother later complained to the police, who recorded this offense as "assault with intent to ravish." The truth, says Wolfgang, is that the "public image of a vicious, violent juvenile population producing a seemingly steady increase in violent crime is not substantiated by the evidence available. . . . it is only the incautious observer who is willing to assert that youth crime is worse today than a generation or even a decade ago."

All this is not intended to suggest that there has been no increase; clearly, in view of the increased birth rates that occurred during and after World War II and the consequent growth in child population, some rise in the absolute amount was inevitable. The "baby boom" has meant that whereas two million persons reached the age of eighteen in 1956, the number for 1965 was four million. Today nearly one-third of the population is under eighteen years of age. Moreover the crime prone part of that population — the eleven- to seventeen-year-old group — has increased disproportionately.

But when we come to ask what precise quantitative and qualitative trends can be discerned on the basis of the statistical information currently available, we find it impossible to provide clear and definite answers. With regard to America, current trends can be assessed on the basis of the statistical evidence available in the reports of the Children's Bureau of the Department of Health, Education, and Welfare and in the Uniform Crime Reports of the Federal Bureau of Investigation. The conclusion to be drawn from the figures supplied by these sources is by no means unequivocal, but there seems to be general agreement on the part of the experts that there has been a real rise in delinquency in the United States which cannot be wholly accounted for by better reporting or better law enforcement. It is extremely doubtful, however, whether it is legitimate to say anything more specific regarding the extent of the rise than to quote the somewhat jejune conclusion of the 1960 report to Congress already cited: "There is evidence that the magnitude of the problem has increased." Or as the President's Crime Commission put it in 1967, "The Commission is of the opinion that juvenile delinquency has increased significantly in recent years." But in view of the inadequate nature of the available records there are no adequate grounds for thinking that there has been any very significant rise in juvenile crime *rates*; such evidence as is available strongly suggests that the overall increase in juvenile delinquency can be largely, if not entirely, attributed to the juvenile population increase.

Regarding qualitative trends, once again few generalizations can be made with confidence owing to the unsatisfactory character of the available data. One type of offense which seems to have increased and to be still increasing in the United States is the stealing or unauthorized borrowing of automobiles. This is directly related to the increase in the number of cars available. Nevertheless it is advisable to be extremely cautious about accepting the crude figures usually cited.

In this connection a distinguished American criminologist, the late Edwin Sutherland, once gave an illuminating example:

> In 1941 a total of 8605 automobile thefts was reported to the Los Angeles police, in comparison to 8424 in 1940. This is a raw, uncorrected increase of 2.15 per cent. When the numbers of thefts is stated in proportion to the size of the population in the two years, however, the theft rate in 1941 is only .49 per cent higher than the rate in 1940. But when the number of vehicles in Los Angeles in the two years is taken into account it may be seen that the automobile theft rate actually decreased between 1940 and 1941. In 1940 there were 154.4 automobiles stolen for every 10,000 motor vehicle registrations; in 1941 the rate was 138.6, or a decrease of 10.2 per cent.

It is also interesting to note that investigations undertaken in Sweden and England suggest that a relatively small group of offenders commit a disproportionate number of car thefts and that the vast majority of automobiles are stolen for temporary use only. Certainly the UCR figures show that the police regularly recover nearly 90 percent of cars stolen in the United States.

It is often suggested that vandalism, by which is meant the deliberate defacement, mutilation, or destruction of public or private property, is a distinctive feature of postwar juvenile delinquency. Thus an American criminologist, Walter Reckless, writing in 1961, said, "Vandalism among youths and juveniles is characteristic of the new era of delinquency in America." He also added that it "has not yet spread to Western European countries." This is odd because Hermann Mannheim, in a 1954 article, "The Problems of Vandalism in Great Britain," had said, "The symbol of delinquency in the present era is the growing pattern of vandalism." The cost to the American public of this type of deliberate damage is probably greater than the combined cost of all other forms of juvenile property offense. This of course is only a guess. Unfortunately the UCRs do not give the figures for vandalism, but in all countries where such figures are available conventional property offenses head the frequency list and invariably constitute a major proportion of the total.

Another group of offenses which has been the subject of a great deal of publicity and public discussion in postwar years is what are called crimes of violence. But the recorded increase in juvenile crime is actually predominantly among property offenses. Although the one-third of the population under eighteen accounts for one-half of the arrests for larceny, burglary, and motor vehicle theft, their contribution to the arrests for homicide, robbery, forcible rape, and aggravated assault constitutes less than one-fifth of the total. Only in regard to assaults does there appear to have been any significant increase in recent years. And in this connection it is important to bear in mind something we have already mentioned. This is the very strong likelihood that one of the main causes for an increase in the recording of violent crime is a decrease in the public toleration of aggressive and violent behavior even in areas where violence has always been regarded as a normal and accepted way of settling quarrels, jealousies, or even quite trivial arguments.

In conclusion it is perhaps sufficient to add that the problem of the extent to which recorded criminality is an indication of actual criminality is an extremely complex one. Where serious attempts have been made to analyze the statistics relating to juvenile crime and arrive at reliable quantitative and qualitative assessments, the figures invariably appear to have exaggerated the extent of the problem. This is not to suggest that juvenile crime does not constitute a serious social problem. It does. No one doubts that the absolute amount of delinquency has increased substantially or that it can be expected to continue to do so for some time to come. But it does seem that much of the uneasiness, apprehension, and anxiety among the adult population and those concerned with the maintenance of law and order has been induced by figures which are far from giving a true representation of the facts. And these figures have been taken to indicate not merely that there are far more young people about today, with all this inevitably implies in terms of friction and nonconformity, but that modern youth is peculiarly irresponsible, immoral, violent, and criminal. The latter proposition, despite its perennial popularity, remains now, as in the past, unsubstantiated.

Causes

It is difficult to read the literature dealing with the causes of juvenile delinquency and survey the mass of confused and contradictory evidence without wondering whether in the present state of our knowledge anything at all useful can be said on the subject.

Barbara Wootton in her justly celebrated *Social Science and Social Pathology* (1959) critically examines and analyzes twenty-one studies selected as being methodologically the best pieces of work available and those most likely to yield reliable evidence regarding the causes of delinquency. Her often quoted conclusion is worth repeating: "All in all this collection of studies although chosen for its comparative methodological merit, produces only the most meagre, and dubiously supported, generalisations."

In our second chapter we discussed causation and we will not rehearse what we said there. Two points, however, must be made which have special relevance to juvenile as distinct from adult criminality. In the first place the fact that a disproportionate amount of crime is committed by the young should not be regarded as a cause for alarm or surprise or a sign that youth today is especially lawless or decadent. As C. H. Rolph has pointed out, "If we ever succeeded in eliminating all juvenile crime, it would mean that 100 per cent of all crime was being committed by adults; which would really be something to worry about."

For the truth is that delinquent behavior of some kind among young people if not universal is at least far too widespread to be regarded as abnormal. Surveys of self-reported delinquency both in Europe and America strongly suggest that delinquent behavior is a normal feature of youth and that most convicted youths are little different in their behavior from their peers who are not caught. Moreover, there is other evidence apart from the self-report studies which indicates that very few young people will not lie, cheat, or steal in some circumstances. The celebrated *Studies in Deceit* by H. Hartshorne and M. A. May, who applied classroom tests to eight thousand American youths from nine to eighteen years of age, demonstrated that only a very small minority behaved honestly (i.e., did not lie, cheat, or steal) in all situations. The vast majority were dishonest. It is in fact perfectly natural for children to lie, cheat, steal, indulge in physical assault, and behave indecently.

The assumption that youth can be discretely divided into the delinquent and nondelinquent is a mistake which has had unfortunate consequences. It appears to have detrimentally affected the type of research done in this field. As sociologists Marshall B. Clinard and Andrew L. Wade have pointed out, "The usual procedure is to take a random and representative sample of delinquents, match it with an equally random and representative sample of non-delinquents, subject them to a variety of diagnostic tests and thus arrive at a 'scientific' formula which supposedly aids the investigator to predict with some degree of accuracy the potential delinquent regardless of type."

It should of course be obvious that grouping all kinds of juvenile deviants and nonconformists into a heterogeneous category labeled "juvenile delinquents" and comparing them with an equally omnibus class labeled "nondelinquents" must inevitably be futile. This is more or less on a level, scientifically, with a medical research project where — to give a hypothetical example — the population was divided into the "diseased" and the "nondiseased" and compared. Quite possibly differentials would be discovered and it might well be found that the diseased differed discernibly from the nondiseased; but such findings would be of no help in formulating specific theories of disease, nor would they facilitate control. This false assumption that the delinquent population is homogeneous has been a persistent source of error in diagnosing and treating juvenile delinquency.

But the basic error is the idea that juvenile delinquency is a pathological phenomenon which requires explanation. The majority of juvenile delinquents both convicted and unconvicted do not subsequently pursue criminal careers; only a minority become recidivists. The fact that in America, as in the rest of the world, only a minority of young criminals become persistent adult criminals indicates that for most young people it is a passing phase of development and not a static condition. This has important practical implications with which we shall deal. In the immediate context it reinforces what we have already said about the inappropriateness of the cause/effect model. For we are not dealing with a specific action, event, or state in regard to which it might be appropriate to ask about causal antecedents but rather with a general developmental process.

It might be said at this point that, although delinquency is an umbrella concept covering an enormous variety of behavior so that to seek a unified causal explanation would be irrational, nevertheless it is reasonable to expect to derive causal explanations for specific types of grossly deviant delinquent activity or for persistent delinquency and adult criminality. As to this we can only say that, while it is reasonable to seek explanations, both logical and empirical considerations disaccord with the curious metaphysical notion that we will one day be able to explain all human behavior in terms of the simple unidirectional cause/effect model employed in that "paradigm of all science" — Newtonian mechanics. "Causation," Leslie Wilkins has said in an excellent critical review of research studies in the field of juvenile delinquency, "is a concept which has little meaning except in terms of something which if changed, changes the outcome." He went on to say, "By this standard, none of the factors discovered in any of the studies to date [i.e., 1963], have been demonstrated to be causes of delinquency." More recently he has suggested that "perhaps the attempts to organize experience into inadequate models is the main factor in the lack of pay-off." It is, surely, a reasonable inference.

So much for our assessment of the problems of juvenile delinquency with which our program must deal; now to the ukases themselves:

1. The jurisdiction of the juvenile courts shall be confined to cases where children have committed acts which would be criminal if committed by adults.
2. Defendants in juvenile courts shall be accorded all the rights guaranteed in the Constitution to criminal accused.
3. Youth service bureaus shall be established in all communities to coordinate all community services for youth and to deal with delinquent and nondelinquent juveniles referred by the police, the juvenile court, parents, schools, and other agencies.
4. The police shall refer to the youth service bureaus all cases other than those involving serious criminal conduct or repeated offenses, which will be referred to the juvenile court, and those minor cases in which outright release by the police is appropriate.
5. In criminal cases referred to them the youth service bureaus shall have authority to refer to the juvenile court within thirty days those with whom it cannot deal effectively.
6. As in the case of adults, unless cause to the contrary can be shown, the treatment of offenders shall be community based.

Juvenile Court or Welfare Board

We must now present the inferential steps by which we reached these political conclusions. We begin with a brief historical excursus on the judicial facilities that we use to handle the juvenile criminal. The point of departure for such a historical consideration is the turn of the century. At that time, the Western world faced two alternative paths of development. One might be called the Chicago path; the other the Scandinavian path. It is necessary to sketch these two paths and to note some of their implications. First, consider the origins of the child-saving movement, especially in relation to the development of the juvenile court, and in particular the Juvenile Court of Cook County, Illinois, which was probably the first such institution in the world. The juvenile court emerged from what was a legal misinterpretation of the *parens patriae* concept. This concept was developed for quite different purposes — property and wardship — and had nothing to do with what juvenile courts do now. Though we keep on prating *parens patriae*, we might as well burn incense. Historical idiosyncrasies gave us a doubtful assumption of power over children. With the quasi-legal concept of *parens patriae* to brace it, this assumption of power blended well with the earlier humanitarian traditions in the churches and other charitable organizations regarding child care and child-saving. The juvenile court is thus the product of paternal error and maternal generosity, which is a not unusual genesis of illegitimacy.

In 1899, then, the Juvenile Court of Cook County was born. Its siblings multiplied rapidly throughout the world, with their procedural informality, inquisitorial as distinct from adversary systems of justice, their surprising power to control the lives of children who have not committed a crime but who are neglected and in need of care and protection, as well as children who are incorrigible, who are truants, or who are thought to be in moral danger. All such courts are equipped with a vast rhetoric of benevolence.

A later development, relevant to this broad historical sweep, was manifested in Illinois in 1953, half a century later, in the creation of the Illinois Youth Commission. The commission has a dual function: to handle young offenders committed by the juvenile courts and to coordinate and organize state efforts to control and prevent delinquency. Nobody doubts the benevolence and good will behind the efforts of the juvenile courts and the state youth commissions. Nor is it possible to doubt the great power they wield over the lives of children and their families. What we should have doubts and also anxiety about are the problems which develop when these types of rescue operations become institutionalized. Too often what happens is that the rescue operations ignore the preferences of those who are to be rescued. And this is a crucial reason for reconsidering what is being done in this area.

An old story makes the point. It concerns three scouts reporting their good deed for the day to the scoutmaster. They had helped an old lady across the street. When the scoutmaster asked, "Why three of you?" they replied, "She didn't want to go." This is the heart of the matter. And it leads us to Mr. Justice Fortas's often quoted statement in *Kent* v. *United States*. He said there is evidence that the child receives the worst of both worlds, that he gets neither the protections accorded to adults nor the solicitous care and regenerative treatment postulated for children. In Chicago, for example, the detention facilities are grossly overcrowded. In 1967 there were 11,000 receptions into the main reception home for the Cook County Juvenile Court; in 1968 there were 10,215. The pressures involved in administering such an overloaded system are enormous. The problems included crowded court dockets, excessive case loads for probation officers (who thereby become little more than bookkeepers), overcrowded institutions, and inadequately paid and insufficiently trained staff.

In the main treatment institution in Illinois, four and a half months is the norm of detention. In most cases this is either too long or too short. How is the norm of four and a half months reached in that institution? Simple enough: you have to find beds for the intake, so you must get rid of some at the other end. Generally speaking, throughout the United States juvenile courts exist in this milieu, not in a milieu of adequacy of treatment resources.

Let us turn now to the other path followed toward solution of the juridical problems in child-saving and the delinquent child — to the Scandinavian welfare boards. The model there is not a modified court, not a benevolent court, not a court with lesser procedural safeguards and a greater interest in the welfare of the child than the adult court has in the adult criminal. The model is quite different. The model is the local community welfare council: a meeting of a few people in the community, knowledgeable in that small community, bringing together the resources of the community. Interested readers may refer to Margaret Rosenheim's *Justice for the Child* (1962), which includes an excellent chapter by Paul Tappan on the Scandinavian welfare boards.

The Scandinavian welfare boards are a serious attempt to deal with the problem of aggressive, nonconforming, delinquent criminal behavior of youths, other than by judicial process. They are a genuine attempt to use the resources of local communities in an administrative board structure. Do they function consensually or coercively? It is a hard question. There certainly are coercive elements, but where possible they try to function with as much family and child consent as can be gained. And they have more chance of gaining it than does the most benevolent juvenile court, for reasons we will offer later.

It has been suggested that this is the path that we should now take, we who have so far followed the court path. For example, the government of Great Britain, in a white paper entitled "The Child, the Family, and the Young Offender," suggested that England and Wales totally abolish all juvenile courts for children under sixteen, recommending instead consensual arrangements from time to time between the child, the parents, and the local welfare authorities. No day in court at all. No judicial hearing. No final formal decision. A variable, changing agreement from time to time. And if ultimately, after protracted informal efforts, this should fail, then the juvenile would be referred to new family courts having general jurisdiction particularly for the sixteen- to twenty-one-year-old group but also handling cases of breakdown of these informal processes for the younger group. These family courts would have the panoply of due process, hearings, counsel, and so forth.

The question is this: Must we choose between these alternatives? We think not, although there are some very responsible authorities who suggest we should. One of the key reasons is philosophic. The child-savers of Chicago at the turn of the century adhered to this critical philosophical position: no formal legal or juridical distinctions should be made between the delinquent child and the dependent or neglected child; they are a unity, a commonalty, to be handled by a single instrumentality. The Scandinavian approach accepts this as true and addresses all treatment of children as a welfare problem. The American juvenile court system also accepts this unity between delinquency and neglect, but addresses it through a court, a modified court, but a court. We submit that this is a false unity and that we should, for the welfare of children and of society, break that unity.

In this we are adopting the recommendation of the President's Crime Commission. Its report states:

The movement for narrowing the juvenile court's jurisdiction should be continued. Specifically, the Commission recommends any act that is considered a crime when committed by an adult should continue to be, when charged against a juvenile, the business of the juvenile court. Serious consideration, at least, should be given to complete elimination of the Court's power over children for non-criminal conduct.

The report proceeds to analyze traffic violations, which the commission says should be out of the court's jurisdiction. The commission felt that there might be grounds for keeping some neglect jurisdiction, but dependency and other family problems should not be within the jurisdiction of the juvenile court. In sum, juvenile courts should confine their attention predominantly to situations where children have performed acts which would be crimes if committed by adults; the other problems of turbulent and troublesome children should be handled by youth service bureaus on the pattern of the Scandinavian welfare council.

What would the consequences of this be? Let us take the Cook County Juvenile Court figures which reflect the pattern all over the country. In 1967, referring to intake processes, the court handled 21,409 cases. Of these, criminal delinquent behavior, such as auto larceny, burglary, robbery, theft, injuries to persons and property, sex offenses, accounted for only 11,452, or just over half of all the cases. The other half was made up as follows: minors in need of supervision, such as runaways, truants, ungovernables, and so on, 5,253; dependency, 3,038; neglect, 1,207; victim of a criminal or a delinquent offense, 15; and what one might call "welfare offenses," 444.

To give another example, in the state of California in 1966 arrests for major offenses equivalent to adult felony offenses accounted for only 17 percent of all juvenile arrests. Arrests for offenses generally comparable at an adult level with misdemeanors accounted for 20 percent. The remaining 63 percent was made up of arrests for "delinquent tendencies," which include such behavior as incorrigibility, waywardness, runaway, and truancy.

Thus the implementation of our ukase would mean that the juvenile court system would apply to about half the present cases that reach the courts and the other half would be cognizable elsewhere.

What would be some of the advantages of this in relation to the delinquent criminal group? We do not think that there is any answer to the proposition that people, adults and children alike, who have been charged with criminal offenses are entitled to due process. If we believe in an adversary system of justice for charges against adults, as a bastion of freedom, it is hard to deny its advantages to the accused child. If an inquisitorial, nonadversary system is right for children, must it not also be right for adults? If benevolence is what guides us, why should benevolence stop short with children. Clearly the implications of lesser due process protections for the accused child are unacceptable.

This, however, does not mean that we cannot retain many of the advantages of the valuable atmosphere and understanding and attitudes of juvenile court judges. We certainly can. But if we are taking such great powers over another citizen, child or adult, it is minimum decency to be sure that the jurisdictional facts on which that power is based are adequately proved. In other words, benevolence within powers otherwise taken is a fine virtue; the taking of power over another because of benevolence without other authorization is a clumsy exaggeration of our own competence.

Let us turn to the other group, the welfare cases — what advantages would there be for the other half? These are the neglected, the truants, the unruly, the sexual experimenters among the poor rather than among the wealthy. It is obviously desirable, where the child has not committed what would be a crime in an adult, to try to work through consent decrees rather than unilateral court orders. There is more hope of involving the family, such as it is, and the child in the treatment plan. Whatever our system, it is desirable to increase the consensual element. Is the day in court appropriate for that? We submit that the day in court itself is inappropriate to the settlement of difficult welfare and family-breakdown issues.

In our view the day in court is appropriate to the decision of the question, Did this child, or did he not, do a given proscribed act? This is the sort of question that lawyers are skilled in determining. We have created adversary systems that do not excessively seek for truth but rather seek to strike a decent balance between the quantum of proof of guilt and the values of individual freedom. Given an affirmative finding of guilt, the lawyer then should be able to relate to available social science information in determining the appropriate sanction to be imposed, not only in the light of the community's needs for protection and deterrence, but also in the light of the capacity of the accused to respond to treatment within available resources for treatment. By contrast, the lawyer is lost in adjudicating and effectively determining a course of action in relation to such matters as allegations of neglect, dependency, incorrigibility, and truancy. There is no issue of fact capable of being determined in such matters. The determining criteria for those conditions relate to the general squalidness of life for the children who are the subjects of such litigation. There is no neat solution to their problem. The best we can hope to achieve is a rough staggering forward in a far from perfect world for a few weeks or possibly months; the least unsatisfactory course of action which might get the child, without too much damage, through the next few weeks or months. Solutions are transitory and changing. Experimentation with various family support or placement alternatives on a temporary testing basis are the normally optimum solutions.

And should we not have *less* power in this field? That is to say, shouldn't we *not* have the power that we have given to the juvenile court over children whose socially harmful conduct has justified the passage of power to us. These are the themes which have justified the effort, in our view a wise effort, to maximize community involvement generally, and which justify the report of the President's Commission recommending that youth service bureaus handle at least half the cases currently handled by the juvenile court.

There are various reasons why we think the youth service bureau idea is a good one. One is linked with the concept of the unit of treatment in relation to a delinquent or neglected child. This point applies for both the criminal child and the neglected child, but we think it has greater application for the latter, since we suspect that we are, at least to a degree, exercising purposes other than the rehabilitative with the criminal child. But if our purposes really are turned totally toward therapy for the individual, then it seems to us we must consider what is the appropriate unit of our treatment. There are some cases, but they are very few, in which we know things to do to and for the child apart from his usual social setting which may facilitate his return to that social setting. These are cases, for example, where the child has capacity for vocational training, where he has a genuine need for the insights and the understandings which psychotherapy may give; but these are the expectations. For the overwhelming run of cases the only viable unit of treatment is the child in his family (if he has a family) and in his social setting. We have no nostrums, no processes, to bring to bear on the child that can effect change apart from his relationship in that social setting. Hence, for such cases, removing the child from his social setting and from his family without consent is on its face inappropriate. Problems remain, however, in defining consent in these types of cases.

One can cheerfully offer the principle that our aim should be to obtain parental and child consent to the temporary or more permanent arrangements that are sought to assist parents in solving the problem that the child presents to them and to the community. And to a degree, in the early stages of such efforts at social adjustment, consent may be an obtainable reality. But in many cases, and perhaps in most that are not quickly solved, it will soon become a cloak for the expression of community or state authority. If there is division within the home between the parents on the proper solutions or even on intermediate steps toward the solution of a problem, one of the parties is likely to see himself, or herself, placed in a coerced situation. Likewise, if the problems are not rapidly solving themselves and if the tensions and pressures of their continuance bear on the family or on the community, it is very likely indeed that the agents of the youth service bureau or the court intake processes will seek to take steps, such as a foster home placement, which the parent or parents may genuinely oppose. The parents and the agent of the court intake service or the youth service bureau will all understand that if no agreement can be reached the case may be referred to a court where the question of consent will change dramatically. This alternative is, we think, unavoidable; all we can do is to try to widen the area of parental and child consent and to recognize that it is, in the more difficult cases, not always genuinely obtainable. The justification for attenuation of consent, if there be justification, lies in the fact that the youth service bureaus have lesser powers over the child and the child's family than does the court.

In regard to criminal conduct by juveniles, on the other hand, we take the view that the child-savers of the turn of the century erred in drawing the line between youthful crime and adult crime and seeking to distinguish the former as, in all cases or even in most cases, not properly the subject of criminal sanctions. We would argue that we should raise the same question for adult and child of any age — did he, with criminal intent, do the prohibited act. It is, of course, true that for extremely young children the fact of their youth would be persuasive evidence of lack of wicked intent; but some experience with children's courts and juvenile institutions leads one rapidly to eschew the belief in the innate innocence of children. Indeed, when one includes the incompetent, the decrepit, and the lost characters that form so much of the grist of the mill of adult courts, one might suspect that there is a lesser quantum of responsibility per hundred in adult cases than in juvenile cases. If this be so, there is no impropriety at all in seeking to divide the present jurisdiction of the juvenile court into that which might be called a young criminal court and that which is mainly welfare, local community, social assistance, or individual assistance jurisdiction.

In the children's criminal court there should be exactly the same due process protections as apply in the adult criminal court. Where there is a disputed issue of fact bearing on guilt or innocence or a disputed issue of fact relevant to adjudication, it is entirely proper that the child should have the same protection as the adult accused of a crime. Likewise, if an adult is allowed counsel to make submissions on the best disposition of his case, there is no reason at all for denying counsel to a child. Indeed, if we seek to deny any of these rights for the child on the ground of the greater efficiency and protective capacity of a different type of adjudicating or disposing system, it will surely be found, as we have suggested above, that the argument is exactly and equally applicable to adult offenders. It may be true that the adversary system is a less efficient system of fact-finding or even of composing contentious community issues than an inquisitorial system; but the argument is equally applicable to adults and children, and we are, it seems to us, for the time being politically captured by public dedication to the rhetoric of the adversary system.

Another advantage of the division of jurisdiction of the juvenile court should be mentioned. It will lead to an increased involvement of lawyers. Lawyers bring a healthy skepticism to our benevolent processes. It is a wise policy in human affairs to trust a man with power only if he doubts himself. And he doubts himself more if others are doubting him, which in the case of lawyers is part of their normal way of life. If you have an adversary system, lawyers have a real contribution to make. A third of all criminal cases in the country are juvenile court cases, which have too long been isolated from the profession. Although we do not regard lawyers as experts in solving all human problems, we do think they are skilled in the solution of many social organization problems. It may be that one of the reasons why the President's Crime Commission talks of the involvement of lawyers as the single most important reform in the juvenile court area is that it will bring to bear a whole new area of professional criticism on the juvenile court system. Quite apart from the consequences in individual cases, it is believed that the political consequences of this new interest in a heretofore hidden social process will be of great importance.

Of course, it is one thing to say the lawyer must come to the court; it is another to describe his role there. It may well be that the lawyer in the juvenile court has to have different shades of energy, different approaches, a different quality about him than he does in the adult court. We do not think these two courts, given the present level of development, can be regarded as the same, nor should they be. How is the juvenile to be represented in, say, a neglect case? Whom does the lawyer represent? For in such cases there are really three parties. What degree of adversary posture should a lawyer take up in a juvenile case when he is reasonably convinced that the child he is representing has indeed committed the crime and is indeed in need of substantial treatment? When he thinks perhaps the only way of getting that treatment is by the use of state resources on a commitment order if the state has these resources?

If the lawyer is to play this enlarged role in the juvenile court (and if he is also to play a role in relation to misdemeanors as well as felonies in adult courts) it may be necessary as a matter of available resources for the lawyers to train subprofessional assistants as have the doctors. At present the lawyer is expected to play the role of doctor and nurse, an impossible burden. And the subprofessional would have an important role quite apart from the pressures of demand on supply. At present in the inner cities of the world, and in particular in the inner cities of the multiracial complex of society of the United States, most lawyers are totally incapable of talking to their clients and their clients are quite unable to communicate with their counsel. An interview between a lawyer and a citizen of the inner area is a wild exercise in the imputation of attitudes. The lawyer projects values and attitudes which the client, if he is swift in the uptake, feeds right back. They both need an interpreter, and the subprofessional can be the interpreter. There are values in the "new careers" idea here as well as the plain fact that we have to create large numbers of new, less-trained counseling and service avocations. The subprofessional can be the fact-finder for the lawyer concerning community pressures as well as the interpreter in the early sorting out of the realities of the case which the lawyer will have to handle.

This is not the place to attempt to give definitive answers to the host of questions which arise in this connection. But there is one question which cannot here be avoided. How will the implementation of this program help to reduce delinquency? In answer to this it must first be said that the primary justification for the division of jurisdiction of the juvenile court is not in terms of crime control or prevention. The justification is rather that such a program represents respect for human rights. It represents an endeavor to fulfill the rhetoric of our system.

Nevertheless it is also possible to provide a justification quite independently in terms of crime control and prevention. We have already indicated that the narrowing of the juvenile court's jurisdiction and the elimination of the court's power over children for noncriminal conduct (i.e., conduct-illegal-only-for-children), such as curfew violation, running away from home, and ungovernability, will reduce that jurisdiction by half and get rid of one-sixth of all "criminal" cases. But much more is involved than merely erasing crime by employing different terms for criminal acts and thus defining them out of existence. Thirty years ago, Frank Tannenbaum, in *Crime and the Community*, emphasized the role played in the development of criminal careers by the stigmatizing pejorative labeling associated with the processing of juveniles by law enforcement agencies. More recently the President's Crime Commission stated:

> Official action may actually help to fix and perpetuate delinquency in the child through a process in which the individual begins to think of himself as delinquent and organizes his behavior accordingly. That process itself is further reinforced by the effect of labeling upon the child's family, neighbors, teachers, and peers, whose reactions communicate to the child in subtle ways a kind of expectation of delinquent conduct.

The implications of this analysis are of considerable significance. Taken in conjunction with the evidence mentioned above, to the effect that the conduct of most delinquents (and certainly most first offenders) is little, if at all, different from that of their peers who are not caught, it strongly suggests that the formation of delinquent careers is a response to the stigmatization and labeling involved in official treatment as a delinquent. As Stanton Wheeler has put it, "Whatever the source of the initial delinquent act, the labeling and stigma that result from the official processing provide an important new stimulus toward delinquency, for the actor is invited, implicitly, to assume a delinquent *role*." Insofar as this is true, the removal of approximately one-half of the subjects of that processing may well be the most far-reaching single measure that could be devised in the field of delinquency prevention and control.

This brings us to another aspect of our program, the provision of youth service bureaus. These community service agencies would act as coordinators of all community services for youth and have as their principal function the control and redirection of both criminal offenders (other than cases of serious or repeated crime) and the provision of services for handling troublesome youths referred by their parents or schools as well as others in need of such services as residential facilities, job placement, vocational training, remedial education, psychiatric therapy, and counseling. The use of community agencies in this way would avoid the stigma associated with the criminal justice system. At the same time all referrals should be on a voluntary basis and the bureau should have the authority to refer to the court only the criminal cases which it cannot deal with effectively.

Our direction that the police should refer to the youth service bureaus cases other than those involving serious criminal conduct — in particular such actions as muggings, holdups, and aggravated assaults or repeated offenses — is not, as we indicate, meant to imply that all other cases should be necessarily referred to the bureaus. There will be many minor cases in which the police should continue to exercise their discretion to dismiss and release offenders. The ultimate object is not only to secure protection for the community against dangerous offenders but also to avoid the destructive labeling likely to provoke rather than effectively control delinquency in less serious offenders.

Because it is generally agreed that "the undesirable consequences of official treatment are maximized in programs that rely on institutionalizing the child," incarceration in institutions should be avoided as far as possible. But there are also other reasons for avoiding institutionalization. The intensification of contact with other offenders, disruption of normal social life, and the costliness of a mode of treatment which on the available evidence is no more effective than alternatives are all relevant considerations. In regard to cost it has to be noted that projections on the basis of present trends indicate that by 1975 the number of juveniles who would be confined would increase by 70 percent. Unless policies are changed, the 44,000 juveniles in state and federal institutions in 1965 will reach 74,000 by 1975. At present rates this expansion would involve construction costs of $600 million and maintenance costs of more than $267 million per year.

Community Treatment

In general our approach to juvenile corrections is the same as to adult corrections: that community programs are to be preferred to institutionalization. The development of alternatives to institutionalization of juveniles is, however, much more urgent than in the case of the adult offender, for population forecasts indicate that the numbers of adult criminals who will be confined in the next ten years will increase only slightly. Fortunately in recent years a variety of experimental programs have been developed for juveniles which avoid the expense and damaging consequences of institutionalization and at the same time provide more effective supervision and guidance than traditional probation and parole practice.

One of the most promising developments in this field are the guided group interaction programs pursued at Highfields and Essexfields in New Jersey and at Pinehills in Provo, Utah. The strategy of guided group interaction is to involve offenders in regular, frequent, prolonged, and intensive discussions of the behavior and motivations of individuals in groups. The underlying theory has already been outlined in chapter 5 and is essentially the same as for group counseling. In the Highfields project, guided group interaction is employed with youths aged sixteen and seventeen in an institutional setting. Although the average period of incarceration is only three to four months, which is about half that for the typical reformatory where the boys otherwise would be sent, evaluation indicates that Highfields is at least as successful as the reformatory, if not more so, and considerably cheaper. In the Essexfields and Pinehills programs the offenders continue to live at home and during the day are gainfully employed in the community. Group sessions take place in the evening after work. The Pinehills experiment involves a design to assess the effectiveness of the project in dealing with persistent offenders and, measured by the percentage of releasees not arrested within six months, has revealed that it is nearly twice as effective as institutionalization.

It is not necessary here to describe in detail all the different types of community programs which have been set up in different parts of the country. They include, in addition to the guided group interaction programs described above and the California Youth Authority's Community Treatment Project dealt with in chapter 5, foster homes, group homes, pre-release guidance centers, and reception center parole. These programs were described by the President's Crime Commission as "perhaps the most promising developments in corrections today." They are promising both because they are examples of innovation and experimentation and because they all represent attempts to treat the juvenile as much as possible in the community to which he will ultimately have to return whatever treatment is given.

It is necessary to say something here about the popular notion that juvenile delinquency could be controlled if sterner and more afflictive penal methods were employed. In fact the available evidence lends no support to this theory. Credulity, however, is not confined to the advocacy of methods when evidence of efficacy is conspicuously lacking; it extends even to a cavalier disregard of counterevidence when that is available. Nowhere is this more apparent than in relation to corporal punishment, which is still used as a penalty in a number of countries. Despite the overwhelming evidence regarding the ineffectiveness of corporal punishment presented in two celebrated English reports — *Report of the Departmental Committee on Corporal Punishment* (1938) and *Corporal Punishment: Report of the Advisory Committee on the Treatment of Offenders* (1960) — the belief that it is a uniquely effective deterrent persists and acts as a spur to recurrent agitation in its favor. It is very commonly recommended as an appropriate punishment for those guilty of crimes of violence, although the idea that to employ violence ourselves is the best way to teach the lesson that violence is wrong is curious, unsubstantiated, and, on the available evidence, quite mistaken.

This is not to say there is anything to recommend the antithetic notion: that psychological or psychiatric treatment would solve all penological problems. This too has no support in factual experiment. As a matter of fact the amount of experimental work done on the effects on offenders of punishment of any kind is extremely limited. This is part of the explanation for the enthusiastic advocacy of various correctional techniques as universally potent modes of treatment for what is wrongly regarded as a single specific condition. Yet prima facie the idea that the vast, undifferentiated, heterogeneous mass of offenders will somehow miraculously respond in an identical fashion to one and the same type of treatment, whether it be physical punishment, stringent discipline, or psychotherapy, is extremely implausible.

Clearly, we should seek to develop specialized forms of treatment for limited groups of offenders. Such measures as are introduced should be kept under constant review and subjected to careful empirical examination designed to evaluate their effectiveness. The existence of different treatment needs among different types of delinquent was demonstrated in a classic experiment some years ago at the United States Navy's Camp Elliott in San Diego by J. D. and M. Q. Grant. By a novel method of group therapy attempts were made to bring about attitudinal and behavioral change in the nonconformist confinees of this institution for navy and marine offenders who presented much the same problem as a civilian prison population. One of the most significant findings was that, although success was achieved by this method with men of high social maturity (as measured by Interpersonal Maturity Scales), low maturity inmates could be actively harmed by the same treatment programs. The obvious implication is that for different types of individuals differential "treatment" regimes are required.

This may not sound like a major discovery; in fact one might be tempted to suggest we have always known that what is good for one type of person may be detrimental to another. Two observations, however, are relevant here. In the first place, even if it is true that we have known this in theory we have largely disregarded it in penal practice. Second, we have not in the past been able to classify individuals in terms of their adjustive capacity or probable response to treatment or to identify the relevant personality characteristics which distinguish those with a low potential for improved behavior.

The truth is that in regard to both programs of general prevention and specific methods of treatment we have so far advanced very little beyond the prescientific stage. It should be remembered that the sciences of human behavior are a relatively recent development which have undergone great changes in the last few decades. These changes have been so radical that as David Wills says, in *Common Sense about Young Offenders* (1962), "We have hardly had time to bring the new discoveries and new attitudes to bear on the problem of delinquency."

But he goes on to say, "One cannot examine the modern scientific literature of delinquency without the feeling that we are on the threshold of the most fascinating and exciting developments." Whether or not that belief is justified depends largely upon the extent to which we are prepared to devote resources to experiment and research. This is a matter to which we referred briefly in our second chapter. We shall return to it again in the final chapter.

Prevention

For the immediate present, however, we are confident that the program outlined will effect a substantial reduction in juvenile delinquency. Two points need to be added. In the first place this chapter does not constitute the whole of our plan for combatting and controlling delinquency. The evidence suggests, we believe, that a great deal of juvenile crime does not arise from deep psychogenic or sociogenic causes but is situational — an immediate response to temptation and opportunity. Insofar as this is true, the technological measures outlined in chapter 4 may have a considerable impact. Automobile theft provides an excellent example of the type of crime which is predominantly juvenile and can be controlled by the use of technology. Eighty percent of the arrests arising out of the more than half a million motor vehicles stolen annually are of persons under twenty-one. No other crime index offense results in such a high percentage of referrals to juvenile court jurisdiction. Yet as we have stated in our fourth chapter we believe that devices designed to make automobiles theft proof could prevent three-quarters of all auto thefts. There is nothing to support the view that illegal use of a car represents a breakthrough of a pent-up urge to illegality which must express itself some way. It is to a large extent a reflection of response to opportunity, and the opportunity can be greatly curtailed. The determined car thief will, of course, not be affected at all; but there are very few determined car thieves among illegal users.

There is, however, no reason why we should limit our preventive efforts to this sort of negative approach. Is there any reason why we should not attempt to provide a reasonable opportunity for youths who lack cars to have cars to drive? In any American city this would be quite easy to achieve. There is no reason at all why we should not establish car libraries in the same way we establish book libraries. A large number of perfectly drivable, if properly maintained and me-

chanically inspected, second-hand vehicles sit in used car lots throughout the city. We could purchase an appreciable number of these and
allow youths to hire the car for a dollar a night or, possibly, two
dollars for the weekend. For those youths who can show genuine inability to raise this amount of money, it should be possible to reduce
the price. The youth would well understand that the safe and careful
return of the car in similar order to that in which it was delivered is
a condition of further hiring. Regular and safe use of the vehicle could
possibly reduce the price for which the youth might hire the car. It
would, of course, be necessary to have adequate insurance cover on
such cars, but the very modest hiring fee paid by the youths should be
sufficient to meet this need. The automobile has become an essential
and integral part of American life, and it is plainly idiotic to expect
children to grow up surrounded by the ordinariness of a motor vehicle
but never allowed, even after the age at which they may be licensed,
to drive one. We do not think the economics of this would be too
difficult to work out and we think it would be an ideal experiment
in a small town. Once the community is genuinely involved in dealing
with the delinquency problem, we may anticipate the development of
a variety of imaginative schemes of this nature.

One final point. We have not dealt in this chapter with the problems of "reducing poverty, discrimination, ignorance, disease and urban
blight, and the anger, cynicism or despair those conditions can inspire."
This should not be interpreted as signifying disagreement with the
view of the President's Crime Commission that to deal with those
problems would be "one great step toward reducing crime." The fact
that, for purposes of exposition, we have deliberately confined our
attention to the criminal justice system does not mean we are under
the illusion that the system operates in a social vacuum. But whatever
large-scale national strategy against crime may be adopted, there will
still be a need for the sort of tactical plan for the prevention and control of delinquent conduct outlined above.

7

Crime and the Psychiatrist

The accused is, we are informed, "psychotic," and should therefore not be convicted of a crime. Further, though "acquitted" because of his mental illness, he is "dangerous" and should therefore be detained until he is both "cured" of his malady and no longer "dangerous." Lewis Carroll, in *Through the Looking-Glass*, offered a fine commentary on the superficialities involved in such a traditional response to the psychologically disturbed offender:

> "What sort of insects do you rejoice in, where *you* come from?" the Gnat inquired.
>
> "I don't *rejoice* in insects at all," Alice explained, "because I'm rather afraid of them — at least the large kinds. But I can tell you the names of some of them."
>
> "Of course they answer to their names?" the Gnat remarked carelessly.
>
> "I never knew them to do it."
>
> "What's the use of their having names," the Gnat said, "if they won't answer to them?"
>
> "No use to *them*," said Alice; "but it's useful to the people that name them, I suppose. If not, why do things have names at all?"

Our program on crime and the psychiatrist is designed both to eliminate our present futile name-calling from the criminal justice system and to engage the psychiatrist in the treatment of certain dangerous criminals, a task he now eschews. We achieve these results by three ukases:

1. The defense of insanity shall be abolished. The accused's mental condition will be relevant to the question of whether he did or did not, at the time of the crime, have the *mens rea* of the crime of which he is charged. His mental condition will, of course, also be highly relevant to his sentence and his correctional treatment if he is convicted.
2. High priority shall be accorded to research aimed at the definition of social dangerousness and the development of prediction tables designed to deal with the "dangerous," psychologically disturbed offender.
3. Special institutions for the treatment of "dangerous" psychologically disturbed offenders, on the lines set out in this chapter, shall be established in all states.

The vast literature dealing with psychiatric or psychoanalytic criminology ranges from detailed studies of particular cases to attempts to explain all criminal behavior in terms of psychopathy. Yet apart from providing a profusion of new labels the practical contribution that psychiatry has made to the problems of defining and treating the offender is very limited. This is in part, but by no means entirely, the fault of psychiatrists themselves. There is no doubt, however, that the leaders in corrections and in criminal law policy accord the psychiatrist a slim role indeed in treating the behavior disorders that come to the courts, the prisons, and other correctional agencies. The slight attention given to the role of the psychiatrist in the report of the President's Crime Commission, *The Challenge of Crime in a Free Society*, and in the same commission's task force report on corrections, is recent testament to this neglect. Let us be clear about this. We are not suggesting that the judges, academic and practicing lawyers, correctional administrators, and criminologists prominent in the criminal justice system are reactionary, or that they fail to keep up with the literature in the social sciences; their attitude to psychiatry is not usually one of ignorance, it is rather a thoughtful rejection. They see psychiatrists, as too frequently psychiatrists see themselves, merely as diagnosticians, classifiers, separating out from the bulk of criminal offenders those whose psychological disturbance is at the level of psychosis. Where, it is asked, are psychiatrists successfully treating criminal offenders? The psychiatrist is useful, it is agreed, in classification and in staff training, but he is not seen as a serious ally in the correctional process.

We do not share this view. We believe there has been gross failure both by leading forensic psychiatrists and by those responsible for the criminal justice system sufficiently to mobilize psychiatric resources for the prevention and treatment of crime. We believe part of the fault lies in our national monomania, our *folie à collective,* concerning criminal responsibility and the defense of insanity. This has distracted us from many important tasks, two of which we shall deal with in this chapter — first, the task of defining the dangerous offender for sentencing and treatment purposes, and second, the task of better mobilizing psychiatric and other clinical resources for the treatment of such criminals. We believe these three themes — the defense of insanity, the definition of dangerousness, and the mobilization of clinical resources for the treatment of criminals who are dangerous and psychologically disturbed — are closely interconnected. The importance of all three issues must be recognized if the psychiatrist is to assist appreciably in efforts to protect the community and to treat the criminal.

Abolition of the Defense of Insanity

Rivers of ink, mountains of printers' lead, and forests of paper have been expended on an issue that is surely marginal to the chaotic problems of the effective, rational, and humane prevention and treatment of crime. We determinedly insulate ourselves from the realities we are facing — the role of psychological disturbance in criminality and the measures we might effectively and fairly use to deal with psychologically disturbed and dangerous criminals. We do not propose here to contribute to the wastage or to pursue the traditional minutiae. Our view is that the defense of insanity itself is moribund and should be interred. We are not suggesting amendments to the rules concerning fitness to plead; that issue is relevant to our present topic, but it is not one we now wish to consider.

The suggestion that the defense of insanity should be abolished is not original. Many authorities including Lady Barbara Wootton, Professor H. L. A. Hart, and Chief Justice Joseph Weintraub of New Jersey among others have advocated its abolition, though for diverse reasons and with diverse substitutes for it. We do not propose to marshal and analyze their reasons and their suggestions. We have put forward a ukase on this topic and we shall here advance some of the reasons underlying it, a few of which are not to be found in the writings of the authorities on this subject.

Why should there be a defense of insanity?

The question strikes deep into the social function of the criminal law. Over the years, we have found the traditional answers less and less convincing — such as the uncritical acceptance of what is by the Royal Commission on Capital Punishment:

> It has for centuries been recognized that, if a person was, at the time of his unlawful act, mentally so disordered that it would be unreasonable to impute guilt to him, he ought not to be held liable to conviction and punishment under the criminal law. Views have changed and opinions have differed, as they differ now, about the standards to be applied in deciding whether an individual should be exempted from criminal responsibility for this reason; but the principle has been accepted without question.

Or the answer in the American Law Institute's Model Penal Code:

What is involved specifically is the drawing of a line between the use of public agencies and public force to condemn the offender by conviction, with resultant sanctions in which there is inescapably a punitive ingredient (however constructive we may attempt to make the process of correction) and modes of disposition in which that ingredient is absent, even though restraint may be involved. To put the matter differently, the problem is to discriminate between the cases where a punitive-correctional disposition is appropriate and those in which a medical-custodial disposition is the only kind that the law should allow.

Or that offered by Sir Owen Dixon:

Now it is perfectly useless for the law to attempt, by threatening punishment, to deter people from committing crimes if their mental condition is such that they cannot be in the least influenced by the possibility or probability of subsequent punishment; if they cannot understand what they are doing or cannot understand the ground upon which the law proceeds.

Or that in the Durham case:

Our collective conscience does not allow punishment when it cannot impose blame.

Our position, putting aside the difficult and important issue of fitness to plead — competency to be tried — is very simple. The accused's mental condition should be relevant to the question of whether he did or did not, at the time of the crime, have the *mens rea* of the crime of which he is charged. There should be no special rules of the M'Naughten or Durham types. The defense of insanity being abrogated, evidence of mental illness would be admissible on the *mens rea* issue to the same limited extent that deafness, blindness, a heart condition, stomach cramps, illiteracy, stupidity, lack of education, "foreignness," drunkenness, and drug addiction are admissible. In practice, such cases are rare, and they would remain rare were mental illness added to the list. There would not merely be a shifting of psychiatric testimony to the *mens rea* issue with the same problems as beset the courts which hear it in the defense of insanity. A quite different issue would be raised, and one traditionally within the competence of the finder of fact. The convicted person's mental condition would, of course, be highly relevant to his sentence and to his correctional treatment if he were convicted.

Historically the defense of insanity made good sense. The executioner infused it with meaning. And in a larger sense, all criminal sanctions did so too, since they made no pretense of being rehabilitative. In the present context of the expressed purposes and developing realities of both the criminal justice system and the mental health system this defense is an anachronism. In the future, this defense would be not only anachronistic, it would be manifestly inefficient as well.

Let us offer a small statistical point before turning to the moral issue. In this country the defense of insanity is pleaded in about 2 percent of the criminal cases which come to jury trial. Overwhelmingly, of course, criminal matters are disposed of by pleas of guilty and trials by a judge sitting without a jury. Only the exceptional case goes to trial by jury. And of these exceptional cases, in only two of every hundred is this defense raised. In the United Kingdom, for the period on which the Royal Commission on Capital Punishment reported, the situation was very similar. The verdict of "guilty but insane" was returned, over a five-year period, in 19.8 percent of murder trials, whereas over the same period it was returned in only 0.1 percent of trials for other offenses. Does anyone believe that this measures the significance of gross psychopathology to crime? Let him visit the nearest criminal court or penitentiary if he does. Is not this defense clearly a sop to our conscience, a comfort for our failure to address the difficult arena of psychopathology and crime?

The practical difference between traditional tests of insanity and modern revisions was recently empirically tested. Various juries were given instructions based on the M'Naughten rules, the Durham test, and the following simple and uncluttered formula: "If you believe the defendant was insane at the time he committed the act of which he is accused, then you must find the defendant not guilty by reason of insanity." The juries failed to see any operative differences in the three instructions. Do we need to labor another century and a half to produce a mouse of such inconsequence?

Yet the moral issue remains central. Should we exculpate from criminal responsibility, or from "accountability" to use the preferable European concept, those whose freedom to choose between criminal and lawful behavior has been curtailed by mental illness? It is too often overlooked that the exculpation of one group of "criminal actors" confirms the inculpation of others. Why not a defense of "dwelling in a Negro ghetto"? This defense would not be morally indefensible. Such an adverse social and subcultural background is statistically *more* criminogenic than is psychosis, and it also severely circumscribes the freedom of choice which a nondeterministic criminal law (and that describes all present criminal law systems) attributes to accused persons.

True, a defense of social adversity would be politically intolerable; but that does not vitiate the analogy for our purposes. Insanity, it is said, destroys, undermines, or diminishes man's capacity to reject the wrong and adhere to the right. So does the ghetto — more so. But surely, you might ask, you would not have us punish the sick? Indeed we would, if you insist on punishing the grossly deprived. To the extent that criminal sanctions serve punitive purposes we fail to see the difference between these two defenses; to the extent that they serve rehabilitative, treatment, and curative purposes, we fail to see the need for the difference. Some reply: it is not a question of freedom or morality, it is a question of stigmatization, and to this we shall return; but let us not brush aside the moral issue so lightly.

In Shavian terms: Vengeance is mine, saith the Lord — which means that it is not the Lord Chief Justice's! It seems to us clear that there *are* different degrees of moral turpitude in criminal conduct and that the mental health or illness of an actor is relevant to an assessment of that degree — as are many other factors in the social setting and historical antecedents of a crime. This does not mean, however, that society is obliged to measure any or all of these pressures for purposes of a moral assessment which will lead to conclusions concerning criminal responsibility.

In a few cases the question of moral irresponsibility is so clear that there is no purpose in invoking the criminal process. The example of accident, in its purest and least subconscious accident-prone form, is a situation where there is little utility in invoking the criminal process. The same is true of a person who did not know what he was doing at the time of the alleged crime. But to exculpate him there is no need for the M'Naughten or Durham rules for he falls clearly within general criminal law exculpatory rules. He simply lacks the *mens rea* of the crime. Thus, it seems to us that all we need to achieve within the area of criminal responsibility and psychological disturbance is already achieved by existing and long-established rules of mental intent and crime, and we would allow a sane or insane *mens rea* to suffice for guilt.

Perhaps an example of this principle may help. The *Hadfield* case will serve our purpose admirably. Hadfield had been severely wounded in the head in the Napoleonic wars and subsequently decided that it was necessary for the salvation of the world that he kill George III. He equipped himself with a blunderbuss and secreted himself in the Drury Lane Theatre in a position from which he hoped to shoot George III as he waddled into the royal box. Hadfield saw the flabby creature in the royal box and discharged his blunderbuss in the direction of the king, unfortunately missing him.

There was no doubt of Hadfield's brain damage or of his psychosis, his gross psychological disturbance. He did, however, clearly intend to kill the king. He had the insane *mens rea* of murder, and indeed of treason. We do not regard the phrase "insane *mens rea*" as a contradiction in terms. Had his psychological disturbance led him to think that he was discharging the blunderbuss to start the performance on the stage, or to burst a balloon, he would have lacked the *mens rea* of murder and of treason. But he saw himself as sacrificing himself for the good of the world — and he may not have been far wrong. We do not deplore the fact that Hadfield was held to be not guilty on the grounds of insanity. We do, however, maintain that there would be no greater injustice involved in convicting in such a case and applying the psychological diagnosis to the decision how to treat the offender than in convicting in any of the other thousands of cases that daily flow through our criminal courts.

Clearly the crucial question in this context is: what are the consequences of the defense of insanity? Is there an operative difference between peno-correctional and psychiatric-custodial processes which renders benefit to the accused who is found not guilty on the grounds of insanity? To this important inquiry we offer two replies. First, the differences if they exist are marginal; and second, the defense of insanity is an extraordinarily inefficient mechanism of deciding on the allocation of psychiatric treatment resources.

The American Law Institute's recommended modification of the M'Naughten rules in its Model Penal Code was accompanied by a recommendation requiring the indeterminate commitment of those found not guilty by reason of insanity. Likewise, within a month of the adoption of the Durham rules in the District of Columbia, Congress provided that being found not guilty on the grounds of insanity should be followed, mandatorily, not in the discretion of the court, by indeterminate commitment to Saint Elizabeth's Hospital until such time as the person so committed could meet the requirements that he prove, beyond reasonable doubt, his freedom from "any abnormal condition" and that he is not likely to repeat the act which resulted in his insanity acquittal. Dr. Winfred Overholser, the late superintendent of the mental hospital to which the recipients of this benevolence in the District of Columbia are sent, put the matter precisely: "The notion that a verdict of not guilty by reason of insanity means an easy way out is far from the truth. Indeed the odds favor such a person spending a longer period of confinement in the hospital than if the sentence was being served in jail."

Facilities and practice differ from country to country, and in this country from state to state. The point we wish to stress is that it is error to *assume* benevolence and to assume that there are more psychiatric treatment resources, better physical conditions, and earlier release practices pursuant to a finding of not guilty on the grounds of insanity than pursuant to a conviction. It all depends. We know of systems where there are more facilities per patient for psychiatric treatment in the penitentiary holding psychologically disturbed prisoners than in the nearby state mental hospitals. Frequently the converse is true.

Let us offer a final point on the sometimes assumed benevolence of the defense of insanity. It is more than a straw in the wind, more than a suggestion that this is not a liberal, benevolent, humanely exculpating defense, when one finds the prosecution alleging at trial the insanity of the accused at the time of the crime while the defense urges his sanity; but this has occurred in both the United Kingdom and this country. Lady Barbara Wootton has discussed at least six cases in which "the witness called by the Crown to rebut evidence of diminished responsibility sought to establish that the accused was in fact insane." And in a judgment in the House of Lords, Lord Denning said: "The old notion that only the defense can raise a defense of insanity is now gone. The prosecution are entitled to raise it and it is their duty to do so rather than allow a dangerous person to be at large."

It might be suggested that our attack on the defense of insanity misconceives the problem. The task of the law, it might be suggested, is mainly to protect the community, and the defense of insanity will indeed permit better psychiatric treatment and, if necessary, longer custodial supervision of the disturbed and dangerous criminal. Later in this chapter we shall deal with the definition and prediction of social dangerousness; in the meantime, it suffices to note that the defense of insanity started on moral premises different from this, and that the defense is both unnecessary and inefficient to achieve this protective purpose.

A more sophisticated critic might suggest that we are missing the point in a different way. Criminal processes are, he might say, public morality plays. They have deterrent purposes, perhaps, but they certainly aim dramatically to affirm the minimum standards of conduct society will tolerate. By public ceremonial and defined liturgy, criminal trials stigmatize those who fail to conform to society's standards. In short, the criminal justice system is a name-calling, stigmatizing, community superego reinforcing system. And, it could be urged, we should not stigmatize the mentally ill. They are mad not bad, sick not wicked; it is important that we not misclassify them. Is there a rebuttal to this defense of the defense of insanity? We believe there is — the fact of "double stigmatization."

Consider the question, Are psychologically disturbed criminals seen by prison authorities only as "criminal," and are the mentally ill who have committed or have been charged with crime seen only as "mentally ill" by the hospital authorities? Or are the former seen as "mentally ill criminals" and the latter as "criminal and mentally ill"? Are the systems separate or confused in the minds of the staff and of the "patients"? It is clear that some belief in the separateness and purity of the two systems infects the position of those who advocate retention of the defense of insanity. Yet the fact is that the prison authorities regard their inmates in the facilities for the psychologically disturbed as both criminal and insane, bad and mad; and the mental hospital authorities regard their inmates who have been convicted of crime or even arrested and charged with crime as both insane and criminal, mad and bad.

In mental hospitals the fact that an inmate was arrested for a crime seriously influences the date of his likely discharge. Note, it is an arrest without a conviction that has this effect. Likewise the conditions of incarceration in the psychiatric divisions of correctional systems are frequently less desirable than elsewhere in the system and the chances of obtaining parole are substantially lower. The truth is that our present intellectually loose approach to this problem inflicts gratuitous extra suffering both on those who are categorized as criminal and mentally disturbed and those who are categorized as mentally disturbed and criminal. The police power of the state and the mental health power of the state are surely sufficient unto themselves, separately, to control questions of dangerousness and the upper limits of power over individual citizens. It is mutually corruptive and a potent source of injustice loosely and thoughtlessly to blend these two powers, and thus to gloss over in each the proper balance between state power and the freedom of the individual.

There is one concept common to both, the concept of social dangerousness. The problem for both the prison authorities and the mental health authorities is reasonably and effectively to make assessments of social dangerousness and to design a process by which that assessment can be fed into the releasing procedure. We do not facilitate this difficult task by making a porridge, a farrago, out of the two powers — the mental health power and the police power — and using this mess to avoid facing and trying to dispose of a genuinely difficult problem.

Thus, in terms neither of the morality of punishment nor of stigmatization is the defense of insanity now essential or operative. Similarly, it is neither a necessary nor effective principle around which to mobilize clinical resources for the rational treatment of the psychologically disturbed criminal actor. It is, however, in our view, a political issue of some difficulty and the politics are concerned with the stigmatizing role of the criminal law.

While the hangman, or in this country the fryman, and the capital punishment controversy lurk in the background, the issue of criminal irresponsibility in relation to homicide is intractable. Yet, in the five years 1964, 1965, 1966, 1967, and 1968, the number of executions in this country was, respectively, 15, 7, 1, 2, and 0. Our ukase on this matter does no more than hasten the inevitable. Moreover, when one looks at the pattern of capital punishment for murder in the world, it becomes clear that this is a rapidly declining sanction. We can reasonably exclude it from our consideration of the future. What remains then is the question of stigmatization of conduct as either wicked or the product of sickness, as either bad or mad. This difference in stigmatization may result in different treatments but the differences are neither essential to our system of criminal justice nor necessarily involved in either our correctional or mental health systems. The essential difference is the difference of nomenclature, of overt public stigmatization.

For our part, we look toward a future in which moral outrage and name-calling will not so significantly influence our reaction to the behavior of others. This is a generation that despoils our natural resources and prepares to terminate human life on this planet; but if the ruination of our environment and the eliminating of our species are avoided, if aggressions are controlled in favor of decency and creativity, we do not believe that systems of justice in which name-calling and vengeance figure so prominently can long survive. If this be so, then the issue becomes one of how we can, as rapidly as the traffic will allow, destigmatize our criminal law processes.

There is a choice. We could follow the pattern of a gradual extension of the exculpatory and allegedly destigmatizing processes of the defense of insanity, opening it more and more widely to cover larger and larger slices of criminal conduct until most criminal behavior is encompassed. Many of those working in this field, men whom we respect, favor that engulfing process. We do not oppose their purpose; but we think their political judgment wrong. It seems to us that we should not make an artificial and morally unjustifiable exception to a false general rule and allow the exception to swallow the rule. It seems to us better to support the advance that is now taking place, certainly in theory and rhetoric, in the treatment of all criminal conduct, and to a degree in correctional practice. In other words, to put it aggressively, we think society will move faster toward a rational system of criminal justice through honesty than by self-deception; and we think it dishonest to creat an artificial, morally unjustifiable, practically ineffective exception to the general rules of criminal responsibility. We think the English judges went wrong in the nineteenth century and that it is time we got back to earlier and truer principles.

We find it impossible morally to distinguish the insane from others who may be convicted though suffering deficiencies of intelligence, adversities of social circumstances, indeed all the ills to which the flesh and life of man is prey. It seems to us that our approach better accords with the total role of the criminal law in society than does a system which makes a special exculpatory case out of one rare and unusual criminogenic process, while it determinedly denies exculpatory effects to other, more potent processes. In the long run we will better handle these problems, as well as the whole and more complex problem of criminality in the community, if we will recognize that within crime itself there lies the greatest disparity of human wickedness and the greatest range of human capacities for self-control.

Our perennial perseverations about the defense of insanity impede recognition of this diversity, since they push us to a false dichotomy between the responsible and the irresponsible. They should be abandoned. One occupation for the energies thus released might be suggested, a task in which the psychiatrist has an important role to play: the defining of those categories of psychologically disturbed criminals who are serious threats to the community and to whom special treatment measures should therefore be applied.

On Defining and Predicting Dangerousness

The policeman, the prosecutor, the jury, the judge, the probation officer preparing a presentence report, the clinician in the diagnostic and classification center, the correctional officer planning the inmate's treatment and custody, the parole board and the parole officer — all, like it or not, must make predictions about the possible social dangerousness of the offender they confront. This is frequently a complex and difficult task to which psychiatric insights are often relevant. It involves at least two interacting issues: what kinds of behavior are sufficiently threatening to be called "dangerous" and with what degree of certainty must the prognosis establish the likelihood of recurrence of the kind or kinds of behavior designated "dangerous" and over what period of time?

The task of conceptualizing and providing methodologically sound processes for reaching decisions on these twin aspects of "dangerousness" is of central importance to the development of the criminal law. It is critical at every level of the criminal justice system. The report of the President's Crime Commission stresses the

> necessity for identifying those dangerous or habitual offenders who pose a serious threat to the community's safety. They include those offenders whose personal instability is so gross as to erupt periodically in violent and assaultive behavior, and those individuals whose long-term exposure to criminal influences has produced a thoroughgoing commitment to criminal values that is resistive of superficial efforts to effect change. . . .

Clearly indicated is the need for an improved capability in the information gathering and analysis process and continued experimental development to improve the predictive power of the information gathered. These needs point to increased manpower and the training requisite for the development of sophistication and skill in the investigative-diagnostic process.

There is another reason, relevant to developments in the field of corrections which we have dealt with at some length in chapter 5, why we must move toward more sophisticated definitions of dangerousness. Certain goals and broad methods of correctional treatment are increasingly accepted. Following the lead of psychiatry we develop community-based corrections emulating the community psychiatry movement. We design an armamentarium of alternatives to prisons, all of which try to treat criminals in the community; specifically, we move toward halfway houses, work-releases, furloughs, and community treatment centers. And the leaders in the correctional field struggle to reduce the duration of the social isolation we call prison in those cases in which it is used. Our attitude to the mega-prison matches the psychiatrist's concern about the continued survival of the mega-asylum, the gross and pervasive state mental hospital. This aspect of the evolution of treatment processes is clear, and we have made it clear that we favor this development; yet the evolutionary pace is inhibited by a mixing of prisoners who are social nuisances with those who are social threats — the poacher with the predator, the sneak thief with the sadist. This Gresham's Law, this principle of the lowest common denominator, limits treatment processes to the needs of the least easily treated. It also besets the police and the courts as well as the correctional system. It is necessary better to discriminate and more meaningfully to diversify our processes.

There are various legal approaches to this task of separating dangerous criminals from less serious offenders. Let us briefly mention several of these in order to sharpen the focus on the challenging psychiatric tasks that remain:

Habitual criminal laws are widespread and long established. "The consensus," writes the director of the American Law Institute, Professor Herbert Wechsler, "is that they are a failure, productive of chaotic and unjust results when they are used, and greatly nullified in practice." They have swept up the persistent social nuisances while leaving the dangerous and serious offenders untouched.

Sexual psychopath laws have spread like a rash of injustice across this country, unjustly commingling the inadequate and aberrant with the dangerous and brutal. Their social and legislative psychopathology is clear; their contribution to the problem of the dangerous offender is slight.

Wherever discretion in sentencing exists, and this is now ubiquitous, the judge may and frequently does fix the sentence at least partly in relation to his view (guided by such advice as he has received) of the future danger the criminal presents to the community.

Wherever discretion in paroling exists, and this is now ubiquitous, the parole board may and frequently does defer the criminal's release if (guided by such advice as it has received) it regards him as a continuing and serious danger to the community. In making this decision, many parole boards are helpfully assisted by parole prediction tables developed for this purpose.

Special quarantine-type legislation, protracting custodial banishment, is also frequently used for persistent petty offenders, professional criminals, multiple offenders, vagrants, prostitutes, alcoholics, and narcotic addicts.

None of these techniques has brought us to grips with the various classifications of dangerous offenders we must reach if our criminal justice system is to have any chance of becoming socially protective. Two major recommendations for this purpose have been made — one by the American Law Institute, the other by the Advisory Council of Judges of the National Council on Crime and Delinquency.

The American Law Institute's Model Penal Code authorizes a trial judge, when sentencing a person convicted of a felony, to extend the term of imprisonment beyond the maximum provided for that category of felon when "the defendant is a dangerous, mentally abnormal person whose commitment for an extended term is necessary for protection of the public." Psychiatric examination "resulting in the conclusion that his mental condition is gravely abnormal; that his criminal conduct has been characterized by a pattern of repetitive or compulsive behavior or by persistent aggressive behavior with heedless indifference to consequences; and that such condition makes him a serious danger to others" is a precondition to the judicial imposition of the extended sentence.

The Model Sentencing Act of the Advisory Council of Judges of the NCCD has as a pivotal classification the distinction between "dangerous offenders" and all others. The former are defined as those who have committed or attempted certain crimes of physical violence and who the court finds to be "suffering from a severe personality disorder indicating a propensity towards criminal activity." Again psychiatric diagnosis and advice to the judge are a precondition to the exercise of this power. Unlike the Model Penal Code, however, a psychiatric recommendation in favor of the longer sentence is not required for such a sentence to be imposed. Furthermore, such a "dangerous offender" may be sentenced to a term of thirty years' imprisonment!

Under these two systems, pouring meaning into the definition of the "dangerous offender" would become an obligation of psychiatrists and lawyers. A third example of the need for this type of definition merits mention. The benevolence of the Durham rules has led to the compulsory hospitalization in the District of Columbia of those found not guilty by reason of insanity until such time as the court concurs in the certification of the superintendent of Saint Elizabeth's Hospital that the detained person "has recovered his sanity, . . . and will not in the reasonable future be dangerous to himself or others." It is a serious moral question whether the power to detain the "no longer insane" in a mental hospital because of his predicted future danger to himself or others is a fertile source of gross injustice; but whether or not it is, here too can be seen the urgent need for psychiatric and legal definition of an operable concept of dangerousness.

To take power over the lives of others on predictions of their future criminality, in particular of the likelihood of future physical injury they may inflict on others, is no light assumption of competence. Those who cautiously and modestly assess their abilities would, it might seem, hesitate in the face of such awesome authority; but neither lawyers nor psychiatrists seem to have been unduly disturbed by such reflections. The distressing moral problem inherent in this situation can be stated as: Whom shall we trust? Our reply, for the time being, is: Nobody. We believe that we can construct an effective and just system of criminal justice without relying on increasing our power over offenders on the grounds of their predicted dangerousness. Within the ambit of power defined by other purposes, mostly retributive, we must frequently relate sentences and parole decisions to our best judgments of the offender's dangerousness; but we should not rely on such inadequate judgments to increase our power over him, to raise the limits of punishment. This rejection of increased power based on predictions of the criminal's dangerousness does not mean that such predictions are irrelevant. Quite the contrary; they can be essential to rational decision making, from arrest to final discharge from parole, but only if we are sincere in our protestations of community protection without injustice to the offender.

The path before us is lengthy and passes through many thickets, clinical and jurisprudential. We wish here to consider only two: the myth of individual clinical judgments and the failure to develop methodologically acceptable means of predicting dangerousness. We must escape that mythology and design morbity tables appropriate to assisting us in predicting the criminal's dangerousness. It is surely clear, without argument, that neither a merely diagnostic classification nor one which is only a synonym for types of symptoms can suffice for purposes of such predictions. In 1958 Dr. Ralph Brancale argued that "an improved methodology in psychiatric work should, in time, dispel the popular notion that psychiatric conclusions are, for the most part, inferential guesses." Eleven years later, so far as predictions of the future danger of an offender are concerned, we are no closer to dispelling that popular notion. In 1966, Dr. Brancale himself wrote (and he and his staff of thirty full-time clinicians at the Menlo Park Diagnostic Center, New Jersey, have vast experience in this work): "Psychiatrically, our course of development has been slow and laborious. The insights which we believe we have gained are not readily confirmed by research methods and the judgments that are made are not always sustained by scientific formulations." We offer these quotations by Dr. Brancale as witness to the need for "research methods" and "scientific formulations"; without them, our emotional reactions to the actualities and threats of crimes of violence will lead us to inflict injustice on individuals and to tolerate superficial and discordant concepts in our system of criminal justice; currently a myth of individual clinical psychiatric judgment, using a complex diagnostic tax-onomy together with a primitive treatment nosology, bedevils psy-chiatry. Let us clarify that opaque condemnation by analogy.

Many readers will remember the heroic days when the weather fore-caster would boldly aver a prediction of "no rain tomorrow." He is more cautious today. The proposition now is that "within a defined geographic area, there is a 10 percent chance of measurable rain." The forecaster does not thereby reveal that he has succumbed to the modern epidemic of pretentious circumlocution; rather, he is making a laudable effort more precisely to state his knowledge. And what is that knowledge? We assume that a fuller statement of his prediction would read, "The configuration of dynamically interacting meteoro-logical processes within a given region which, to the best of our knowl-edge, create the weather conditions we now see and have observed over the past days and hours, giving these factors the weight which experience and our understanding of their operation leads us to allot to them, most closely resembles a category of weather experience in the past on which, during the immediately subsequent day, it rained measurably in another defined region in one in ten cases." And few people today would plan any outdoor activity on the advice of a weather predictor who, fresh for each case and judging only by his own vast experience and deep intuition, looked at those factors which he believed most significantly affected the weather and struck what he asserted to be an individual, personalized weather prediction.

The same is, we believe, true of psychiatric predictions of danger-ousness. If, of course, a hurricane is marching steadily in one's direc-tion, it requires no great prescience to predict tomorrow's weather. There are cases of equal obviousness in predicting serious criminality; but they are rare. The usual case demands, it seems to us, prediction in terms of probability based on existing categories of experience. These categories should not be expressed only in a multiplicity of lengthy case histories; they should also be reduced to a summariza-tion of experience in a more precise and quantified form.

One should not place great reliance on psychiatric predictions of social dangerousness until they have been expressed in the form of prediction tables, which are really only "experience tables," and which are available for critical testing by other than the predictor. The raconteurs, the narrators of the individual case history, may greatly contribute to our understanding of the dynamic interaction of individual and social processes, but such solitary insights can only in the most exceptional cases form the basis of predictions of social dangerousness on which the law should rely. Control over another man's life is too serious a matter to be posited on other than tested, evaluated, refined experience — on carefully validated prediction tables.

The mechanics of the preparation of prediction tables are well established. There have been some false leads in criminology but, overall, the movement from prediction tables to base expectancy rates and the testing of alternative treatments in relation to those rates is the most promising methodological tool we have developed. It is no substitute for clinical judgment; it is rather a necessary precondition of clinical judgment. Until this hard work has been done, we would most strenuously oppose any sentencing or paroling process structured around psychiatric predictions of dangerousness. To this extent, we regard the provisions which we have discussed in the Model Penal Code and Model Sentencing Act as based on false assumptions of knowledge; accordingly, they should be vehemently resisted.

Such an approach to predicting dangerousness does not, of course, grapple with the quite separate and equally important question of defining "danger." For this purpose: danger of what type of criminal behavior? What *types of risk* should the community bear? But it does lead us to the central policy issue thereafter: what *degree of risk* should the community bear in relation to the countervailing values of individual freedom? It leads to the determinative and difficult policy question: how many "false positive" predictions (he will prove to be a danger, but does not) are justified for the sake of avoiding the "true positive" predictions? This is a sociolegal question, not one within the psychiatrist's particular competence. We cannot, however, even reach that question, let alone answer it, until psychiatry has more amply contributed the data within its competence relevant to posing the question for diverse categories of offenders. Psychiatrists must do the hard statistical work; they cannot slough it off by superficial assumptions of the sufficiency of clinical insights; nor can they rely on those in other disciplines to do that hard statistical work for them.

To put the argument in a slightly different form, we are submitting that, just as it is impossible to consider an individual case in a social vacuum, so it is impossible to make "individual" predictions. Every consideration of the individual is inevitably a consideration of the ways in which and the extent to which he conforms to and varies from a class or classes of people about whom we have defined experience. So guided, if our experience is ample and quantified, and our perceptions of his similarities to and differences from that class precise, we may be able to state that "this offender belongs to a group of whom X in every hundred commit a crime of defined gravity within Y months or years." Of course, even such knowledge, validated and refined, does not provide individual prediction. It leaves open the question, already referred to in chapter 3, whether he is a "false positive." Any individual who falls within a predictably dangerous group may be among the ten in one hundred who do not act out their dangerous potentialities rather than among the ninety who do.

Nevertheless, his "risk category" properly remains of importance to our many unavoidable decisions of how and for how long (within existing powers) to treat him. We can state probabilities based on experience and go slightly further by explaining our reasons for attributing this particular offender's qualities to those of the groups which make up the categories of experience which we are bringing to bear on this predictive task. The psychiatric literature has not, to our knowledge, supplied this necessary basic data for categorizing offenders as dangerous for purposes of sentencing, of allocating our sparse treatment resources, and of determining release procedures. The value of such an effort is clear; not only will it improve our capacity within our existing powers better to protect the community from violent recidivists but also it will set us free better to treat other offenders. Further, we will less frequently segregate the harmless on a false unity that sees the violent criminal as the prototypical criminal and assimilates the treatment of all to the treatment of the prototype.

On Mobilizing Clinical Resources

Though our definitional skills may not yet be capable of precisely isolating the group or accurately predicting its behavior, no one with experience in the criminal courts or the penitentiaries doubts that there is a group of dangerous criminals whose treatment requires the skills and insights of the psychiatrist. Yet few psychiatrists are engaged in this work.

A cynical friend of ours, a European psychiatrist who has spent two years in this country, assures us that American psychiatrists do not treat psychotics. They treat neurotics and diagnose psychotics (whose treatment is delegated to others). It is a harsh and overstated allegation, but it is not without a kernel of truth. When we visit the mega-mental-hospitals for psychotics we find few Board-certified psychiatrists at work in them. On the other hand, in the great teaching hospitals and in the ample diagnostic facilities, fully qualified and excellently trained psychiatrists are to be found aplenty. If this be the overall pattern of our allocation of psychiatric resources, we should not be surprised at the meagerness of those resources now available for the treatment of dangerous, psychologically disturbed criminals. Let us consider the statistics of this parsimony.

There are today more than 1,300,000 persons in the correctional system. This does not include those awaiting trial; it is made up of convicted adult felons and misdemeanants and young persons adjudged delinquent. It includes those on probation, those in correctional institutions, and those on parole or similar aftercare. To supervise and care for these 1,300,000 convicted offenders, there are today more than 125,000 people employed in correctional work. Only one in five of these correctional employees has treatment and rehabilitation as his primary function. The remaining four are custodial and maintenance personnel. How many of the 20 percent of "treaters" are psychiatrists?

There would seem to be about fifty-six psychiatrists employed full time in the approximately 230 adult correctional institutions in this country. Others, of course, are in consultative relationships with correctional systems. Of the fifty-six, eighteen are in the federal prison service. Another large group is to be found in the service of the Californian Adult Authority. The remainder are scattered sparsely elsewhere. And even these figures conceal the degree of scarcity of psychiatric *treatment* resources in corrections, since most of the energies of those psychiatrists who are working in the correctional system are devoted to diagnosis and classification. As the American Bar Foundation's *Mental Illness and the Criminal Law* puts it:

> Administration of criminal law is plagued by an
> overemphasis on diagnosis and a corresponding
> underemphasis on treatment. In one clinic, the ratio
> of diagnostic interviews to treatment interviews
> approached 100 to 1. The case histories of persons
> coming through our courts tell of frequent and
> numerous recommendations for therapy, but seldom is
> the suggestion of therapy actualized. Some diagnostic
> work is absolutely essential in the criminal process,

given the constitutional requirement of competency and the fact that some defendants will continue to raise the defense of insanity. Yet the problem of increasing the frequency and quality of treatment is not insuperable.

The situation is well described in the task force report on corrections of the President's Crime Commission. After considering the general problem of the lack of resources for the treatment of special offender groups, the report continues:

> This is perhaps most dramatic in the case of mentally disturbed offenders, where the shortage of clinical personnel even for the treatment of the general population has meant that offenders, who generally come at the end of the line of social priorities, have received few of the benefits of recent advances in the treatment of mental illness. Referral to civil mental hospitals is often attempted by correctional officials who are unable to undertake treatment themselves and for whom the mentally disordered offender often creates severe disruption in handling other offenders. But to the mental hospital the criminal offender may present unwanted custodial problems, and in some cases treatment there may also be nearly non-existent.

The task force and the commission make one recommendation relevant to this wasteland. They suggest that "one approach which does hold general promise of providing a better basis for resolving these problems is the pooling or joint operation of facilities for them. Already a few small States, for example, send their female prisoners to adjoining States. Other minority offender groups, notably the mentally disordered and retarded, could also profit from the more specialized handling which pooling facilitates." This is certainly a sound suggestion but it is not in our view as promising as the model which we have adopted and will detail here.

In surveying this desert we should mention other oases and other springs which may be relevant to its reclamation. Special institutions for sexual psychopaths are to be found, as also are facilities for defective delinquents. The former seem to us to suffer the inevitable disadvantage of being based on an indefensible artificial isolation of one type of offense. Nevertheless, among the prisoners sent to such institutions are some who are seriously disturbed and dangerous offenders who fall within a more rational classification of offenders suitable for psychiatric treatment. Much the same is true of the mentally retarded who commit crime and receive the double stigmatization applied under some defective delinquency statutes. For example, the Bridgewater Institution in Massachusetts and Patuxent in Maryland take such offenders and provide a therapeutic milieu for them.

Other such facilities are often, however, merely custodial and segregative. The promise in the law of special treatment for the "sexual psychopath" and the "defective delinquent," which alone could justify such legislation, is belied by the reality of protracted segregation without treatment. The task force on corrections recognized this iniquity. "There is a decided danger that the existence of special facilities will imply a comparable existence of special expertise, encouraging society to shuffle off on correctional institutions problems that should be dealt with elsewhere. There are many indications that this has been the result, for example, of schools for defective delinquents and programs for sexual psychopaths."

The California Medical Facility at Vacaville, which opened in 1955, is a 2,000-bed institution providing psychiatric and medical treatment as well as the usual diagnostic and classification services. The Patuxent Institution in Maryland, which also opened in 1955, likewise provides treatment for psychologically disturbed and dangerous offenders. These institutions are oases in the desert, of importance to the future treatment of that category of offender. But they are exceptional. The problem of the absent psychiatrist persists. We are reminded of the nonbarking dog in Conan Doyle's "Silver Blaze": Why do psychiatrists only bark diagnostically, concerning dangerous criminals? Why are they not involved in treating dangerous criminals?

The treatment of criminals is, of course, hard and often unrewarding work. Salaries are exiguous and the emotional satisfactions of effecting a cure are not the common experience of the practitioner. The patients are not a particularly attractive group; it is difficult to divest oneself of one's emotional responses to the brutal and injuring criminal. Yet this cannot be the whole story, since many psychiatrists, without thereby swelling their bank balances, work with less than charming patients. Nor should a lack of likely treatment success be accepted as an explanation of the absence of the psychiatrist from this work, since some evidence indicates that they might well be quite successful.

If one looks at the most distinguished institution in the world devoted to this type of work — Herstedvester near Copenhagen in Denmark, of which a full account may be found in *Treating the "Untreatable"* by Herstedvester's superintendent, Dr. Georg Stürup — one finds it reasonable to expect that psychiatrically controlled treatment will measurably and substantially better protect the community and observably and appreciably assist the offenders themselves, in substantial numbers, to a less self-destructive and happier life. Herstedvester takes the most severely disturbed, idiosyncratic, dangerous (but nonpsychotic) offenders in Denmark. Keeping this group in detention less than two and a half years, the institution achieves a success rate slightly better than 50 percent in terms of subsequent maintenance of these offenders in the community without conviction of crime or need to return them to the institution. The success rate speaks only to the first release. When subsequent releases are taken into account, a more encouraging pattern emerges. The percentage who are returned after their second release (which usually follows about one year of detention in Herstedvester) is also about 50 percent and this rate remains roughly constant for each successive parole. Thus, taking a group of extremely difficult cases, Herstedvester has only 10 percent in custody after ten years; the remaining 90 percent manage to live in the community and to avoid serious criminality.

Salaries and the difficulty of the task cannot in themselves explain the failure of psychiatrists to be attracted to this work in the United States. Salaries are just as meager for diagnostic work in the correctional field, and here the scarcity of clinical resources is not so acute. Furthermore, diagnostic work has no success-satisfaction whatsoever. A more cogent explanation of this imbalance, in our view, is the fact that for too long a period of years concentration on treating this type of psychiatric disorder has lain outside the normal career line of the young and ambitious psychiatrist. One can earn a national reputation by being the first director of an institution like Patuxent or Herstedvester, but the role of the successor is much less attractive. Positions lower in the hierarchy of these institutions are apparently not regarded as providing that diversified clinical experience which the young and ambitious psychiatrist should have. It is a specialized task outside the recognized mainstream of professional advancement in psychiatry.

Let us add another reason which is not as unimportant as at first it may appear. Correctional institutions tend to be situated in distant corners of far-flung Siberias. Political pressures often lead to their establishment in remote areas of declining agriculture, scanty industry, and burgeoning unemployment. Living in such banishment, a psychiatrist is not in the center of a stimulating cultural life, and the alternative of spending much of his time in protracted commuting is less than enchanting.

For these reasons, and possibly for many others, psychiatrists are not in practice involved in the treatment of psychologically disturbed, serious offenders; but psychiatrists particularly those at the thresholds of their careers, are far from uninterested in this work. A recent survey revealed that of 11,000 members of the American Psychiatric Association, 975 listed "forensic psychiatry," which presumably includes institutional as well as court work, among their top three major interests. Very many would be likely to find it of interest and of value to their development to spend two or three years giving much of their time to the treatment of this group.

The intellectual game of the moment is model building. The most superficial thought can be cloaked in sophistication by being described as a "model." But as we shall indicate in our final chapter on research this approach can perform a valuable function. Let us, therefore, describe a model designed to bridge the chasm between the need for psychiatrists to be involved in the treatment of dangerous criminals and the existing motivations of some psychiatrists to devote some of their energy to this type of work without stunting their professional and personal growth or curtailing the range of their clinical experience. The model is designed to put this work on the career line of the younger, ambitious psychiatrist. It is also designed as the prototype for establishments in every state, as indicated in our ukase.

The model is a hundred-bed security institution ("security" for this purpose can be achieved without obtrusive walls). It lies within walking distance of a psychiatric teaching hospital or of a major psychiatric facility with both inpatient and outpatient services. The institution has five twenty-bed wards or houses; there is also a small administration and reception block, with a few separate rooms in it to serve as both hospital rooms and punishment-isolation rooms.

The institution will have a medical director. It is important that he also have duties at the nearby teaching hospital or psychiatric facility.

The assistant director will be assigned to the institution from the Department of Prisons. He will be an experienced correctional administrator with some training in and sensitivity to the social sciences. He will work full time in the institution and will bear the burden of its administration. It must be stressed, however, that ultimate responsibility resides in the medical director, since everything that occurs in the institution is "treatment." There is no problem of custody, of discipline, or of maintenance that is not also a treatment issue.

The model institution will require five half-time psychiatrists who are also employed in the nearby psychiatric facility. The understanding must be that their work in the model institution is a passing stage in their career, that they spend two, three, or four years in this role. Each of these psychiatrists will undertake responsibility for one of the five wards or houses. He will be assisted by two or three social workers and the necessary subprofessional staff. Psychological services, as required, will be provided by the proximate psychiatric facility. If the proximate facility is a psychiatric teaching hospital, then assignment to this prison should be part of the internship experience of psychiatrists.

The facility will not need educational programs, either scholastic or vocational. It must, however, have some industrial activity of the carpentry or print-shop kind, and it is important that whatever type of factory is built here should provide reasonably demanding and full-time activity. The inmates will not be employed specifically in housekeeping and maintenance duties in the institution. They will be responsible for the maintenance of their houses, but this will be an off-hours duty. There will be a central kitchen for the whole institution but each of the five houses will have its own dining room. There will need to be some recreational and exercise facilities, but these need not be lavish. Indeed, economy will characterize the entire architectural approach to this institution. It cannot be a spacious institution, since it will be built on much more expensive land than is usually used for correctional institutions.

Pending a more meaningful definition of the disturbed and dangerous group, what prisoners will be sent to the model institution? In general, those whom nobody else wants; those whom other institutions reject because they are too disruptive, too turbulent, too unpromising; but not those who are certifiably insane under the civil commitment processes of the state, or those similarly certifiable as being retarded.

They will need to be serving sentences with at least two years to run at the time of their transfer to the model institution and must also have some realistic hope of parole release within that period, if this is recommended by the medical director. The prisoner will have no choice whatsoever about his being placed in this model institution, and once he is so placed it shall be clearly understood that this institution will maintain responsibility for his custody and treatment until his sentence and any parole revocations that follow it have expired. This model institution will be, for him, the end of the correctional road. It should be both a threatening and a promising end.

We will exclude no category of offender from this institution. We do not think it peculiarly suited to the particular problems of the offender whose criminality is the product primarily of addiction, alcoholic or narcotic, but we would not want to define any exclusionary principle along these lines. Likewise, the institution should neither be devoted to serious sexual offenders nor should it exclude them. The principle of selection will be the seriousness of the threat that the offender poses to the community and the extent to which the treatment resources in the institution may reasonably be expected to bear upon that offender's problems. It seems likely that such institutions will not be particularly well suited to the treatment needs of the subcultural offender, as distinct from the idiosyncratic offender, to the extent that such a distinction can be drawn. Likewise, they will not be likely to succeed with the habitual offender who has had repeated and protracted institutional experience and whose life pattern has made him substantially unfit for existence outside an institution. But, all in all, the most positive criterion for selection of an inmate will be the urgent strength of the desire of the warden of another institution to get rid of him!

The medical director will have authority to permit the inmate to work outside the institution when that is appropriate treatment. He will control furloughs and trial releases. He will also, where geography makes it possible, rely on parole and aftercare services by a staff owing allegiance to the institution and trained in its methods. He will have the power expeditiously to revoke trial leave or parole in some cases and to use the model institution for short-term treatment of the parolee during the period of his resettlement in the community.

We have not discussed the therapeutic milieu that should be created in these institutions, the inmate group interactions, staff and inmate relationships, treatment methods, and similar basic processes. These lie outside our competence. The model is sketched, in this unfinished form, to indicate broadly the means by which psychiatry can be more deeply involved in the treatment of severe criminal behavior disorders. The group needing treatment is manifest, and there will be no difficulty in mobilizing psychiatrists to work in such institutions.

While the psychiatrist is confined to the pure and distant work of diagnosis and staff training, the potentiality of his contribution to social protection will never be tested. And, since these functions are inextricably intertwined, his absence from the scene of actual treatment will impair his value in diagnostic and training functions. We shall not produce an American August Aichhorn of adult corrections until psychiatrists are involved in this work. They are unlikely to become involved unless we offer new, less remote, more career-related venues for their involvement.

Finally, there are two collateral advantages of establishing such institutions which may be mentioned as political assets. They will take a great deal of weight off other correctional institutions in the state. The treatment accorded to all inmates in an institution is too often that appropriate to the most difficult group. By removing the hardest and most troublesome cases, we will ease the task of other institutions. Second, such model facilities can be changed and adapted to fit the crime and population patterns of different regions and cities of the country. The model is a testable one, a model capable of evaluation. It can be structured in such a fashion that, unlike most other correctional experiments, it could prove to be a failure; only thus can it ever prove to be a success.

Conclusion

The view has been, and in some quarters still is, held that all or at least a majority of offenders are psychologically ill or abnormal and that psychiatric treatment would solve all our problems of penology. The evidence to support such a view is lacking and the contributions that psychiatrists have made to the problems of treating offenders have been extremely sparse. Forensic psychiatry has largely consisted of classifying offenders and participation in court proceedings when the defense of insanity has been raised. Our ukases are designed to ensure that the psychiatrist will make a much more meaningful and ample contribution to the needs of the criminal justice system. They are not intended, however, to set a limit to that contribution. For as more psychiatrists are attracted to, and involved in, the treatment of offenders, here, as in other fields, they will develop more adequate and effective treatment methods. And, at the same time, as experience is expressed in prediction tables susceptible of validation and progressive refinement, psychiatrists will be able to operate on a sounder and more objective basis than individual clinical insight. The role of the psychiatrist in corrections and community protection is currently of minor significance. It can become of substantial importance.

8

Organized Crime and God

And, if any more proof is needed, I possess invisible horns.

Henrik Ibsen, *Peer Gynt*

In chapter 2 we have spoken of myths which exercise a powerful influence on the ways in which we think and act in the criminological field. In this chapter we deal with one of the most seductive and persistent of those myths, the demonology of organized crime. This is the notion that behind the diverse phenomena of crime there exists a single, mysterious, omnipotent organization which is responsible for much of it. It is an idea which has long exerted a powerful influence on the minds not only of journalists but also of law enforcement agents and serious students of crime.

We issue two ukases designed to strengthen law enforcement and to exorcise the myth of organized crime. We stress, however, that these two ukases are not to be implemented until those set out in chapter 1 have been in force for a period of one year.

1. All special organized crime units in federal and state justice and police departments shall be disbanded.
2. Those employed in such units shall be transferred to other duties but shall suffer no reduction in salary status or seniority.

A perplexing and elusive problem does indeed confront anyone seeking information about organized crime. It concerns the concept "organized crime" itself. A curious feature characterizes almost all the literature on the subject, up to and including the task force report on this topic published by the President's Crime Commission. This is that a large proportion of what has been written seems not to be dealing with an empirical matter at all. It is almost as though what is referred to as organized crime belonged to the realm of metaphysics or theology.

The analogy with theology is quite striking. Nor is it merely a matter of occasional similarities or likenesses but rather of a systematic resemblance recurring in a wide variety of different sources. The parallelism is so pervasive that it is difficult to dismiss it as altogether fortuitous. But before considering its significance we may as well illustrate it.

Take first the question of the existence of organized crime, a matter about which, like the existence of God, doubts have been expressed. On this subject Estes Kefauver, in *Crime in America*, based on testimony taken at the hearings and on reports of the Senate Crime Committee in 1950–51, writes as follows:

> A nationwide crime syndicate does exist in the United States of America, despite the protestations of a

strangely assorted company of criminals, self-serving
politicians, plain blind fools, and others who may
be honestly misguided, that there is no such
combine. . . . The national crime syndicate as it
exists today is an elusive and furtive but nonetheless
tangible thing. Its organization and machinations
are not always easy to pinpoint. . . . However, by
patient digging and by putting together little pieces
of a huge and widely scattered puzzle, the picture
emerges. . . . Behind the local mobs which make up
the national crime syndicate is a shadowy,
international criminal organization known as the
Mafia, so fantastic that most Americans find it hard
to believe it really exists.

Now, apart from the bizarre nature of its content, one of the most remarkable facts about this quite categorical statement, which occurs in
the first chapter of Kefauver's book, is that the evidence necessary to
substantiate it is never produced. Indeed Daniel Bell in *The End of
Ideology* comments as follows:

Unfortunately for a good story — and the existence
of the Mafia would be a whale of a story — neither the
Senate Crime Committee in its testimony, nor
Kefauver in his book, presented any real evidence
that the Mafia exists as a functioning organization.
One finds public officials asserting before the Kefauver
committee their *belief* in the Mafia; the Narcotics
Bureau *thinks* that a world-wide dope ring allegedly
run by Luciano is part of the Mafia: but the only other
"evidence" presented — aside from the incredulous
responses both of Senator Kefauver and Rudolph
Halley when nearly all the Italian gangsters asserted
that they didn't know about the Mafia — is that
certain crimes bear "the earmarks of the Mafia."
[Bell's italics.]

Others have been equally skeptical. Thus, Burton B. Turkus, in *Murder Incorporated*, written at the time the Senate Crime Investigating
Committee was publishing its findings, said:

If one such unit had all crime in this country under
its power, is it not reasonable to assume that
somewhere along the line, some law agency — federal,

state, county or municipal — would have tripped it up long before this? No single man or group ever was so clever, so completely genius, as to foil all of them forever. . . . In fact, as a factor of power in national crime, the Mafia has been virtually extinct for two decades.

Gus Tyler, editor of *Organized Crime in America*, prefaces the section devoted to the Mafia with an essay in which he says that the Mafia, "whose existence is assumed by some government agencies," is "a still unproven fact." He adds, however, that "while the existence of the Mafia is still legally conjectural, theories of its existence cannot be ignored."

But the "theories of its existence" prove upon examination to consist of little more than a series of dogmatic assertions. Thus, the *Final Report of the California Special Crime Study Commission on Organized Crime* in 1953 speaks of the Mafia, which it says is "now known as L'Unione Siciliana," as "the most sinister and powerful criminal organization in the world [with] headquarters on at least two continents." But after giving a somewhat desultory account of a variety of "illegal enterprises" and making further reference to "a criminal organization extending all over the world," the report falls back on the argument that "the study of these crimes over the years shows a definite pattern, the repetition of which in case after case cannot be laid to coincidence." This incidentally bears an extraordinary resemblance to one of the best known arguments for the existence of God: "the argument from design" in the form in which it was used by the eighteenth- and nineteenth-century rationalist theologians. But it is neither probative nor particularly persuasive.

Another respect in which assertions about the existence of organized crime in general and the Mafia in particular resemble statements about the existence of God is that in neither case is it clear what would be regarded as constituting significant counterevidence. Thus, in the *Third Interim Report of the Special Committee to Investigate Organized Crime in Interstate Commerce* (i.e., the Senate Crime Investigating Committee or the Kefauver committee), it is said: "Almost all the witnesses who appeared before the committee and who were suspected of Mafia membership, either denied that they had ever heard of the Mafia, which is patently absurd, or denied membership in the Mafia."

The only exception to this which stood up under cross-examination was a witness who said "that the Mafia was freely discussed in his home when he was a child." It is not at all clear what the significance of this childhood reminiscence is supposed to be. What is perfectly clear, however, is that *whatever* witnesses said would have been construed as evidence *for* the existence of the Mafia. Acknowledgment of membership in or awareness of the existence of the Mafia would have been accepted at face value. Denials, on the other hand, merely demonstrate that the Mafia "is a rare 'secret' society whose existence is truly secret," secrecy being enforced by "Mafia killings" which themselves "are surrounded with the secrecy which has proved to be most difficult to penetrate."

But even when organized crime is not identified with the Mafia, it is still referred to in terms which imply divine attributes such as invisibility, immateriality, eternity, omnipresence, and omnipotence. Thus, the President's Crime Commission task force report on organized crime says that "organized crime affects the lives of millions of Americans, but . . . preserves its *invisibility*." Again, organized crime is said to have its own discipline but "the laws and regulations they obey, the procedures they use, are private and secret ones that they devise themselves, change when they see fit, and administer summarily and *invisibly*." Moreover, "Agents and employees . . . cannot implicate the highest level figures, since frequently they have neither spoken to *nor even seen them*." Another task force report, *Assessment of Crime*, states that "organized crime thrives on *invisibility*. . . . No one knows whether it is getting bigger or smaller." And F. J. Cook, in *The Secret Rulers*, speaks of "a secret organization, an *invisible* government of crime." (Our italics.)

As for immateriality, we are also told by the President's Commission:

> But to discuss the impact of organized crime in terms
> of whatever direct, personal, everyday effect it has
> on individuals is to miss most of the point. Most
> individuals are not affected in this sense, very
> much. . . . Sometimes organized crime's activities
> do not directly affect individuals at all.

And one writer, "the former attorney for an illicit New York organization," is quoted as speaking in mystical terms of "a mysterious, all pervasive reality."

The task force report on organized crime also emphasizes the perpetually enduring nature of organized crime: "Organized crime maintains a coherent, efficient organization with a *permanency of form that survives changes* in working and leadership personnel." And Gus Tyler, in "The Roots of Organized Crime," speaks of "its *eternal life* . . . an institutional longevity extending far beyond the natural life span of its more mortal leadership." (Our italics in both quotations.)

With regard to omnipresence and omnipotence, Robert F. Kennedy said: "The insidious influence of organized crime can reach into almost every facet of our life, corrupting and undermining our society." The task force report goes further and states, "Organized criminal groups are known to operate in all sections of the Nation." D. R. Cressey, writing of "the American confederation of criminals," in his paper "The Functions and Structure of Criminal Syndicates," which is printed as an appendix to the task force report, says that "while organized criminals do not yet have control of all the legitimate economic and political activities in any metropolitan or other geographic area of America," they have started "to undermine basic economic and political traditions."

As with the Deity, however, direct knowledge of this phenomenon is apparently not vouchsafed to us. "While law-enforcement officials now have detailed information about the criminal activities of individual men," Professor Cressey writes, "knowledge of the structure of their confederation remains fragmentary and impressionistic." He goes on to say, "Our knowledge of the structure which makes 'organized crime' organized is somewhat comparable to the knowledge of Standard Oil which could be gleaned from interviews with gasoline station attendants." But there is nothing tentative about his explicit statement, "In the United States, criminals have managed to organize a nation-wide illicit cartel and confederation." And in a lengthy chapter beginning, "The structure of the nationwide cartel and confederation which today operates the principal illicit businesses in America, and which is now striking at the foundations of legitimate business and government as well came into being in 1931," sufficient baroque detail is provided to suggest that interviews with gasoline station attendants may not be totally uninformative for those with ears to hear.

Yet, as Professor Cressey acknowledges, "some officials, and some plain citizens, remain unconvinced." And, although he regards skepti-

cism as "misplaced," he does not, like Senator Kefauver, define un-
believers as criminals, self-servers, blind fools, and so on. Which is,
in the circumstances, prudent. For when only "fragmentary and impressionistic" data about an "elusive and furtive" phenomenon are
available for judgment, it is unwise to assume that doubt must be dis-
ingenuous or perverse.

Thus, as an instance for the sort of thing which might occasion
doubt on the part of a plain citizen, consider the tenets of the code
which Professor Cressey says "form the foundation of the legal order
of the confederation." He states frankly that he was "unable to locate
even a summary statement of the code" and that his statement of it
is based only on "the snippets of information we have been able to
obtain." Yet, on this presumably exiguous basis, he constructs a code
which, in regard to form and content, compares favorably with more
easily accessible examples of such systems of general rules regarding
conduct.

The sinister underworld code which "gives the leaders exploitative
authoritarian power over everyone in the organization," reads like the
product of collaboration between Rudyard Kipling and Emily Post.
Most of it would not appear incongruous if embroidered on a sampler.
Organized criminals are enjoined to "be loyal members of the organization," to "be a member of the team," to "be independent," and yet
not to "rock the boat." At the same time, they are told to "be a man
of honor" and to "respect womanhood and your elders."

The organized criminal "is to be cool and calm at all times"; "is not
to use narcotics . . . not to be drunk on duty . . . not to get into
fights. . . ." "He does not whine or complain in the face of adversity."
"The world seen by organized criminals is a world of graft, fraud, and
corruption, and they are concerned with their own honesty and manli-
ness as compared with the hypocrisy of corrupt policemen and corrupt
political figures."

In a world of corrupt police and politicians, it must be difficult to
preserve these standards. But Professor Cressey explains that, by a
"process of recruitment and indoctrination," the leaders of organized
crime "have some degree of success" in inculcating "a sense of decency
and morality — a sense of honor — so deep that there will be absolute
obedience." It is no surprise to be told that Mr. Vito Genovese, who
is said to have been, in 1957, leader of the "All-American 'Commission'" which is "the highest ruling body in the confederation," was

"invested with charismatic qualities by his followers. He was almost revered, while at the same time being feared, like an Old Testament divine. Even his name had a somewhat sacred quality."

The truth is that this sounds very much like what Gus Tyler calls "the fantasy of the Mafia" and Daniel Bell refers to as the "myth of an omnipotent Mafia" all over again. Indeed, Professor Bell, in a subsequent article entitled "The Myth of Cosa Nostra," seems to have been one of the few persons to have remained unpersuaded by the later evidence which we shall critically examine in some detail. For others, however, the same sparsity of data supports an equally grandiose inferential superstructure. "Since we know so little," Professor Cressey says, "it is easy to make the assumption that there is nothing to know anything about." But the scarcity of hard facts does not appear to constrict him unduly. And although some of what he says sounds plausible in a nonderogatory sense, when it comes to the question of the *existence* of "the American confederation of criminals" he uses a form of argument which comes close to what one might call logical legerdemain.

The argument is worth examining briefly. Under the heading "The Structural Skeleton," Professor Cressey provides an outline of the "authority structure" or " 'organizational chart' of the American confederation." Twenty-four criminal "families," each with its "Boss," are said to operate under the "Commission," which "serves as a combination board of business directors, legislature, supreme court and arbitration board." After giving some details of "the formal structure of the organization," Professor Cressey deals briefly with street-level operations and more informal functions. He then concludes briskly:

> The skeleton has more bones than those we have
> described, as our discussion of informal positions and
> roles indicates. *The structure outlined is sufficient
> to demonstrate, however, that a confederation of
> "families" exists.* [Our italics.]

It scarcely seems necessary to point out that, if "to demonstrate" here means "to prove by reasoning" or "to establish as true," the existence of the confederation cannot be said to have been demonstrated.

It may be said here, parenthetically, that the details of criminal hierarchies given by Professor Cressey and others in the literature on organized crime are curiously reminiscent of the details of celestial hierarchies to be found in the literature of angelology. Both the "Lord of Hosts" and the "Boss of all Bosses" stand at the apex of a pyramidal structure. Just as the "Lord of Hosts" is attended by superior orders of angelic beings like archangels and seraphim, so the "Boss of all Bosses" has his attendant counsellor (or *consigliere*) and underbosses (or *sottocapi*). The cherubim and ordinary angels are paralleled by the lieutenants (*caporegime*) and soldiers, lower-echelon personnel who, like the lower orders of angels, may have particular missions as agents, messengers, guards, and enforcers. Possibly in the light of this analogy, Professor Cressey's description of Vito Genovese, sometime "Boss of all Bosses," as "like an Old Testament divine" may not seem altogether incongruous.

At this point, it is necessary to define the question at issue a little more precisely than has been done so far. In the first place, there is no doubt that small groups of criminals organized for carrying out particular kinds of crime have existed for centuries. Such groups operated in the Elizabethan period and have been described in some detail in A. V. Judges's recently reissued *The Elizabethan Underworld*. It would be generally agreed that "similar groups exist today for purposes of bank burglary, shoplifting, confidence games, picking pockets and stealing automobiles." Organized crime at this level, it is said, in Sutherland and Cressey's well-known textbook on criminology, "involves association of a small group of criminals for the execution of a certain type of crime, together with the development of plans by which detection may be avoided, and the development of a fund of money and political connections by means of which immunity or relative immunity may be secured in case of detection." It is only necessary to say that, about the existence of organized crime in this sense, there is general agreement.

It should be clear, however, that the concept of organized crime with which we are dealing relates to something of different character from that just described. We are here concerned with what Sutherland and Cressey call the "organization of the vices." In this connection, they say:

> The most widespread organization of lawlessness is in connection with the vices. Relatively few people demand that burglars, pickpockets and confidence men engage in crime, but many persons demand opportunities for illicit sexual intercourse, gambling and consumption of narcotics. . . . This provides

> a basis for extensive organization which involves the
> places of vice, the patrons, the real estate dealers,
> the manufacturers of commodities used in the vices,
> the police and courts, the politicians, and sometimes
> a much wider public.

Here, too, there would be little dispute. In the field of what we may call "service" crime involving the supply of consumer goods and services for which there is a widespread demand, it would be surprising if there did not develop, as in legitimate business, what Harvard economist Professor Schelling, in "Economic Analysis and Organized Crime," refers to as "large-scale continuing firms with the internal organization of a large enterprise, and with a conscious effort to control the market."

The question we are considering, however, is whether in addition to such "large-scale continuing firms" located in various parts of the country there is a national syndicate which dominates organized crime throughout the country — one large nationwide criminal organization which controls the majority, if not all, of the local undertakings. For the concept of organized crime which was presented in the evidence given by Attorney General Robert F. Kennedy before the Permanent Subcommittee on Investigations of the Committee on Government Operations (McClellan committee) in 1963 involves "a private government of organized crime, a government with an annual income of billions — run by a commission [which] makes major policy decisions for the organization, settles disputes among the families and allocates territories of criminal operation within the organizations."

Now — when the existence of some social phenomenon or complex of phenomena is asserted, it is reasonable to ask, "What difference does it make?" For, however elusive and invisible and impalpable a social phenomenon may be, the assertion that it exists must, if it is to be regarded as significant, imply the presence of some concrete conditions, some specific actions, events, or series of events in our society which constitute evidence for it. Otherwise one is entitled, in the present context, to ask a question analogous to the sort of question posed by skeptics in theological discussions: How does this elusive, invisible, impalpable organization differ from an imaginary organization or from no organization at all?

To pursue the theological analogy for a moment, one can go further. For an assertion to be empirically meaningful, it must also constitute a denial of whatever would be incompatible with its truth. For, if there is nothing which an assertion denies then there is nothing which it asserts. So the agnostic or the skeptic asks the deist: "What would have to occur or to have occurred to constitute for you disproof of the love of, or of the existence of, God?" It is therefore relevant to ask also in *this* context: What would count as evidence against the assertion that an all-American crime syndicate exists? What would constitute disproof of, or be regarded as sufficient reason for withdrawing, that assertion? Is there anything which might conceivably count against it and, if so, what?

This brings us to the problem of defining an objective approach to the question whether an all-American criminal cartel and confederation exists. What sort of argument may be adduced as, if not being fully probative, at least having a significant bearing on the question at issue? The principal question which we have to ask is, What kinds of evidence are available and may be regarded as providing a means of ascertaining the truth in this matter? Clearly of crucial significance in this context must be the evidence upon which the attorney general based his contention that such a criminal government and such a nationwide organization existed.

The nature of that evidence became clear as the McClellan committee hearings proceeded. For, at those hearings, as Senator McClellan himself put it: "For the first time a member of the secret underworld government, Cosa Nostra, testified under oath describing the operations of that criminal organization, and the misguided and dedicated loyalty of its members." The witness referred to was Joseph Valachi, a sixty-year-old man with a long criminal record, at that time serving a life sentence for murder and a twenty-year sentence for a narcotics offense.

Of the significance attached to Valachi's evidence there seems to be no doubt. The attorney general described his disclosures as "the biggest intelligence breakthrough yet in combating organized crime and racketeering in the United States." William George Hundley, head of the Justice Department's organized crime section, was even more revealing. He said:

> Before Valachi came along *we had no tangible*
> *evidence that anything like this actually existed.*
> He's the first to talk openly and specifically about the
> organization. In the past we've heard that so-and-so
> was a "syndicate man" and that was all. Frankly I

always thought it was a lot of hogwash. But Valachi named names. He showed us what the structure is and how it operates. [Our italics.]

It becomes necessary therefore to examine Valachi's testimony critically. In this connection, it must be remembered that, prior to giving evidence, Valachi, who the year before (in June 1962) had murdered a fellow prisoner, was, according to his own statements, in fear of his life. He claimed that his former criminal associates intended to kill him. His feelings for them were no less inimical. When asked why he had decided to cooperate with the Department of Justice, he replied: "The main answer to that is very simple. Number one: It is to destroy them." With such an objective in view, the witness could not be regarded as totally disinterested. Moreover, on his own evidence, he clearly did not regard veracity as always obligatory when speaking to law enforcement agencies.

In the circumstances, it is understandable that Senator McClellan attached importance to securing some corroboration for Valachi's testimony. Thus, in opening the hearings, he said: "We believe a substantial part of his testimony can and will be corroborated." And, in closing them, he said: "The corroboration furnished by law enforcement officers makes Valachi's testimony more credible and important." We may ask therefore how far that verdict is borne out. For in such a case as this, the corroborative process assumes unusual significance.

Let us take first a point of detail which has already attracted some comment. What was the name of the organization about which Valachi testified? According to Valachi, it was Cosa Nostra. He was asked if the organization was "anything like the Mafia, or is it part of the Mafia, or is it the Mafia?" He replied:

> Senator, as long as I belong to this Cosa Nostra, all
> I can tell you is that they never express it as a Mafia.
> When I was speaking, I just spoke what I knew. . . .
> I know this thing existed a long time, but in my
> time I have been with this Cosa Nostra and that is the
> way it was called.

On this, F. J. Cook, in *The Secret Rulers*, comments: "There is a consensus among the nation's best investigators, men with the most intimate knowledge of the underworld and its rackets that they had never heard the name before Valachi used it. . . . This has cast some doubt upon the validity of Valachi's story."

It is not a doubt which troubles Mr. Cook, however. "Regardless of name," he says, "the vital fact remains: the criminal organization exists. . . . The name itself is secondary. What matters is the reality of a secret organization, an invisible government of crime." Yet for those more skeptical than Mr. Cook and concerned about the *corroboration* of Valachi's testimony, it is not a matter which can be passed over so lightly. For the fact is that on this point Valachi's evidence was never corroborated, although a large number of expert witnesses were examined on this subject. "It is a name I am not familiar with," said the New York City police commissioner, Michael J. Murphy. "I have never heard of such a name; no sir," said the Rhode Island state police superintendent, Colonel Walter E. Stone. "Not by the name 'Cosa Nostra,'" said the Boston police commissioner, Edmund L. McNamara. "We in Detroit apply the name 'Mafia,'" said George C. Edwards, Detroit city police commissioner. Nor were any of the Italian-speaking experts on organized crime who testified more enlightening on the point.

Senator McClellan took the view that "whether he calls it Cosa Nostra or the Mafia makes no difference." Commissioner Edwards of Detroit said, "The last thing I am interested in doing is debating nomenclature." Yet, it is doubtful whether so cavalier an approach to the evidence can be justified in this case. For, apart from the state and local police forces, according to the attorney general, "over 25 various investigative bodies of the Federal Government" were pooling their information "in the organized crime section." It seems a little surprising that out of all those who appeared before the committee not one person was found to confirm Valachi's evidence on this matter.

But if the question of nomenclature is regarded as of no great significance, there are what may be seen as more substantial matters about which the state of the evidence is equally unsatisfactory. Take, for example, the question of initiation rites, about which a great deal has been written in the literature. The attorney general told the McClellan committee: "They literally take an oath and they have the blood-letting. I think it will be described to you before the committee, but those who are members of this organization, take the oath."

When he testified on this, Valachi described a ceremony at which thirty-five or forty persons were present in the course of which he took an oath ("I repeated some words they told me, but I couldn't explain what he meant"); burned a piece of paper ("Well then he gave me a piece of paper, and I was to burn it"); had his finger pricked ("With a needle and he makes a little blood come out"); and repeated some more words ("I never asked what it meant").

Now the purpose of this meeting, according to Valachi, was, "To make new members and *to meet all of them.*" Yet, later, when questioned, Valachi, although he claimed to have proposed others for membership, twice stated that he couldn't remember being invited to participate at any other initiation ceremony. No member of the committee thought to ask him how it was that subsequently — from 1930 onward — no new member was ever to meet *him* at an initiation ceremony. They appeared to be satisfied with his statement: "Let me explain it this way. You are only made once; that is all. If you live a hundred years, it will be just that once." Yet, earlier he had stated that the purpose of these meetings was "to meet the others that were in that family." It remains only to add that, although Valachi stated, "That is the same ceremony today, what I described in 1930," on this matter, too, there was no corroboration. The nearest the committee came to securing corroboration was a statement from Detroit Police Commissioner Edwards: "We would not be in the slightest surprised at the form of initiation which was described here, but we, unfortunately, do not have in our possession someone who could testify directly."

We come now, however, to what is unquestionably a matter of substance, to that part of Valachi's testimony which dealt with the membership and organizational structure of the Vito Genovese "family" in New York to which he belonged. It was in this connection that his evidence was said to be most valuable and reliable. John F. Shanley, deputy chief inspector in the Central Investigations Bureau, which is the intelligence unit concerned with organized crime in the New York City police department, stated, "His strength is in the Genovese chart, his greatest strength," the chart referred to being one prepared by the Central Investigations Bureau showing details of the Vito Genovese "family." It is important, therefore, to see how far Valachi's evidence was corroborated by the police. In this connection, the evidence given by Deputy Chief Inspector Shanley reveals that the information given by Valachi coincided with that put forward by the police in a number of respects. Yet, an examination of the record reveals other facts which make it clear also: (1) that it would have been very surprising indeed if the police evidence had not agreed with that of Valachi, and (2) that to talk of the police evidence as *corroborating* Valachi's testimony is totally to misrepresent the situation.

In order to demonstrate this point, it is necessary only to reproduce two brief passages from Deputy Chief Inspector Shanley's testimony. The first passage is taken from the beginning of that testimony:

The Chairman	Have you gone over the information that the committee has obtained and conferred with the staff regarding it, and also with this witness, Joe Valachi?
Mr. Shanley	I haven't conferred with the witness.
The Chairman	You never conferred with the witness?
Mr. Shanley	No, sir.
The Chairman	So, what you are going to testify here is not a result of any conference you have had with Valachi?
Mr. Shanley	No, sir.
The Chairman	Very well, you may proceed.

The second passage occurs toward the end of Deputy Chief Inspector Shanley's evidence, after he had produced the chart referred to above and testified about the Genovese "family." It runs as follows:

The Chairman	Senator Muskie, you have a question?
Senator Muskie	You testified earlier, Inspector Shanley, that you had not personally talked to Mr. Valachi.
Mr. Shanley	That is right.
Senator Muskie	Yet these charts are based heavily on his information, am I correct?
Mr. Shanley	That is correct.
Senator Muskie	What was the source of your access to his information.
Mr. Shanley	The Committee.
Senator Muskie	These hearings?
Mr. Shanley	Yes, sir. We received the information prior to the hearings.
Senator Muskie	Would it have been possible for you to reconstruct these charts without his testimony?
Mr. Shanley	No, sir.
Senator Mundt	Mr. Chairman.
The Chairman	Senator Mundt.
Senator Mundt	While we are talking about the value of the charts, you have been in the hearing room, I think, Inspector, since the very beginning of the Valachi testimony. Is that right?
Mr. Shanley	Yes, sir.

It is necessary only to add that sedulous reproduction is not the same thing as substantiation. Nor is it sufficient merely to assert as Mr. Shanley did that Valachi's information possessed "an apparent authenticity that is hard to doubt." Mr. Shanley appears to have felt that the impossibility of verifying much of what Valachi said did not necessarily detract from its credibility or value. For he said:

> The specific information that he gave, this will be pursued. But even if this specific information does not pan out, it *would not necessarily detract from the effectiveness of the information*, because the lapse of time, as you well know, goes for the defendant and what happens in 10, 20, 30 years is that the witness is not available, memories fade, locales change. In New York, some of the things this man is talking about no longer exist as to locale. The buildings are torn down. Physical evidence has gone. [Our italics.]

It never became clear exactly what he meant by "effectiveness" in this context.

There is, however, one example in the transcript of the McClellan committee hearings which throws some light on the credibility of Valachi's evidence and the reliability of the sources from which he derived his information. That is the case of Abe Reles. Early in the hearings, Valachi cited Reles's death as an example of the way in which "the organization" was able "to kill somebody when they are in prison if they want to." He testified as follows:

Mr. Valachi   There was another, Abe Reles. He was also supposed to testify. He fell out of the window.
Senator Brewster How did he fall out of the window, do you know?
Mr. Valachi   They threw him out.

Later in the hearings, the committee returned to this point. Senator Javits read out the passage quoted above and then asked:

Senator Javits   Who threw him out?
Mr. Valachi   There was the rumor that they threw him out.
Senator Javits   Who is "they"? You used the word.
Mr. Valachi   Let us put it this way, whoever was in charge.
Senator Javits   That is on the gang side; is that right:
What was the rumor, as you knew it?
Mr. Valachi   That the police threw him out.
Senator Javits   That was the rumor as you knew it?
Mr. Valachi   Yes.

Senator Javits	Do you know any more about it?
Mr. Valachi	No; that is all.
Senator Javits	Did you hear that confirmed in prison or in any way?
Mr. Valachi	The boys talked about it; that is good enough for me.
Senator Javits	The boys in prison?
Mr. Valachi	No, the boys outside.
Senator Javits	The boys in your gang, is that right?
Mr. Valachi	Yes.
Senator Javits	Any particular boy?
Mr. Valachi	Well, now, I would say in general conversation here and there. When you have a conversation, it is pretty solid.
Senator Javits	You believed it?
Mr. Valachi	Yes, anything I hear.

Eight days later, the committee was to hear more about the death of Abe Reles. Picturesque stories about "the organization" were one thing; allegations against the police were a different matter. Deputy Chief Inspector Shanley, who had been so impressed by the "apparent authenticity" of Valachi's information, reappeared, speaking in a somewhat different vein.

The Chairman	Very well. Is there anything further?
Mr. Adlerman	I think that Inspector Shanley has something that he would like to put into the record, a statement he would like to make.
Mr. Shanley	I have here a grand jury presentment in the matter of the investigation of the circumstances surrounding the death of Abe Reles on November 12, 1941.

Shanley then read a statement to the effect that the grand jury, after examining 86 witnesses, viewing 127 exhibits, and hearing scientific reports from the FBI, had concluded that

> Abe Reles met his death while trying to escape, by means of a knotted sheet which was attached to a wire, which wire was in turn attached to the radiator in his room. He fell to his death, while suspended from or supporting himself in this sheet, when the wire parted as a result of the strain of his weight on it. We find that Reles did not meet with foul play and that he did not die by suicide.

We turn now from "the corroboration furnished by law enforcement officers [which] makes Valachi's testimony more credible and important," to what, in the circumstances, is the only other criterion of validity available, that is, the internal consistency of the evidence. Here there are a variety of matters which might be considered. In view, however, of the great emphasis that is always placed, in the literature, on the strictness of organizational discipline and the obvious necessity for this if such an organization is to cohere and continue to exist, it is interesting to examine first the evidence on this topic.

In this connection, Senator McClellan spoke in his opening address of "the strict discipline imposed upon the members." He said: "This tightly knit association of professional criminals demands and gets *complete dedication and unquestioned obedience* by its members to orders, instructions and commands from the ruling authority or boss or bosses thereof." Subsequently, many witnesses were to refer to this. Thus William H. Schneider, commissioner of police of Buffalo, spoke of the syndicate as "a multibillion dollar syndicate which depends on brutal assault and murder as its means of *cold, dispassionate discipline*" (our italics). Valachi was asked about this by Senator McClellan.

The Chairman	. . . [T]hat [i.e., Cosa Nostra] is an organization, is it that requires *absolute obedience and conformity* to its policy as handed down by those in authority? [Our italics, again.]
Mr. Valachi	Yes, sir.
The Chairman	Is that correct?
Mr. Valachi	Yes, sir.

It is interesting to compare these statements with some passages in Valachi's later testimony. It appears that, because of "the heat of the narcotics prosecutions, and the investigations and the publicity" in 1957, "those in authority" decreed that there was to be no more dealing in narcotics among members of Cosa Nostra. As Valachi put it: "No narcotics. You are in serious trouble if you were arrested for narcotics. You had to prove to them — you have another trial after having a trial with the government." His examination on this topic ran as follows:

Mr. Valachi	After Anastasia died in 1957, all families were notified — no narcotics.
Mr. Adlerman	Who laid down that rule?
Mr. Valachi	That was a rule that was discussed by the bosses themselves.
Mr. Adlerman	Was that the consigliere and the bosses themselves made that rule?
Mr. Valachi	That is right; that covered all families.

It is instructive to read what came next:

Mr. Adlerman	Was the narcotics trade one of the principal money-makers for the members of the Cosa Nostra?
Mr. Valachi	Yes, it was.
Mr. Adlerman	And was this rule disregarded to a large extent?
Mr. Valachi	You mean there were lots of people in business?
Mr. Adlerman	That is right.
Mr. Valachi	Yes, sir.

Valachi went on to say that even some of "the bosses" violated the rule and he was then asked:

Mr. Adlerman	What was the reason why the members, the soldiers and so forth, and even some of the bosses disregarded the rule?
Mr. Valachi	Because of the moneymaking, the profit in it.
Mr. Adlerman	There was big money?
Mr. Valachi	They would chance their own lives.
Mr. Adlerman	And there was a conflict between the desire to make money and the desire to obey the rules; is that right?
Mr. Valachi	Well, they just defied the rules.
Mr. Adlerman	They defied the rules?
Mr. Valachi	That is the way I can explain it that way.

In the light of what had been said earlier about "complete dedication and unquestioned obedience," it was not an entirely satisfactory explanation. But then no explanation, however ingenious, could encompass the logically impossible task of reconciling the development described with the concept of a ruthless, unquestionable authority imposing "cold, dispassionate discipline" and securing "absolute obedience and conformity." Indeed, the evidence casts doubt also on the validity of the attorney general's belief that "Cosa Nostra . . . establishes an allegiance for its members that is higher than family, country and religion. It becomes the primary allegiance of the member." Not quite the *primary* allegiance apparently. Yet, Senator McClellan was still talking a week later about "Cosa Nostra . . . and the misguided and dedicated loyalty of its members."

It is, in fact, extremely difficult to understand what membership of the organization was supposed to entail in the way of either rights or duties. When Valachi was describing his initiation, he was asked:

Senator Mundt	In executive session you said when you had your hands all clasped together and repeated some words in Italian

	or Sicilian, that what it meant was "One for all and all for one."
Mr. Valachi	Yes; that is the way I explained it.
Senator Mundt	One for all and all for one.
Mr. Valachi	That is right. But I didn't know the words, Senator. You remember, I didn't know the words.
Senator Mundt	That is right, but you said that is the reaction you got.
Mr. Valachi	That is correct.
Senator Mundt	All right, then you became there a full-fledged member.
Mr. Valachi	Yes, sir.

It would seem reasonable to assume that the slogan, if Valachi understood it correctly, implied some kind of mutual aid and protection. Certainly Senator McClellan had told the committee, "The benefits of membership . . . are a share in its illicit gains from criminal activities and protection from prosecution and the penalties of the law." Later Valachi was asked:

Senator Mundt	I want to ask you a couple of questions dealing with the first part of your testimony. You belonged to Cosa Nostra for about 30 years?
Mr. Valachi	Since 1930.
Senator Mundt	What was your average income from your criminal contacts during those 30 years, your average annual income?
Mr. Valachi	Senator, I wouldn't be able to tell you. Sometimes I was doing bad, sometimes I was doing good.
	. . . .
Senator Mundt	What I am trying to establish is that you were working as a soldier in this family, I am trying to determine what your income was as a soldier working for Genovese.
Mr. Valachi	You don't get any salary, Senator.
Senator Mundt	Well, you get a cut then.
Mr. Valachi	You get nothing, only what you earn yourself. Do you understand? . . .
Senator Mundt	You say the only thing you got out of your membership and for carrying out your assignments that Genovese gave you was protection?
Mr. Valachi	Yes. . . .

So much then for Senator McClellan's "share in its illicit gains." What about "protection from prosecution and the penalties of the law"? Deputy Chief Inspector Shanley had told the committee that "the family will help with lawyers, bail bondsmen, et cetera, if anything goes wrong."

The following passages are relevant here:

Senator Javits	Were you represented, for example, by lawyers in that time when you were picked up?
Mr. Valachi	When you are picked up, sometimes yes; sometimes no. Sometimes you don't even require a lawyer.
Senator Javits	How did you seek the help of your family when you were picked up?
Mr. Valachi	I used to get my own help. What family do you mean?
Senator Javits	The family to which you belonged, the Genovese family.
Mr. Valachi	I never bothered them. If I got picked up, I got myself out, I got my own lawyers.
Senator Javits	Did they give you any protection in the 35 years?
Mr. Valachi	No.
Senator Javits	They did not furnish lawyers?
Mr. Valachi	Never.
Senator Javits	Or bondsmen?
Mr. Valachi	Never, I got my own bondsmen, my own lawyers.

. . . .

Senator Javits	Do you attribute the fact that you were not convicted of a crime for 35 years to your membership in this family? Do you connect the two at all?
Mr. Valachi	No.
Senator Javits	You were just lucky?
Mr. Valachi	That is right.
Senator Javits	And you changed the nature of activities?
Mr. Valachi	Put it that way.
Senator Javits	So your membership in the family had nothing to do, in your opinion. . . .
Mr. Valachi	I was never in a position, if I was I would tell you, Senator, I was never in a position where the family helped me.

In his evidence before the McClellan committee, the attorney general spoke of the commission ("We know that Cosa Nostra is run by a commission") as a body which "makes major policy decisions for the organization, settles disputes among families and allocates territories of criminal operation within the organizations." It sounds like a very businesslike and efficient operation on the part of men about whom the committee was later told, "Frequently they don't make out in the legitimate business" because they are "not very smart businessmen." But it is hardly consistent with Valachi's testimony. He was asked:

Senator Curtis   In that connection, did they divide up the territory? Even though you operated on your own, you knew where you could operate?

Mr. Valachi   No, you see, Senator, you take Harlem, for instance. We have about four families all mixed up there. *There isn't any territory.* You find Brooklyn gangs in New York and New York into Brooklyn. They get along very well. If anything, you have in Brooklyn, in fact they help protect it for you. *I would not say it is territories.* You take for instance in Harlem, we have about three families bumping into one another. You have the Gambino family, the Lucchese family, and you have the Genovese family right in Harlem. . . . You have three families right there. You have members there from all different groups. [Our italics.]

We may deal briefly with one other matter and then leave the McClellan committee. Senator McClellan told members, "the penalty for disloyalty or any serious deviation from the precepts, rules and dictates of the order is usually death." But what were the precepts and rules of the order? We have already noted Professor Cressey's remarkable "code of good thieves everywhere." What did Joseph Valachi have to say on the subject? He stated that at the time of his initiation he was told that he must never divulge the secrets of the initiation ceremony or of the organization. On this point, he said:

   . . . As to what I am telling you now, I need go no further to say nothing else but this here, what I am telling you, what I am exposing to you and to the press and everybody. This is my doom. This is the promise I am breaking. Even if I talked, I should never talk about this, and I am doing so. That is my best way to explain it.

His examination continued as follows:

The Chairman   . . . Were any of the rules explained to you there, or were they explained to you later?

Mr. Valachi   Just two rules at this time.

The Chairman   Just two at that time?

Mr. Valachi   At this time.

The Chairman   What were they?

Mr. Valachi   One was the secret which I was just telling you about, and the other rule was, for instance, a wife, if you violate

	the law of another member's wife, or sister, or daughter, these two rules were told; in other words, you had no defense.
The Chairman	You have no defense?
Mr. Valachi	These two main rules. If you give away the secret or you violate — at this time that is all of the rules I was told.
The Chairman	Those two?
Mr. Valachi	At this time.
The Chairman	If you violated the family relationship of a husband and his wife, and if they were members of Cosa Nostra; is that all?
Mr. Valachi	If they were members. If they were members of Cosa Nostra.
The Chairman	You were prohibited from violating the rules of family relationship?
Mr. Valachi	That is right.
The Chairman	Those two at that time?
Mr. Valachi	That is right.

But, although Valachi testified that later on he "learned the rules," the only other example he gave was, "For instance you can't hit another member with your fist." He admitted having broken this rule himself when he found his partner "was stealing most of the profit." Senator McClellan seems to have scented another rule at this point, for he asked: "Was that against your code, to steal from each other?" But Valachi's reply was somewhat equivocal. "Well yes," he said, "against my code it was." And that was all the committee learned about "the code" which, according to the President's Crime Commission task force report on organized crime "gives the leaders exploitative authoritarian power over everyone in the organization."

Of the three rules he mentioned, Valachi had avowedly broken two. Was he unusual in this? He was certainly not unique in becoming an informer. According to the attorney general, the *main* thing that distinguished him was that he was willing to "come and testify in public." Over two years later, J. Edgar Hoover told a House of Representatives appropriations subcommittee that "*all the Valachi informa- tion . . .* had been obtained from informants of the Bureau" prior to the McClellan committee hearings. But, apart from this sort of dis- loyalty, did the chivalric code of "one for all and all for one" otherwise prevail? Almost everything in Valachi's testimony suggests the opposite. He spoke of vicious power struggles and murderous internecine con- flicts like the Masseria-Maranzano war and the Gallo-Profaci feud. He spoke of "the bosses" as being "very bad to the soldiers and they have been thinking for themselves, all through the years." He portrayed Professor Cressey's "almost revered" Vito Genovese as mean, murderous, and megalomaniacal. If there existed anywhere among organized criminals that "sense of decency and morality — a sense of honor," which Professor Cressey remarks as characteristic of them, it seems to have escaped Joseph Valachi's notice.

In sum then, what can be said about the Valachi evidence? In the first place, the attorney general's assertion that "for the first time an insider . . . has broken the underworld's code of silence" was misleading. It was contradicted later both by the attorney general himself and by J. Edgar Hoover. Apart from his willingness to testify in public, only one feature of the Valachi testimony was unique. What that was is clear from the attorney general's statement:

> You look back on organized crime and people who
> are talking about organized crime, somebody might
> talk about a particular criminal act. What we have
> always lacked is somebody who could come in and
> tell the whole picture. Now he tells it . . .

In short, what Valachi added to the already available evidence about particular crimes and criminals was the story of the syndicate, its organization, its operations, and its membership.

What was his evidence on that subject worth? A great deal of it was the loosest kind of hearsay. Valachi believed and repeated on oath, as matters of fact, "anything" he heard in conversation "here and there" with his fellow criminals. Despite what Senator McClellan said about his evidence being corroborated, it was not corroborated on any points essential to the hypothesis we are considering. It was consistent neither with itself nor with other evidence that was presented to the committee. Valachi both contradicted himself and was contradicted by others. Moreover, what the attorney general called "the biggest intelligence breakthrough yet" appears to have produced nothing in the way of tangible results.

Two and a half years after Valachi testified, J. Edgar Hoover was asked before the House of Representatives appropriations subcommittee mentioned earlier:

Mr. Rooney (Chairman)   Has Valachi been of any assistance to the Bureau in the prosecution of any criminal as a result of which there has been a conviction?

Mr. Hoover   There has been no person convicted as a direct result of any information furnished by Valachi.

And four years later, the President's Crime Commission task force report on organized crime described the situation regarding organized crime in precisely the same terms as those used by the attorney general before the McClellan committee. Almost the only development reported is that "FBI intelligence indicates that the organization as a whole has changed its name from the Mafia to La Cosa Nostra." The report is not very clear on this point but seems to suggest that the name was changed at some time between 1951 and 1966. Even this contradicts Valachi, who maintained that it had been called Cosa Nostra ("they *never* express it as a Mafia") when he joined in 1930.

There is one other piece of "evidence" which should be mentioned here before we conclude. This relates to what J. Edgar Hoover called the "meeting of hoodlums at Apalachin, N.Y.," which has been referred to somewhat more grandly by others as the "Crime Convention at Apalachin" and the "historic rally of the Mafia at Apalachin." Senator McClellan says of it: "The meeting gave to millions of Americans their first clear knowledge that we have in this country a criminal syndicate that is obviously tightly organized into a secret brotherhood which none of its members dare betray, and which has insinuated its tentacles into business and labor and public life at high levels." But, whatever else can be derived from the mass of confused and contradictory evidence available regarding Apalachin, it is certainly not "clear knowledge."

There seems to be general agreement that on 14 November 1957 a number of individuals, most of whom had criminal records relating to the kind of offense customarily called "organized crime" gathered at the home of Joseph Barbara in Apalachin, New York, and that the gathering was interrupted by the police. But, beyond that point, the evidence becomes extraordinarily confused. Indeed, even such basic information as how many persons were present at the gathering is lacking. Thus, Senator McClellan in his book *Crime without Punishment* states that "*fifty-eight* men were picked up on the Barbara estate or in the immediate surrounding countryside." *The Report of the State of New York Joint Legislative Committee on Government Operations* on "the Gangland Meeting in Apalachin, N.Y." states, "On November 14, 1957, *about* 65 individuals gathered at the home of a man named Joseph Barbara, in Apalachin, N.Y." The task force report on organized crime talks of "the meeting in Apalachin, N.Y., of *at least* 75 criminal cartel leaders." Attorney General Robert Kennedy testified to the McClellan committee: "In 1957, *more than a hundred* top racketeers met at the now infamous crime convention at Apalachin, N.Y." (Our italics in each quotation.)

Where such discrepancies exist about a matter which is, at least in principle, subject to quantitative measurement, it is not surprising that there is disagreement about less objective features. The following brief passages by two authors, both of whom derived their information from, and cite as their authority, the Federal Bureau of Narcotics, give almost totally disparate accounts of such matters as the weather, the number, dress, demeanor, and spirits of the guests at Apalachin. Frederic Sondern, in his *Brotherhood of Evil: The Mafia*, says that, of the *"more than sixty"* persons present, many were engaged in "conclaves" inside Barbara's house. He continues:

> Others were grouped around the huge stone barbecue pit. . . . The weather at Apalachin was unusually mild for November and most of the guests were dressed in immaculate light suits of Italian silk, white on white shirts and highly polished shoes of soft leather. The majority were in their late fifties and early sixties — dignified, even pompous. All seemed to be in a decorous good humor.

Renée Buse, on the other hand, in *The Deadly Silence*, says:

> It was an odd day for a barbecue. The sky was gray. The November temperature hovered just above freezing. Cold, damp rain-winds swirled through the barren trees. The *hundred-odd* men who stood in uncomfortable clusters around the barbecue pit were quiet, even glum. Somehow, the party spirit had failed to penetrate. Dutifully the guests ate and drank . . . but their loud, Broadway type sports jackets, their thin, pointed shoes, and their pasty complexions bespoke their awkward discomfort.

It is true that this discrepancy is not a matter of great significance. Such differences could easily be due to one informant having drunk from the "selection of choice wines," which Sondern says was available, more "dutifully" than another.

But discrepancies regarding more substantial matters are less easy to discount. Consider, for instance, the question of the nature of the gathering at Apalachin. John T. Cusack, district supervisor for the Federal Bureau of Narcotics, testified before the New York State Legislative Committee that "the meeting at Apalachin, New York, should be considered a meeting of the Grand Council" of "the Mafia Society." Attorney General Robert Kennedy, in his evidence to the McClellan committee, cited "the meeting at Apalachin" as an example of a meeting of the commission which runs Cosa Nostra and "makes major policy decisions for the organization." But he also testified that "membership in the Commission varies between 9 and 12 active members." He made no attempt to reconcile this evidence with his earlier statement that "more than a hundred top racketeers" were present at Apalachin.

Senator McClellan allowed himself a rhetorical flourish. "The meeting of the delegates to the Apalachin convention," he says, "suggests a lawless and clandestine army . . . at war with the government and the people of the United States." He failed to mention, however, that not one of these lawless warriors was armed, and that only one (a parole violator from New Jersey who should not have left the state) was wanted anywhere by the police.

What business was conducted at Apalachin? Renée Buse, who says that the Federal Bureau of Narcotics commissioner H. L. Giordano's "desire to have the story told accurately" made his investigation possible, describes a hearing of an appeal to "the Bosses" by Carmine Lombardozzi against conviction by "a kangaroo court of his peers . . . for having tried to muscle into another man's exclusive jukebox territory" as being the principal business in progress when the police closed in. Frederic Sondern, whose accuracy is vouched for by the former Federal Bureau of Narcotics commissioner H. J. Anslinger, states:

> The business of the meeting at Barbara's —
> according to well placed informers who have pieced
> the picture together for the Treasury Department's
> agents — *concentrated on two questions* crucial to
> the future of big organized rackets, narcotics and
> gambling.

But another well-placed informer, Joseph Valachi, testified to the McClellan committee:

> The meeting *was held for two main reasons* that I
> know of. One was to talk about the justifying of the
> shooting of Albert Anastasia. The other one was that

> they were going to talk about eliminating some
> couple of hundred new members. [Our italics in both
> quotations.]

Valachi, incidentally, stated that Vito Genovese "called the meeting at Apalachin," whereas Sondern says that the McClellan committee "had very reliable information" that "William Bufalino . . . was responsible for organizing — for his close friend and associate of many years, Don Giuseppe Barbara — the whole Apalachin meeting." Giuseppe, he says, "was a capo mafioso of the first order, of unusual experience, wisdom and authority."

It scarcely seems necessary to multiply examples. When, subsequently, twenty of those present at Apalachin were charged with "conspiring to obstruct justice and commit perjury," the government frankly admitted at the outset of the trial "that it would not be able to show what was going on at the meeting." Regarding this trial, the task force report on organized crime says: "In 1957, twenty of organized crime's top leaders were convicted (later reversed on appeal) of a criminal charge arising from a meeting at Apalachin, N.Y." It is characteristic of the inconsequential way in which the whole subject is treated in both official and unofficial reports that the defendants are said to have been convicted in 1957 of charges on which they were not even indicted until May 1959. But the report is accurate in stating that all the convictions were reversed on appeal.

What remains after one penetrates the fog of senatorial fustian and journalistic rhetoric? Professor Cressey is unusually restrained on this question. "No one has been able to prove the nature of the conspiracy involved," he says. But, he adds reasonably enough, "no one believes that the men all just happened to drop in on the host at the same time." Professor Bell says: "The accidental police discovery of a conference of Italian figures, most of them with underworld and police records at Apalachin, New York, in November, 1957, revived talk of a Mafia." But, he says, the " 'evidence' that many gangsters congregate . . . by itself does not prove much; people 'in the trade' usually do." A reasonable explanation seems to be that it was, as suggested by *Time* magazine reporter Serell Hillman, who was assigned to check the story over some weeks, a meeting "of criminals in various cities and areas, who run their own shows in their own fields but have matters of mutual interest to take up." One thing is certain: the information available about Apalachin provides no serious evidence that "a single national crime syndicate" dominates organized crime in America; nor does it make this seem probable.

Yet, if the evidence for the existence of an all-American crime confederation or syndicate is both suspect and tenuous to the point of nullity, it is clear that for the believer there is nothing which could count decisively against the assertion that it exists. Indeed, precisely those features which in ordinary discourse about human affairs might be regarded as evidence in rebuttal are instantly assimilated as further strengthening the case *for* the hypothesis. The absence of direct evidence, apart from Valachi's inhibited garrulity and remarks of other unspecified informants, merely demonstrates to the task force on organized crime "the fear instilled in them by the code of nondisclosure." Thus, denials of membership in, or knowledge of, the syndicate can not only be dismissed as self-evidently false but also adduced as evidence of what they deny. If there is gang warfare, this indicates to J. Edgar Hoover that "an internal struggle for dominance over the entire organization" is going on and also provides for the McClellan committee "a somber illustration of how cruel and calculating the underworld continues to be." If peace prevails this may be taken either as evidence of the power of the syndicate leadership and the fear in which it is held, or alternatively as reflecting the development of "the sophisticated and polished control of rackets that now characterize that organization."

It is said that "practically all" the members of the organization "are of Sicilian birth or ancestry." Professor Cressey, for example, speaks of "the Italian-Sicilian apparatus [which] continues to dominate organized crime in America." But counterevidence relating to the activities of those from other ethnic backgrounds (e.g., Meyer Lansky, said by J. Edgar Hoover to be "generally recognized as one of the most powerful racketeers in this country") can easily be accommodated as illustrating the "characteristic Mafia method of utilizing non-Sicilian associates where it serves its criminal objectives." In the end, it is difficult to resist the conclusion that one is not dealing with an empirical phenomenon at all but with an article of faith, transcending the contingent particularity of everyday experience and logically unassailable — one of those reassuring popular demonologies which, William Buckley has remarked, the successful politician has to cherish and preserve and may, in the end, come to believe. In the circumstances therefore it is necessary to say something about the nonevidential and irrational considerations — what may be called the mythopeic factors which operate in this field. It is reasonable to assume that a powerful influence is the fact that there is a considerable folklore relating to organized crime. Much of the literature on the subject consists of myths and folktales. The point is made in Earl Johnson's article, "Organized Crime: Challenge to the American Legal System":

> America has a new folklore. This folklore has grown
> up around organized crime. Next to Westerns,
> war and sex, it is probably the chief source of
> material for TV plots, books — both fiction and
> non-fiction — and newspaper exposés. The names of
> "Scarface" Al Capone, Frank "The Enforcer" Nitti,
> Tony Accardo, Frank Costello, and "Lucky" Luciano
> have become as familiar to most present-day
> Americans as Pocahontas, Jesse James, "Wild" Bill
> Hickok, Paul Bunyan, or Nathan Hale.

The significance of this development has nowhere been fully analyzed, but in the light of the functionalist interpretation of myth made by anthropologists, it would be unwise to dismiss it as of little account. Malinowski, for example, holds that "myth fulfills in primitive culture an indispensable function: it expresses, enhances and codifies belief; it safeguards and enforces morality." Nor is this something confined to primitive cultures, although the character of the myths will obviously be different in different cultures. In regard to our own society, Ruth Benedict has pointed out that "the fundamental opposition of good and evil is a trait of occidental folklore that is expressed equally in Grimm's fairy tales and in the *Arabian Nights*. . . . it determines some of the most deeply seated world views of western religions and western civilizations. The opposition of God and the devil, of Christ and Antichrist, of heaven and hell, is part of the fundamental intellectual equipment of those who participate in these civilizations." It is probable that a large part of the appeal of such television series as "The Untouchables," "Target: The Corrupters," and "The F.B.I.," to mention only three, rests on the fact that they dramatize the struggle against organized crime in terms of this fundamental myth. In this, too, it seems likely, lies some of the appeal of televised and reported congressional investigations, newspaper accounts of "crusades" against organized crime, and a vast literature dealing with law enforcement efforts against it.

Another function of mythology, however, is that it provides an explanation, in that it helps to introduce some intelligible order into the bewildering diversity of phenomena surrounding us. Thus, it is said, "In anthropology there is general agreement that a myth" may be concerned with "the nature and meaning of the universe," and, "In political science and sociology the meaning of the term is sometimes extended to include the whole world picture held by a social group." Ruth Benedict says also that "man in all his mythologies has expressed his discomfort at a mechanistic universe and his pleasure in substituting a world that is humanly motivated and directed." But all myths are not of a cosmic character and discomfort can be induced just as much by an apparently formless and unstructured field of experience as by the theory that all natural processes are mechanically determined. Yet, whether alarm and uneasiness are induced by an apparently chaotic upsurge of crime and lawlessness, or whether explanation in terms of anonymous and intangible "social forces" is found unsatisfying, it is likely that the attribution of responsibility to a group of identifiable human agents for a large proportion of the disturbing happenings could be both intellectually and emotionally reassuring. Similarly, it may be that part of the popularity of what has been called the Lombrosian myth in criminology and its success in shifting attention from crime as a social phenomenon to crime as an individual phenomenon may have been due to the fact that crime was seen as "humanly motivated and directed" rather than as a function of abstract social processes.

Yet something more than a demand for simplicity and order is involved. In this connection, the way in which anger and distress lead to a demand for the identification of a responsible individual or group, which is brought out by G. W. Allport in his discussion of the psychological process of "scapegoating" in *The Nature of Prejudice*, is directly relevant to our discussion. "The common use of the orphaned pronoun 'they,'" says Allport, "teaches us that people often want and need to designate outgroups — usually for the purpose of venting hostility." And Daniel Bell attributes part of the attractiveness of the "theory of a Mafia and national crime syndicate" to the fact that there is "in the American temper, a feeling that 'somewhere,' 'somebody' is pulling all the complicated strings to which this jumbled world dances. In politics the labor image is 'Wall Street' or 'Big Business'; while the business stereotype was the 'New Dealers.'" In the field of crime, the national crime syndicate provides a specific focus or target for fear and discontent.

There is, of course, nothing exclusively or peculiarly American about this process. The popularity of conspiracy theories throughout history reflects a general human tendency. The objectification and institutionalization of fear reactions is not a native American development. Thus, the English Popish Plot of 1678, which was supposed to involve a vast Jesuit conspiracy, occurred before the Salem witch trials of 1692. And Pope Innocent VIII's denunciation of those who had the "unblushing effrontery" to contend that witchcraft was not a real thing preceded them by more than two centuries. Yet, as Richard Hofstadter demonstrates in his brilliant essay "The Paranoid Style in American Politics," American history is singularly rich in examples of "conspiratorial fantasy." Hofstadter does say that "the paranoid style is an international phenomenon." But he also admits "it can be argued . . . that certain features of our history have given the paranoid style more scope and force among us than it has had in many other countries of the Western world." It is relevant to note here that, in describing "the basic elements in the paranoid style," Hofstadter says "the central image is that of a vast and sinister conspiracy, a gigantic and yet subtle machinery of influence set in motion to undermine and destroy a way of life."

So much having been said about irrational factors which may be regarded as conducive to the acceptance of the notion of an all-powerful syndicate dominating American crime, it remains true that the validity of an idea and the reasons for its popularity may be quite independent of one another. Thus, one of the principal forms of the scapegoat theory rests on the "frustration-aggression hypothesis." Very briefly, this theory asserts that frustration generates aggression which becomes displaced upon scapegoats, and that the displaced hostility is rationalized and justified by blaming, projecting, and stereotyping. But, as Allport and others have pointed out:

> What seems like displacement may, in some instances, be an aggression directed toward the true source of the frustration. . . . The scapegoat theory, like all other theories of prejudice, should make certain that it is not misapplied to cases of realistic social conflict.

In this context, however, we have to face the fact that quite apart from the paucity and dubious character of the available evidence it is inherently improbable that organized crime is for the most part in the hands of a monolithic nationwide crime syndicate, controlled by a single "commission." As T. C. Schelling says in "Economic Analysis and Organized Crime," printed as an appendix to the President's Crime Commission task force report on organized crime, "A large part of organized crime involves selling commodities and services contrary to law." But "not all businesses lend themselves to centralized organization," and "the inducements to expansion and the advantages of large-scale over small are especially present in some markets rather than others." It is conceivable, of course, that the economy of the underworld is totally different from that of legitimate business. But it seems reasonable to assume that, as Professor Schelling says, "a good many economic and business principles that operate in the 'upper-world' must, with suitable modification for change in environment, operate in the underworld as well, just as a good many economic principles that operate in an advanced competitive economy operate as well in a Socialist or a primitive economy." In other words, the assumption that — despite the diversity of the activities involved and the absence or presence of the market characteristics which would be likely to determine whether or not, or to what degree, organization would be likely to occur — one vast criminal monopoly has developed with the profits pouring into "the treasury of the Cosa Nostra" seems extraordinarily fanciful.

In conclusion, two things can be said. In the first place we note that the task force on organized crime recommended that the "relevant disciplines such as economics, political science, sociology and operations research" should "begin to study organized crime intensively." As to this, we have to acknowledge that too little is known about the "organized" aspect of the crime problem. But we would remind researchers that here as elsewhere, it may be salutary to bear in mind the principle expressed in the celebrated Scholastic dictum which has become known as Occam's razor: *entia non sunt multiplicanda praeter necessitatem* (entities ought not to be multiplied except out of necessity). It is said that when Napoleon I asked why God was not mentioned in his *Traité de la mécanique céleste* (1799–1825) Laplace replied: "Sire, je n'avais besoin de cet hypothèse." It seems likely that what Laplace found in the sphere of cosmology will also obtain in the more mundane field of criminology; there are hypotheses that we do not need.

Our second point is this: As long as we are determined to continue our futile efforts by means of the criminal law to prevent people from obtaining goods and services which they have clearly demonstrated they do not intend to forgo, criminals will supply those goods and services. And insofar as the market is of a character in which combination and organization is profitable they will organize. As we have indicated in our first chapter the way to eliminate organized crime is to remove the criminal laws which both stimulate and protect it.

9

Research

It is worth noting that research commands only a small fraction of one percent of the total expenditure for crime control. There is probably no subject of comparable concern to which the Nation is devoting so many resources and so much effort with so little knowledge of what it is doing.

Report of the President's Crime Commission

Billions of dollars are spent annually by government and private organizations on research in the physical and biological sciences. Approximately 15 percent of the Defense Department's annual budget is allocated to research. In the manufacturing industry generally, the average allocation for research is 3 percent, although in developmental areas a much higher allotment is made. But the expenditure for research in the behavioral and social sciences, particularly in the field of crime and criminal justice, is so small as to seem derisory.

For this neglect we pay a price. Our operations on all levels are vitiated by ignorance. As Rupert Cross has pointed out, underlying nearly everything we do in the sphere of crime control is "a mass of unexplained and unfounded assumptions." And as nature abhors a vacuum just as much here as in the field of physics the lacuna is rapidly filled. Politicians who would be reluctant to pose as experts in biochemistry or astrophysics do not hesitate to peddle fashionable nostrums and panaceas for the crime problem. Guided by an extraordinary amalgam of blind prejudice, random benevolence, and naïve surmise, we launch into extemporaneous improvisations which with the passage of time harden into inviolable institutions.

Possibly our lack of knowledge is to be attributed to intellectual sloth combined with a scarcity both of people interested in criminological research and of sufficient funds for such work to be pursued. After all, many people become interested in the crime problem largely for humanitarian reasons, and this applies as much to the trained social worker as to the lay volunteer. Others are interested only to the extent that they find employment in this field which, if not highly profitable, is at least reasonably secure. It is not sensible to look to such people for critical, methodologically sophisticated assessments of their own work. But no such excuse can be offered for senior officials in police and prison departments who use substantial community funds and considerable resources of personnel without insisting upon research that evaluates what they are doing. The demands of sound business practice alone should have led such departments to test critically the marginal return, in crimes prevented, from the various methods and techniques they employ. It is obviously wise business practice to try to discover the return from your investment. When the investment is in the happiness of law-abiding sections of the community, the prevention of social suffering, and the confidence of all people in their physical safety and the protection of their property, such an effort is overwhelmingly necessary.

It is impossible to ignore the fact that what is required here is a national effort. The President's Crime Commission task force on science and technology pointed out that while more than 200,000 scientists have applied themselves to solving military problems "only a handful are working to control the crimes that injure or frighten millions of Americans each year." Our ignorance is so extensive and so little is known about many basic questions that a major research and development program into the problems of crime and its control is urgently required. For the impediments of inadequate theory and the gaps in our knowledge may well prove more intractable than the political exigencies and the chronic shortage of men, money, and materials which usually obstruct progress.

This is not the place to consider in depth or detail all the areas in which scientific research and technological development may be expected to make contributions to the better understanding and control of crime and to improving the effectiveness of the criminal justice system. There is no doubt that modern technology could immediately provide an enormous amount of equipment which would vastly improve the operations of criminal justice agencies. Thus the task force on science and technology listed the following as among "the more important possibilities."

1. Electronic computers for processing the enormous quantities of needed data
2. Police radio networks connecting officers and neighboring departments
3. Inexpensive, light, two-way portable radios for every patrolman
4. Computers for processing fingerprints
5. Instruments for identifying criminals by voice, photograph, hair, blood, body chemistry, etc.
6. Devices for automatic and continued reporting of all police car locations
7. Helicopters for airborne police patrol
8. Inexpensive, reliable burglar and robbery alarms
9. Nonlethal weapons to subdue dangerous criminals without inflicting permanent harm

10. Perimeter surveillance devices for prisons

11. Automatic transcription devices for courtrooms

Although many of the devices listed are in existence and even commercially available, in most areas they are very expensive, their potential value in reducing crime is unknown, and only a research, development, test, and evaluation program could determine whether investment of resources in them would be worthwhile. It is therefore clear that, as far as technology is concerned, until a government-sponsored program involving requirement studies, cost-effectiveness analyses, and careful field evaluations is undertaken the application of modern technology to controlling crime must be restricted. Moreover, lacking the findings of such a program, it is not possible to indicate here exactly which new equipment and procedures should be developed and adopted.

We shall therefore confine our ukases on research to administrative and budgetary propositions which require little defense. The commentary on these ukases, however, will take up some of the major issues in research with which the research agencies, so established and funded, should deal.

1. Criminal justice agencies such as state court and correctional systems and large police departments shall develop their own research units.

2. In every appropriation for any agency or institution connected with the criminal justice system at least 5 percent of the total shall be allocated for research purposes.

3. All new crime prevention or correctional methods and practices shall be subject to critical evaluation.

4. The federal government shall establish a National Foundation for Criminal Research charged with the responsibility of stimulating and coordinating research, development, test, and evaluation projects in the field of crime and its control. Primary components of the research program shall be: (a) systems analysis studies; (b) field experimentation in police and correctional areas; (c) prediction research; (d) evaluative research in both police and correctional areas; (e) deterrence research; and (f) equipment system research and development.

Systems Analysis

The great range of our ignorance and the enormous potential of research and development confront us with a problem of priorities which is not easily soluble. For this reason one of the most important contributions of the President's Crime Commission was its recognition that the techniques of systems analysis can be applied to the overall criminal justice system and to the operations of its three main subsystems — the police, the courts, and the correction agencies. One of the principal advantages of systems analysis, which has been applied to such complex systems as national economies and air traffic systems, is that it provides a means for determining which of a number of alternative courses of action will provide maximum effectiveness for a given cost.

The essence of this technique is to construct a mathematical description or model of the system in the light of which it is possible to conduct simulated experiments which may indicate how the real life system may be better organized and operated. This sort of experimentation by the manipulation of models is particularly appropriate in the criminal justice area, where intervention in the complex of actual operations is often impractical. Unfortunately at present much of the data required for a complete analysis is not available. But once the necessary information is obtained — and modern information technology makes this possible — it will be possible to estimate both the costs of present operations and the consequences and possible benefits of any proposed changes in the system.

It is true that there are a variety of intangible social costs and nonquantifiable considerations, such as justice and individual liberty, which cannot be treated in this way. But systems analysis enables us to see clearly those aspects which can be measured and in the light of cost-effectiveness measures to make decisions which take them into account. Whereas in the past we have had to make decisions when even those considerations which are susceptible of numerical treatment have been assessed only by guesswork, it is now possible to design rational strategies which can be evaluated in the light of whatever basic objectives (e.g., reduction of crime, justice for individuals, etc.) we have.

Our science and technology program must therefore begin with systems analysis studies. For it is only on the basis of such studies that rational decisions can be made on which areas are most critical for research and which of all the possible lines of development open to us are likely to make the most effective contribution to improving the working of the criminal justice system and controlling crime.

Nevertheless, we need not await the results of such studies before we begin scientific investigation and research. There is no reason why evaluation, controlled testing, and experimentation should not be used inside the present system, for to do so may enable us to effect immediate operational improvements. Indeed, in our view evaluative research into ongoing systems and controlled experiments with new methods and techniques must be an integral feature of the criminal justice system in all its branches. This point will be developed more fully, but first we must deal with the question of research into the causes of crime and also with prediction research.

Etiological Research

In view of the fact that criminological research is frequently divided into two parts — namely, the causes of crime and the treatment of offenders — it is necessary to add something to the remarks in earlier chapters on the subject of research into the causes of crime. We are concerned here with the prevention of crime. It does not appear to us that further research adding to what Hermann Mannheim has called "the apparently chaotic lists of potentially causal factors found to bear a statistically significant correlation to crime" is in the least likely to aid in that task.

We do not go so far as to say that the search for the causes of crime (in whatever meaning is attached to that expression) must be abandoned. We say only that in the light of experience of very extensive research in that area the value of this sort of investigation for treatment and prevention purposes is likely to be very limited. It might of course be justified in terms of such ends as the disinterested pursuit of truth, the achievement of theoretical insights, or the acquisition of knowledge for its own sake without reference to any practical purposes or consequences.

There is, as it happens, considerable difference of opinion among criminologists about the distinction between "pure" and "applied" criminology. Thorsten Sellin distinguishes the work of the scientist aiming "at the discovery of constants in the relationships among certain defined facts" and that of the technologist concerned with the "adaptation of knowledge to the social needs of the moment." He argues that the term "criminology" should be used to designate only the former. On this issue Marvin Wolfgang, in his paper "Criminology and the Criminologist," concurs with Sellin. Mannheim, however, disagrees, saying that he cannot accept Sellin's conclusion that "the term criminology should not include these technological aspects." Indeed, he goes on to say that it is both "difficult and invidious to distinguish between the scientific and technological side of criminology."

This may sound like the kind of pedantic question which academic persons find amusing as a form of intellectual exercise but which serves no other purpose. Thus, the dichotomy of pure and applied sociology has been a controversial issue since the days of August Comte. But it is hard to discern that it has served any useful function other than to keep academics employed. In any case, it is certainly unnecessary to enter here into an analogous discussion about criminology.

In this context it might be sufficient to state simply that we are concerned with "applied" criminology and that we are prepared to fund and encourage studies directed to practical ends. In passing, however, we may say that we are inclined to agree with Mannheim that "practical needs are particularly strong in the study of crime and punishment," and with Leon Radzinowicz that "to rob it of [its] practical function is to divorce criminology from reality and render it sterile." Some years ago, addressing the Second United Nations Congress on the Prevention of Crime and the Treatment of Offenders, Radzinowicz summed up the matter well: "We should not allow ourselves to be intimidated by those who contrast, with a supercilious air, so-called pure research with applied research. The latter, if well conducted, will not only increase the social utility of criminology but will bring with it a refinement in method and a more exact perception of the things which matter." It is necessary to add only that the considerable investment in etiological research in the past would be difficult to justify in terms of social utility.

Prediction Research

Although causal research has been unproductive, research into prediction, which has sometimes been interpreted as a search for causes, has produced what is probably criminology's most distinctive contribution to knowledge in the social sciences. But prediction tables are not lists of causal factors and do not provide an explanation of criminal behavior. They are "practical devices to facilitate decision and action," as Mannheim puts it. The assumption involved in prediction studies is that, as a statistical proposition, offenders with a number of similar characteristics will act in similar ways when placed in similar situations. To this end, the personal and social characteristics of offenders which are discovered to be significantly related to success or failure after treatment are classified and converted into scores. These scores form the basis of prediction tables to which we can turn as a guide to the kind of treatment which will most probably result in a favorable outcome for the offenders with personal and social characteristics similar to, or varying in some degree from, the one whose case we are considering. The tables cannot predict with certainty for the individual case; their very nature precludes this. Their aim is to reduce the margin of uncertainty in which we are forced to operate. It has repeatedly been stressed that the tables are not intended to replace the decision-making function; rather they are to aid decision making, serving as one important index of future behavior which should be weighed with other available indices.

We shall not outline the different approaches to the construction of prediction tables which have been adopted; a most comprehensive historical survey of such tables, both American and European, is to be found in Mannheim and Wilkins's *Prediction Methods in Relation to Borstal Training* (1955); but rather we shall comment briefly on the areas they cover and their practical utility. Attempts have been made to develop tables for the following uses: (1) identification of predelinquent children; (2) disposition of cases in the juvenile court; (3) selection of adults for probation; and (4) timing of parole from reformatories and prisons and selection of cases for parole.

Significant among such studies are the American studies by Ernest Burgess, who studied the factors making for success or failure on parole; by Sheldon and Eleanor Glueck, who have carried out the most comprehensive studies in America; by Lloyd Ohlin, when he was with the Division of Correction of the State of Illinois, whose work deals with the parole discretion; and the English work of Mannheim and Wilkins.

Broadly speaking, these tables have been devised on the basis of follow-up studies or of comparisons between delinquent and nondelinquent groups. The tables have varied in the number of factors used as a basis for prediction, from the Burgess technique utilizing as many as twenty-one factors to the Glueck technique of five or six factors. Examples of the kind of factors found to be significant are work habits prior to prison, seriousness and frequency of earlier crime, penal experience prior to prison, economic responsibility preceding sentence, and mental abnormality on admission to prison.

The tables have also varied methodologically in the ways in which the significance of factors have been assessed and converted into scores. Earlier studies were able to distinguish the two extremes of success and failure but left a middle group of doubtful cases. Later efforts have been directed toward minimizing this area of uncertainty.

The general application of such tables, which are constructed on the basis of experience with certain subjects under certain conditions, has rightly been questioned. Conditions may change by the time the tables are used to predict the outcome of the treatment of later offenders; or the original group of offenders may have been unique in some important respects. But cross-validation studies, repeated assessments of validity, and the development of prediction measures for specific groups of offenders would go a long way to meet these difficulties. In these areas further research is necessary. At present, though all available prediction methods have relatively low predictive power, they have been used with some success in making selections for parole and in reducing costs of confinement in institutions by releasing those with a high probability of success earlier than originally scheduled.

Much more research needs to be done if we are fully to exploit the potential of prediction techniques. Thus, let it be supposed that from a group of one hundred children we can select with far more success than by the operation of chance those who are likely to be delinquent in the future. Does it help to guide our conduct toward the predicted delinquents? It does if, and only if, we can minimize their actual delinquency by varying our conduct toward them — but this is entirely speculative. It is the vital link in the equation; yet no one tests it. As in so many other areas of social activity we are content to let our good intentions substitute for knowledge — we want to treat them, to minimize delinquency among them, but we hesitate to test whether we can succeed or not. We seek to predict precisely the behavior of a defined group; having predicted, we need to test the precise degree to which we can disprove our predictions. The methodology of this is simple though rarely applied. A group of "predicted delinquents" is randomly divided into a treatment group, receiving the treatment thought likely to reduce their anticipated delinquency, and a control group, receiving the traditional attention or lack of attention. Such experimentation, which in some circumstances is ethically justifiable, tests both the prediction and the treatment thought specific for the group so predicted. It has not yet been done.

Now take the parole prediction example. Assume that we consult the table and discover on carefully refined, cautiously validated experience that a man of the type we are considering for parole has an 80 percent chance of committing a crime; that is to say, of the one hundred like him previously released, eighty did commit a crime. We do not know whether he is one of the twenty or one of the eighty, but the risk gives us pause. Should it lead us not to parole him but to keep him until his maximum term expires? Should we release 80 percent failure risks later than 50 percent risks? These questions raise value judgments to which the prediction table is of distant rather than close relevance. What we should like to know, but no one has sought to tell us, are answers to questions like these: Given he is in the group with an 80 percent failure risk, does that risk decline or increase if we keep him longer? Does it vary with the conditions or type of supervision? Do these conditions tend to reduce the risk? Prediction tables so far developed tell us no more than the likelihood of failure or success of different types of criminals or delinquents (actual or potential) subjected to a given type of treatment or lack of treatment. They do not tell us of the likelihood of failure or success of a defined type of offender subjected to different treatments or lack of treatment or which methods of treatment are the most effective for which types of offenders and how long they should be applied for the optimum effect.

How, then, can these fundamental questions be answered? What types of research might bear directly upon them? The next section is addressed to this problem.

Evaluative Research

We have made it clear that in our view criminological research has too long concentrated on the search for that will-o'-the-wisp, the causes of crime, and much too little attention has been given to research into treatment methods. If the evolution of criminal sanctions is to be adapted to the needs of community protection, it is essential that we evaluate different correctional methods in their application to different categories of offenders. In short, we need gradually to develop a *treatment nosology* of offenders. We must know which of our available methods work best with a range of classifications of types of criminal. When Gil Blas joined the medical profession, he was armed with the alternative remedies of bleeding or drenching. All authorities agreed that these were medically sound and effective treatments, and established diagnostic techniques, backed by a considerable literature, facilitated the important choice between them. Critical evaluation of their true effects faced active opposition from the conventional wisdom. The situation is not dissimilar to current penal practice.

Parenthetically it may be noted that the handicaps of a defective theory and of scanty information about our penal methods, to which we have referred above, have not precluded the development of an appreciably powerful and effective penal reform movement. There is no paradox here, however, since the mainspring of penal reform has been neither empirically validated knowledge nor a developed theory. Decency, empathy, the ability to feel at least to a degree the lash on another's back, the removal occasionally of our customary blinkers to human suffering, a respect for each individual springing from religious or humanitarian beliefs — these have been the motive forces of penal reform, not any validated knowledge concerning the better prevention of crime or recidivism. We have built an intellectual superstructure to our developing sense of identity with all fellow human beings, criminals and delinquents not excepted, but it is an edifice of rationalization. Perhaps this is an overstatement; perhaps a more precise analysis of the relationship between mind and heart in penal reform is that our uniform experience, critically analyzed, seems to be that we can indulge our sense of decency, of reducing suffering even of criminals, without any adverse effect on the incidence of criminality. The history of penal reform thus becomes the history of the diminution of gratuitous suffering.

Capital punishment moves from being the basic punishment for all felonies to an exceptionally inflicted indecency in which we place little trust and have little confidence. But the change is not the product of research studies. The same is true of all the ornate and obscene forms of corporal punishment which constitute our heritage of penal sanctions for noncapital offenses. That convicts ceased to be transported to the southeastern shores of this continent and to the pleasant sunny climes of Australia had little to do with any assessment of the effectiveness of the sanctions of transportation in deterring men from criminal conduct.

Yet again, many of the indignities and cruelties of that American invention, the prison, to be found in the original Auburn and Pennsylvania systems have been eliminated or ameliorated, not because of developing knowledge about the more effective prevention of crime or of recidivism but because they inflict needless suffering. The crime and recidivist situations at least did not deteriorate upon our casting aside the gallows, the lash, the lock-step, the broad arrow, and the rules of solitude and silence. And much yet remains to be done along these lines. The diminution of gratuitous human suffering, gratuitous in the sense that no social good whatsoever flows from it, that it in no wise diminishes the incidence or seriousness of crime and delinquency, remains an important purpose of penal reform. One does not have to travel far anywhere in America to find thousands of convicted persons, adult and juvenile, subjected to needless suffering and for grossly protracted periods. And not only is such suffering useless; it is harmful to us. It tends to increase the social alienation of those we punish beyond our social needs, and it is highly probable that we pay the penalty of increased recidivism and increased severity of the crimes committed by those who do return from such punishment to crime. Studies of inmate culture have confirmed the alienating effect of the prison, the creation of a community of self-identified aggrieved. Inmate culture is highly effective in communicating criminal and anti-conventional values in a situation ideal for their transmission and consolidation. The prison engenders more than social alienation; it fosters and confirms maladjustment.

These, then, have been our main guidelines to penal reform: the humanitarian diminution of gratuitous suffering and the self-serving reduction of social alienation. It is clear, however, that these guidelines are gradually becoming insufficient. New directions must be charted. The Swedish adult correctional system to which we refer in chapter 5 provides an excellent case study of this impending need. In terms of the amelioration of penal conditions little remains to be done there. In Sweden there is as little interference as reasonably possible with the convicted criminal's life, an energetic attempt is made to preserve his social ties by probation systems, and, if it should be necessary to incarcerate him, this is done briefly and in conditions of reasonable comfort with as little disruption of social ties as possible. No large penal institutions; regular home leave; over a third of prisoners held in open conditions lacking bolts, bars, and walls; adequate work and vocational training; a sense of near equality in the relationships between prisoners and staff — these have become the hallmarks of the

Swedish prison system. Along this path, in Sweden, they have gone about as far as they can go, but not quite. There are still a few remaining lockups to be eradicated; there still remain a few needless indignities and hardships.

Nevertheless, in general, the guidelines of empathy and minimizing alienation have served to their limit. Further guidance will not come from the heart; the head must be more directly engaged. And that means a program of research and training which is in Sweden hardly officially envisaged, let alone pursued. The same is true, though at a much earlier stage of development, in this country. Take, for example, the halfway-house movement which is spreading so rapidly. It shortens prison sentences, it sometimes serves as an alternative to institutionalization, it provides a bridge between the institution and the community, it supports probation and parole arrangements for some offenders, and there is great enthusiasm for it. Yet there is no established information showing that it better protects the community or better reforms criminals than the sanctions it is supplanting. We are enthusiastic about it because it assists us to avoid harm, not because we know that it assists us to achieve positive good. It was for the same reason that we eliminated the lash.

But it should not be said that no evaluative research at all has been done. Certain follow-up studies have sought to determine the different rates of success and failure of different treatment measures applied in the same locality. Mannheim's *Juvenile Delinquency in an English Middletown*, the reports of the Cambridge Department of Criminal Science entitled *Detention in Remand Homes* and *Attendance Centres*, and M. Grünhut's *Juvenile Offenders before the Courts* are English examples of such studies. But none attempts to relate the twin variables of the type of treatment and the type of criminal to the likelihood of successful treatment. If we find that treatment A "succeeded" with group Y in so many cases, and treatment B "succeeded" with group Z in so many cases, we have a narrative and not a functional relationship. Thus, in Grünhut's study, probation is shown to have a higher success rate than placement of offenders in an approved school. But this means very little. Probation was probably selected by the courts because the case was of insufficient gravity to warrant placing the offender in an approved school or because the court, on the advice of the probation officer, thought the offender was a "better risk" and therefore did not require committal to an institution. Admittedly, no correlation has been established between seriousness of crime and unreformability on probation, but too many selective factors operated on the two groups subjected to different treatments for any confident conclusions to be drawn evaluating the two methods and their applicability to different types of offenders. There are too many unexpressed variables at work for this kind of research to be regarded as a critical comparative assessment of treatment methods.

There have been a few efforts at more direct evaluative research. Two pioneer projects were the Cambridge-Somerville study and the Highfields study. Both encountered severe methodological difficulties but both confirm the economic and social value of such evaluative research. Further studies of this nature have been conducted by the United States Office of Naval Research and are being pursued by the British Home Office Research Unit and by the California Department of Corrections. In California in particular, experiments have been made, one of which is referred to in chapter 5, where offenders have been allocated at random to different treatments in accordance with a rigorous research design. And, in the long run, effective evaluative research demands clinical trials, and even the methodologically sophisticated techniques of association analysis and predictive attribute analysis cannot avoid this, although such clinical trials themselves raise important and difficult issues of principle.

In medical research the clinical trial is well established and has proved of great value in the development of therapeutic methods. Where there is genuine doubt as to the choice between two or more treatments for a given condition, efficient experimentation requires that the competing methods be tested on matched groups of patients. The new treatment will be given to one group of patients while the traditional treatment will be given to another group of patients, matched so far as possible in all clinically significant respects with the first group. A careful follow-up of the success of the two treatments then gives a foundation on which further testing will provide more secure knowledge, when statistically significant differences are found and validated, upon which the new treatment may be accepted, rejected, or modified. Frequently the new treatment, even if found to be of therapeutic value, does not entirely supplant the old; a common result is that for certain types of conditions within a group being tested the new treatment is found to be more effective while for others the old method for the time being is to be preferred. And thus gradually, and in relation to defined conditions, treatment methods improve and are more selectively applied.

We must, in like manner, experimentally control some criminal sanctions in the cause of the advancement of knowledge and the rational application and development of correctional methods. We must subject criminals of similar personality structures, home backgrounds, and environmental circumstances to deliberately different methods of treatment. Unless we do, we shall have no more than reasonably cogent surmises to guide us; unless we do, we shall continue to lack the minimum knowledge necessary for developing a rational correctional system from our present diversity of sanctions consequent upon the abatement of imprisonment. Whenever a judge or a classification committee or a parole board or a correctional administrator faces a serious choice between competing treatments or punishments, we have an ideal situation for running a clinical trial. There are, quite literally, thousands of such choices taken every day in most judicial and correctional systems, and few are guided by other than surmise and conjecture. In all such situations statistically matched groups of offenders can be treated by two or more competing methods and their comparative success rates assessed with different types of offenders in each group. Only thus can the exercise of that same choice in the future be rationally guided.

Typically, a clinical trial involves defining a group of criminals by age, sex, offense, personality, and home circumstances, the absence of any gross psychological abnormalities, and their rough suitability for two (or more) alternative methods of punishment. Then, as criminals so defined are convicted, they are subjected to the alternative treatments guided only by the demands of a random sampling process (or possibly a more sophisticated matching technique). Extensive information about them and their correctional treatment is obtained and recorded; thereafter, their relative success rates are assessed, and by association analysis information emerges concerning the suitability of various subgroups within the larger group for the two treatments. This result itself requires validation and retesting by further clinical trials, and thus the twin variables of criminal and treatment are gradually related.

The analogy between the doctor's "treatment" and the court's or penal administrator's "treatment" is imperfect. The subject of medical diagnosis is better defined than is the social disease of crime, and in the former the patient consents to treatment, whereas the criminal does not. Problems of abuse of human rights thus obtrude when it is sought to apply the clinical trial to correctional practice. Is it justifiable to impose a criminal sanction guided by the necessities of research and not the felt necessities of the case? Emotionally a negative reply is appealing, but, given certain safeguards, an affirmative answer is wise and does not involve any abuse of human rights. First, we do not have to apply such methods at the stage of judicial sentencing; they can well operate within what the judge determines to be the just and appropriate sentence in each case. Second, by applying a principle which may be called, for want of a better phrase, "testing down," any abuse of human rights can be avoided.

Correctional sanctions already include the possibility, and indeed the fact, of wide diversities of treatment within the judicially imposed sentence. A defined term in "prison" becomes a commitment to possibly extremely different institutions with profoundly different reformative processes and substantially different degrees of social isolation. A sentence of "probation" can lead to close personal supervision or to the most perfunctory experience of occasional reporting. The range of subtreatments within each correctional treatment is very wide, so wide that ample room for evaluative clinical research into those subtreatments exists without interference with judicial processes. Of course, as information relevant to sentencing emerges from such administratively created clinical trials, it must be fed back into the judicial process and will then create yet new opportunities for further evaluative research.

By "testing down" we mean that the new treatment being studied should not be one regarded in the minds of the criminal or the community at large as more severe than the traditional treatment with which it is being compared. To take a group of criminals who would otherwise be put on probation and to select at random some for institutional treatment would risk an abuse of human rights; but to select at random a group who would otherwise be incarcerated and to treat them on probation or in a probation hostel would seem to us not to risk any abuse of human rights. On this principle it would be possible to develop all that we need for many decades by way of research evaluating our correctional methods.

There are many methodological problems in evaluative research. One of the most intractable is defining precisely the treatment method being studied. Probation, for example, is such a potpourri of methods of social casework and individual control that it would be grossly unwise merely to compare probation with any other treatment — "probation" is not a defined treatment; it is rather a convenient name for a considerable diversity of treatments. And there are other difficulties. But the method lies within our research skills and the case for its application is incontrovertible, once it is admitted that we should seek to know which of our diverse treatment and punishment methods best serve our various social purposes.

Our third ukase provides that no new correctional practice should ever be introduced without at the same time plans being made and applied for its critical evaluation. The purposes behind its introduction should be capable of formulation. Insofar as they involve any reformative aim or any aim of special deterrence (and they should involve one or the other), those aims can be tested. If a new reformative method is applied without evaluative testing, it will very probably appear to be successful, since a strong tendency will operate to apply it to those offenders who in any event are the most likely to reform. If we are not perennially to delude ourselves in this way, every penal experiment requires concomitant evaluative research, with the new method being applied randomly within a defined group for whom it is thought to be a suitable sanction and who otherwise would have been dealt with more severely.

What is true of any new treatment method applies also to all existing treatment methods, and it is only the inertia of correctional practice that conceals this fact. It is foolhardy to risk a guess as to the cost of a research program, independent of a close study of the realities of practice in the area to be studied; but, taking the risk, we are confident that when 5 percent of the annual budget devoted to applying criminal sanctions, not including capital costs, is made available for research evaluating those same criminal sanctions, it will be possible to attune those methods rapidly to social needs and within a very few years to diminish suffering from crime, to save a great deal of the present waste of human and financial resources in untested correctional methods, and to produce a return, even in terms of finances, greatly in excess of the investment. Put more concretely: we submitted that, for example, half the time of all probation officers is now wasted by the application of their services to those who do not need them (and who should be bound over or on suspended sentence or supervised by other than skilled caseworkers) and to those who will not respond to their efforts (and who need more forceful casework supervision than the average probation officer can provide); and that it would be quite possible in a few years of evaluative research greatly to reduce that wastage, and at the same time better to protect the community.

Evaluative research is essential to progress in the field of criminal justice and corrections. Correctional administrators must come to see the research worker as an ally rather than as an irresponsible critic, untroubled by the cares and duties of office; and a major effort must be devoted to this type of research, of immediate practical value alike to those who need to create new correctional methods and to those who must make the difficult choices in the application of such methods as are already available. Criminological research must be directed to acquiring such evaluative information, which must be regarded as of primary importance and not as a distraction from the search for causes. Ultimately, it is perhaps true that completely effective treatment presupposes adequate diagnosis; but the present treatment problem is pressing and important, the need for knowledge is great, and, as in medicine, we can with some success treat many conditions whose etiology remains obscure. Further, once research is directed to evaluating our correctional methods it may very well, as has happened in medical research, produce, as a by-product, etiological information of value to a more adequate understanding of crime and criminals.

Deterrence Research

What then are the limitations on the process of evaluating and applying treatment methods to offenders in terms of their effectiveness in preventing recidivism? We must recognize our present penal reform movement as an uneasy series of compromises between punitive aggression and rehabilitative empathy and build toward correctional systems, for adult and young offenders, rationally related to our social purposes. Penal reform must stretch beyond its traditional humanitarian purposes to achieve a larger social protection from crime. And this means that we must take into account more than the response to treatment of the convicted offenders. In particular we have to consider the question of deterrence, which although it figures prominently in academic and juristic discussions of punishment has been largely ignored as a subject for empirical investigation.

Sir Arthur Goodhart wrote some years ago that if punishment "cannot deter, then we might as well scrap the whole of our criminal law." Indeed, every criminal law system in the world, except the Greenland Criminal Code, has deterrence as its primary and essential postulate. It figures most prominently throughout our punishing and sentencing decisions — legislative, judicial, and administrative. We rely most heavily on deterrence; yet we know very little about it.

Ignorance of the consequences of penal sanctions on the community at large is a constant inhibitor of rational action. Punishment sometimes deters, sometimes educates, sometimes has a habituative effect in conditioning human behavior; but when and how? Our ignorance is a serious obstacle, whatever our regulatory objectives. We are hesitant to think only in terms of what the individual convicted offender needs to turn him away from crime because we fear that to do so would sacrifice the general deterrent, educative, and habituative effects of our penal sanctions. Thus, if penal policy is to become rational, it is essential that we begin to learn the extent to which our diverse sanctions serve prospective public purposes apart from their effects on the sentenced criminal; without this knowledge, striking a just balance between social protection and individual reclamation is largely guesswork.

The deterrence argument is more frequently implicit than expressed, the debate more frequently polarized than the subject of a balanced discussion. When we listen to the dialogue between the punishers and the treaters, we hear the punishers making propositions based on the assumption that our penal sanctions deter others who are like-minded from committing crime. And we hear the treaters making propositions concerning the best treatment for a given offender or class of offenders which are based on the assumption that our penal sanctions do not deter at all. There is rarely any meeting of the minds on the issue central to the discourse. And it is not as if such knowledge is unobtainable; it has merely not been sought with anything like the energy and dedication that has been given to the expensive expeditions that have searched for the source of criminality. The polar argument becomes a bore; a modest beginning on the search for more knowledge becomes a compelling need. We have endured a surfeit of unsubstantiated speculation, continuing quite literally since man first laboriously chipped out his penal codes on tablets of stone or scrawled them on chewed and pounded bark. It is time we did better. To do so it may be wise first to get our terms clear, then to assess what we now know, and then to suggest a strategy for our search.

Definitions

Criminologists draw a distinction between special and general deterrence which is helpful to our purposes. By special deterrence they refer to the threat of further punishment of one who has already been convicted and punished for crime; it may be the same medicine that is threatened as a method of dissuading him from recidivism or it may be a threat of a larger or different dose. Special deterrence thus considers punishment in the microcosm of the group of convicted criminals. General deterrence looks to the macrocosm of society as a whole (including convicted criminals). It would seem hard to deny that for some types of crime and for some types of people the individual superego is reinforced and to a certain extent conditioned by the existence of formal punishments imposed by society and that we are influenced by the educative and stigmatizing functions of the criminal law. Further, it seems reasonable to aver that for some people and for some types of crime the existence of punishment prevents the potential offenders from becoming actual offenders, by the very fear of the punishment that may be imposed upon them. These two broad effects can be regarded as processes of general deterrence.

If research is to be done in his area, however, it is necessary to draw further distinctions; and more narrowly defined concepts than "special deterrence" and "general deterrence" (in its two aspects of coercion to virtue through threat, and persuasion to virtue by consolidation of social values) are required. Let us now mention two of these: the channeling effects of threats and the concept of "marginal deterrence."

It is misleading to ask simply, Does the threat of punishment operate or not operate? It may well have *channeling* effects that are not measurable in terms of the threat succeeding or not succeeding in absolute terms. Consider a typical example. Traveling at 60 miles an hour you approach a 50-mile-an-hour speed-limit sign and reduce your speed to 49 miles an hour. The general deterrent threat has operated absolutely in your case. But the car behind glides by, its driver having seen the sign and reduced his speed from 70 to 55 miles an hour. The threat has had an influence on his behavior, a channeling effect. The car behind him, which you had both passed when it was traveling at 45 miles an hour, now increases its speed to 50 miles an hour. The general deterrent threat has had a quite different channeling effect on the behavior of the driver of that third car. These channeling effects of threats on behavior must be borne in mind throughout studies in this field.

The second further concept is of even more importance; it is the concept of marginal deterrence. The question, Do criminal sanctions deter? which is often raised in philosophical discussions cannot be answered in categorical terms. Moreover, it is not difficult to find examples of the threat of punishment under the criminal law clearly influencing human behavior — consider your income tax return. The practical issue is usually, Would a more severe penalty attached to that criminal prohibition more effectively deter? In the capital punishment debate, the real issue is not whether the death penalty is a deterrent to homicide or attempted homicide but whether it is a more effective deterrent than the alternative sanction of protracted imprisonment. It is the marginal increase in severity which is at issue. Hence the key question in deterrence research is whether variations in the severity of threatened sanctions will affect a given crime rate. It is only to the extent that we must increase punishment to achieve a larger deterrent effect, imposing a punishment more severe than would otherwise be imposed, that any conflict can arise between deterrence and the other purposes of punishment. Hence the central importance of the concept of marginal deterrence and of research into marginal deterrence.

Special Deterrence

Let us first consider existing knowledge of special deterrence and then turn to what we know about general deterrence. There are very few empirical studies in special deterrence. The reason for this is, of course, the prodigious difficulty of isolating the threat effect — either of a repeated or of a more severe penalty — from the many other effects of the criminal sanction. We refer in chapter 6 to the evidence on the ineffectiveness of corporal punishment as a deterrent contained in the report of the Departmental Committee on Corporal Punishment (1938) and the report of the Advisory Council on the Treatment of Offenders (1960). But one must resist the temptation to extrapolate such findings beyond their proper base. Some 70 percent of first-timers in prison all over the world do not return. A proponent of special deterrence could strenuously contend that this is a consequence of the special deterrent effect of the imprisonment and not of any reformative process that might have been applied to the offender while he was incarcerated. Again we face a situation where research rather than speculation is required.

Yet research in this area presents formidable problems. Nearly twenty years ago one of the authors conducted a small empirical study in special deterrence. He studied the question whether the length of the periods of imprisonment imposed on 302 confirmed recidivists had any effect on the duration of their subsequent periods of freedom. The group had a total of 2,720 periods of imprisonment and 2,720 subsequent periods of freedom prior to their last period of incarceration. It emerged that the length of each period of penal confinement had no measurable effect on the subsequent interval between discharge and reconviction.

Can we say, then, that since the length of time an individual spent in prison appeared to have no influence on the length of time he spent out of prison, special deterrence was inoperative on the individuals covered by the study? Unfortunately it is not as simple as that. Thus criminals tend to get longer prison sentences as their careers in crime get longer and their status as criminals becomes more confirmed. Since those individuals are more confirmed criminals when they are serving long sentences than they are at the stage in life when they are serving short sentences or receiving probation, it is plausible to suppose that the periods of time they would spend out of prison after longer prison sentences would be shorter than the periods of time that they have spent out of prison earlier in their careers when their commitment to crime was not so manifest. It also should be noted that it is more likely the police will pick up an individual with a long criminal record as a suspect, and it is more likely that police will have an accurate idea of what kind of crime an individual is apt to commit if he has a long record of prior convictions. To the extent that detection has any bearing on how long an individual spends out of jail, this means that criminals would spend less time out of jail during the later stages of criminal careers because they would be caught more quickly. One must also take into account the possibility that longer sentences of imprisonment have an injurious effect on a man's capacity to live without crime in the community. So the apparent ineffectiveness of the long sentences may have been due to the deleterious effect of long-term imprisonment overcoming the possibly special deterrent effects of the more protracted sentences. Thus the apparent lack of relationship between the severity in the punishment that we impose in habitual criminal situations and the results we seem to obtain is not a total rebuttal of the argument that long sentences in prison may make future criminal threats more frightening to criminals and may deter them from future criminal activity for some periods of time. One would be wrong to allege that it disproves the special deterrent effects of such punishment. There are too many variables that may be involved. We cannot, by such simple techniques, reach confident conclusions about special deterrence.

For our part, though we favor experimentation and research in special deterrence, we do not regard it as of equal importance to research in general deterrence. It seems to us that the general sentencing pattern which is emerging in this country does not place great stress on special deterrence; much more emphasis is placed on general deterrence. Within correctional systems the emphasis today is more often on rehabilitation. Special deterrence is not much considered except when the correctional officer faces a disciplinary problem within a prison: then special as well as general deterrent purposes can be heard resoundingly to dominate decisions.

General Deterrence

The capital punishment controversy has produced the most reliable information on the general deterrent effect of a criminal sanction. It now seems to be widely accepted that the existence or nonexistence of the sanction of capital punishment as an alternative to protracted imprisonment for convicted murderers makes no difference to the homicide rate or to the attempted homicide rate. Suppose this is true; there is a temptation to extrapolate from this to other crimes and to deny the operation of marginal general deterrence in them as well. This temptation should be resisted, for it is easy to demonstrate contrary situations for other crimes where increased sanctions (maintaining stable reporting, detection, arrest, and conviction rates) lead to reduced incidence of the proscribed behavior. For example, parking offenses can indeed be reduced by an increased severity in sanctions if one is determined about the matter, and, to take a current example, experience in the United Kingdom leads compellingly to the view that the use of the breathalyzer and a more extensive application of criminal sanctions to drunken driving can by a general deterrent process substantially reduce the mortality and morbidity rates from drunken driving.

There is, however, a trap in this example, since what emerges is that in the recent United Kingdom breathalyzer program the size of the punishment has remained constant; all that has varied, and varied substantially, is the definition of the crime and the method of detecting the offense and prosecuting it to a conviction. It is, of course, truistic that the variables of detection rate and conviction rate will interrelate with the severity of the sanctions, and that we must bear these relationships in mind whenever we are seeking to assess the consequences of various deterrent strategies in the criminal justice system. The available evidence, apart from that relating to capital punishment and drunken driving and certain studies of parking offenses and of bad check laws, does not provide a great deal of insight into our problem. We need knowledge of the marginal deterrent effects of criminal sanctions in channeling human behavior by the threat of punishment. The literature does not take us any distance. Empirical research is a necessary means but its methodology is not obvious. Even the conceptual framework for acquiring knowledge of the consequences of threats on human behavior has not been devised. Some possible avenues of research may, however, be briefly referred to and some of the difficulties mentioned.

Jurisdictions frequently modify their penal sanctions, and it might be thought that historical or retrospective studies of the consequences of these modifications would guide our search. The problem is, of course, that useful comparisons of a rate of crime before and after the changes in punishment policy depend in each case on the assumption that any changes noted in the rate of a particular threatened behavior can be attributed to a specific shift in a facet of punishment policy, and to that change exclusively. The world rarely holds still for the researcher in this way. Moreover, social conditions which cause non-experimental changes in penal sanctions will also affect movements in the crime rate.

A particular danger associated with the retrospective study of changes in the levels of punishment is that increases in penalties are frequently associated with increased levels of enforcement and with extended publicity campaigns about the evils of the behavior being punished. Also, such changes are often introduced in response to abnormally high rates of criminal behavior of the type which is now to be more severely punished. Hence, quite apart from the increased severity of the sanction to be imposed, the rate for that type of crime may be expected to "regress" to more typical levels. Difficulties in drawing firm conclusions from such retrospective or historical studies have been explored in detail in the literature on capital punishment.

The comparative study is the next obvious method of searching out data on the marginal deterrent effects of punishment. Comparison can be made between crime rates in areas with more severe penalties for a given type of prohibited behavior and crime rates in areas with less severe penalties for that behavior. Such comparative exercises would be reliable if we could find a set of areas with different punishment policies toward a particular criminal act and yet so similar in every other way that the differences observed between the two crime rates could reasonably be attributed to the differences in punishment policy. Again, our observations are confounded by a myriad variables. Such comparative studies may of course be valuable, as they have proved to be in relation to capital punishment; but they run the substantial risk of attributing differential results to false causes, and this risk must be carefully guarded against.

Survey research is a third method of studying the marginal effects of general deterrence. Threats can hardly operate on those who do not know about them. It is possible to test the relationship between knowledge of threats and attitudes to behavior, and to make tentative assumptions about the effects of such attitudes on behavior itself. Hence, reliable information about public knowledge of, and attitudes and responses to, elements of a threat and punishment system is a valuable addition to our store of knowledge about deterrent processes. Survey research may be directed at representative samples of the population as a whole or at samples of distinct subpopulations whose responses to punishment policy can be assumed to be different from those of the general population and whose involvement in criminal activities is extensive enough to make distinct subgroup responses of particular significance to effective criminal regulation.

Historical, comparative, and survey methods can all throw light on our central question; but more important than all of these is the field experiment. Here, as elsewhere in criminology, the field experiment designed to test the consequences of increased or reduced severity of a punishment for a given type of human behavior has substantial political obstacles to its acceptance and implementation. Nevertheless, only field experiments provide sufficient opportunity for varying a single component in the deterrence strategy — say, an increase in the maximum punishment that the court may impose — and thus for evaluating in detail the relationship of that component to the rest of the threat and enforcement system.

Not only are field experiments politically unpopular but they are also extremely expensive. Further, there are serious ethical and legal problems in their implementation, though it is our view that such obstacles are not at all insuperable, particularly if the variation in punishment imposed in the experiment is downward rather than toward more severity.

Yet it is not always necessary to require manipulating legislative prescription of penalties to achieve field experiments. Legislatures are hesitant to collaborate, and our hypotheses concerning the marginal general deterrent effects of sanctions are probably insufficiently sound to warrant large-scale experimentations. Opportunities for smaller experiments — soundings in deterrence — exist which may provide the knowledge on which the serious experimental studies of deterrence can in the future be based. Some such empirical soundings in deterrence have already been made at the Center for Studies in Criminal Justice in the University of Chicago. Studies are in progress, or have been made, of the deterrent effects of differential threats governing insufficient-fund checks for large and small amounts; of the effects on driving behavior of compulsory attendance at driving school as a court sanction; of the efficacy of different threats and different educative techniques on false fire alarms from fire alarm boxes proximate to Chicago public schools; of the effects on two groups of traffic offenders in a large city of punishments differing considerably according to which court the offenders were by chance taken to. In all these cases research opportunities were found and are being explored.

The need for this sort of research is great; our ignorance seriously impedes effective social control. It may also impede the acceptance of more humane and more effective treatment methods. The common assumption is that deterrence and reform represent some sort of natural antinomy. Whether they conflict in fact will be known only when we better understand our capacity to influence human behavior by threats and by retraining programs and when we understand the proper limits and roles of each. We are in the prehistory of such studies.

Conclusion

Our present position is aptly summarized in a passage from the President's Crime Commission task force report on science and technology. Speaking of the need for research, the report says:

> The criminal justice system may be compared to a blind man far down the side of a mountain.

If he wants to reach the top, he must first move.
And it matters little whether his first move is up or
down because any movement with subsequent
evaluation will tell him which way is up. A step by
step process of experimenting, evaluating, and
modifying must be undertaken. Both innovation and
the subsequent evaluation of its consequences are
essential to climbing up.

There is one respect in which this metaphor is misleading. We are not after all quite blind. It is fashionable to bewail our ignorance of effective crime prevention techniques; of successful correctional methods; and of deterrence, both of people in general and of offenders as potential recidivists. But although in this chapter we have emphasized the deficiencies in our knowledge and the need for research, the truth is that we know a lot better than we do.

It is perverse to pretend that we do not know how to deal with crime much more effectively than we do deal with it. Nor is it true that lack of money is the major obstacle to improving the operations of the criminal justice system. "The inertia of the criminal justice is great," says the President's Crime Commission report. And it is inertia far more than ignorance or inadequate resources which impedes action. Given the disposition to act resolutely along the lines of our program, crime need no longer be a major source of public alarm and concern. The problem of crime like the problem of disease is not in any final sense soluble. But it can be subjected to effective control. We cannot expect more; there is no reason why we should be satisfied with less.

Drunken driving, 62–63, 72; conditional consent, 75; controls in other countries, 73–75; effect of alcohol, 73; European Council of Ministers of Transport, 72; punishment of, 64

Drunkenness: cost of, 6; effects of, 6–7; extent of, 6; not criminal offense, 3, 7–8; treatment of, 8

Due process. *See* Juvenile courts

Durham rule, 177

Durkheim, Emile, 48

East, Dr. Norwood, 126

Edwards, George C., 214

Effectiveness of Punishment and Other Measures of Treatment, 120

Embezzlement, 46

Emergency telephone communications, 103. *See also* Police

England, Ralph W., 135

Eriksson, Torsten, 132

Essexfields, 168

Etiological research, 241–42

Evaluative research: clinical trial, 249–50; examples of, 248–49; leading to etiological information, 253; limitations of, 253; methods for, 250–52; necessary basis of correction, 252; need for, 249; shortcomings, 248

Exclusionary rule, 100–101

Federal Bureau of Prisons, 136

Federal Parole Board, 136

Federal Prison Industries, Inc., 130

Female staff. *See* Penal institutions

Ferracuti, Franco, and Wolfgang, M., *The Subculture of Violence*, 67

Feshbach's "substitution hypothesis," 84

Field experiment, 260–61

Fines, 142

Firearms. *See* Guns

Folklore. *See* Organized crime

Forcible rape, 60–61

Fornication. *See* Sexual behavior

Fortas, Abe, 158

Fox, Sir Lionel, 116

Frankfurter, Felix, 139

Freedman, Dr. Lawrence, 85

Freund, Ernst, 4

Fry, Margery, 43

Furloughs for prisoners, 128–29

Gallup poll on gun control, 68

Gambling, 3, 5, 10–12

General deterrence: capital punishment, 258; definition, 255; distinct from special deterrence, 255; examples, 258–59; field experiment, 260; research, 259–61; studies in progress, 261

Genovese, Vito, 208–10, 225. *See also* Cosa Nostra

Glaser, Daniel, *The Effectiveness of a Prison and Parole System*, 117–18

Glueck, Eleanor, 78, 243

Glueck, Sheldon, 78, 243

Goodhart, Sir Arthur, 253–54

Grant, J. D., 170

Grant, M. Q., 170

Greenwald, Harold, *The Call Girl*, 23

Grendon Underwood, 125–26

Group counseling, 133

Group therapy, 134

Grünhut, M., *Juvenile Offenders before the Courts*, 248

Guided group interaction programs, 168

Guns: control of, 63, 68–71; number in U.S., 64; sales of, 63, 68; use in crimes, 63–65; use compared with other weapons, 65–66

Guns (magazine), 69

Hadfield case, 180

Halfway hostels, 128–29

Handguns, 63, 67, 70

Hart, H. L. A., 4, 123, 176

Hartshorne, H., and May, M. A., *Studies in Deceit*, 154
Herstedvester, 126
Highfields, 168
Highlands study, 249
Hillman, Serell, 229
Himmelweit, Oppenheim, and Vince study, 84
Hofstadter, Richard, "The Paranoid Style in American Politics," 233
Home protection systems, 104–5
Homosexuality. *See* Sexual behavior
Hood, Dr. Roger, 118
Hoover, J. Edgar, 225–26
Hubert, Dr. W. H. de B., 126
Hundley, William G., 212–13

Illinois Criminal Code (1961), 27
Imprisonment: conditions of, 124; correctional function of, 115–19; curtailment of, 123; effect of, 115; as last alternative, 123; term of, for felony, 12
Incest. *See* Sexual behavior
Index crimes, 31, 56
Insanity defense: abolition desirable, 176–81; consequences of, 180; moral issue, 178; in relation to social adversity defense, 179; ukase abolishing, 174; use in past, 178
Institutionalization, 124, 167
Institutional treatment, 123–34
Insurance companies, 39

Johnson, Earl, "Organized Crime: Challenge to the American Legal System," 231
Johnson, Lyndon Baines, 113
Judges, A. V., *The Elizabethan Underworld*, 210
Justice, cost of administering, 39
Justice Department, 71
Justitia, 138–39
Juvenile courts: deleterious effects, 166; due process, 161–64; jurisdiction, 3, 160–61, 164; *Kent v. U.S.*, 158; labeling, 166–67; versus welfare boards, 157–58
Juvenile delinquency, 3; adult attitudes toward, 148; auto theft, 151–52; car libraries, 171; category not homogeneous, 155; cause/effect model, 155–56; control of, 169; definition of, 146–47; HEW report on, 146; international problem, 148; labeling, 166–67; non-unitary relationship to "dependence," 159; publicity of, 150; rate, 148–51, 153–54; testing, 155; vandalism, 152
Juvenile Delinquency and Youth Crime, 143
Juveniles' correctional services, 143–44

Kadish, Sanford, 21–22
Kefauver, Estes, *Crime in America*, 203
Kefauver Committee, 205
Kennedy, Robert F., 207, 227–28
Kenney, J. P., 58–59
Kinsey Institute study: on homosexuality, 19; on pornography as causal factor in sex offenses, 23; on prostitution, 20–21; on statutory standards for sex laws, 16
Knives: federal prohibition of, 71; number of, 71; switchblade, 71; ukase prohibiting, 64; use in crimes as alternative to guns, 66–67

Langholmen, 133
Larceny, 56
Lawyers, 164–65
Lorenz, Konrad, *On Aggression*, 77

Macaulay, Lord, 27
McClellan, Senator John L., 212, 226, 228

— on crime: causes of crime not to
be studied, 30; compensation for
victims of violent crime, 30;
cost of crime, 30; cost of crime
related to systems analysis, 30;
crime prevention program, 30;
crime prevention and technology,
92; criminal justice agencies
with research facilities, 239;
employment redistribution in crime
units, 203; incidence of crime, 30;
total figures prohibition, 37
— on crime and the psychiatrist:
abolishment of the defense of
insanity, 174; research on defining
the socially dangerous, 174;
treatment of socially dangerous
persons, 174
— on crime and research: appropriations for research, 239; establishment of National Foundation for
Criminal Research, 239; evaluation
of correctional methods, 239
— on disorderly conduct and
vagrancy, 3
— on drunken driving, 64
— on firearms: mail-order sales
prohibited, 63; possession of
military weapons, 64; registration
and licensing of, 63; use of in
committing crime, 63; use of in
resisting arrest, 63
— on gambling, 3
— on juvenile courts: defendant's
rights in, 156; jurisdiction of, 3,
156
— on juvenile delinquency, 3
— on knives, 64
— on narcotics and drug abuse, 3
— on police: academies for, 92;
disbanding of organized crime
units, 203; citizen's complaints
against, 92; mobility of, 92;
recruitment of, 92; relinquishment
of traffic law enforcement, 92;

salaries of, 91–92
— on public drunkenness, 3
— on sexual behavior, 3
— on Standing Law Revision Committee, 27
— on youthful offenders: treatment
of, 156; youth service bureaus, 156
Uniform Crime Reports (UCR):
crime rate, 31, 34; disorderly
conduct, 12; index crimes, 56;
juvenile delinquency rate, 151;
prostitution, 21; rape, 61; robbery
rate, 60
Unitary state correctional systems, 112
United States Department of Health,
Education, and Welfare, 120
United States Office of Naval
Research, 249

Vagrancy, 3, 12
Valachi, Joseph: Apalachin, N.Y.,
228–29; Cosa Nostra, 212–15,
217–18; on Vito Genovese, 225;
testimony, 213, 215–17, 219–22,
225
VERA Foundation Manhattan Bail
Bond Project, 115
Vice legislation, 108–9
Victim: contributions to crime, 40;
compensation, 38, 40, 42–45;
murder, 41; non-homicide cases,
41; public aid, 40; sex crimes, 40;
subject of studies, 40
Violence: censorship of, 80–85;
idealization of, 83–84; in media,
80, 83; part of culture, 55;
prediction of, 77–80; prediction
by parole boards, 79; preventive
intervention, 77–80
Violent crime in England, 33
Visiting privileges, 128
Vollmer, August, 89, 109
Wade, A. L., 55
Walker, Nigel, 62, 118, 142